EDUCATE.IE

SHAKESPEARE

SERIES

KING LEAR

educate.ie

Dedication

For my sisters Sinead, Noreen, Eimear and Aoife, my brother John and my nephew Jody.

Acknowledgements

I would like to thank my inspiring students and supportive colleagues, past and present, at Yeats College, Waterford.

A very special thank you to my wonderful friends and everyone at Educate.ie, particularly Síofra Ní Thuairisg for her editing.

Thanks also to Janette Condon for her invaluable advice on the initial manuscript, to Jane Rogers and Terry Fitzgerald for their editorial input, and to Peadar Staunton and Peter Malone.

– Mary Barron

EDUCATE.IE
SHAKESPEARE
SERIES

–THE TRAGEDY OF–
KING LEAR

INTRODUCTION & NOTES BY
MARY BARRON

educate.ie

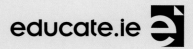

PUBLISHED BY:
Educate.ie
Walsh Educational Books Ltd
Castleisland, Co. Kerry, Ireland
www.educate.ie

ASSOCIATE EDITOR:
Janette Condon

PRODUCTION EDITOR:
Kieran O'Donoghue

DESIGN/ILLUSTRATIONS:
The Design Gang, Tralee

PRINTED AND BOUND BY:
Walsh Colour Print, Castleisland

PHOTOGRAPHS –
Main theatre production photographs by Karl Hugh (courtesy of Utah Shakespeare Festival, USA). Other production images courtesy of the Royal Shakespeare Company, photographer Manuel Harlan. See page 270 for full list of actors.
   Other photographs/images courtesy of Shakespeare Globe Theatre, BigStock, Istock, Stockbyte/Getty.

The author and publisher have made every effort to trace all copyright holders. If any have been overlooked we would be happy to make the necessary arrangements at the first opportunity.

ISBN: 978-1-908507-44-0

CONTENTS

PREFACE

This edition of Shakespeare's King Lear *has been designed with you, the student, in mind. The text is packed with notes, summaries, character studies and sample essays – in short, everything you need for exam success.*

While it is true to say that every word in King Lear *is significant, all of the play's most important quotations have been underlined. This is to draw your attention to those that are most meaningful, which will help you to decide which quotations you need to memorise. When you are doing that, you should try to choose quotations from a range of characters and themes. Choose multifunctional ones when possible. A quotation such as 'Come not between the dragon and his wrath' could be used not only for character questions on King Lear or Cordelia, but also for stylistic questions on animal imagery.*

For ease of reference, each act is colour-coded, and the notes include an explanation of each scene, as well as a longer analysis of each act. These notes are presented in a concise, focused way so that you can learn them confident in the knowledge that you can use all the material there in the exam.

Many scenes have been translated into modern English. Although Shakespeare's language is very eloquent, it is also interesting to see how these words might be spoken today. These scenes are useful for revision and will help you to get to know the text really well, though of course they are not meant to replace the poetry of Shakespeare's own dialogue.

There are detailed character studies here, too. You will have formed your own impressions of the characters by the time you have finished studying the text. Considering your opinions and these notes together will help to give you a well-rounded view of the characters in the play.

All of the important themes in King Lear *are explained thoroughly in the notes. As well as that, there is a comprehensive section on how to answer exam questions, and there are many helpful sample essays for you to emulate in your own writing. Most important,* King Lear *is a brilliant, complex play, written by a playwright at the height of his powers, so enjoy the play and form your own opinions of it.*

Mary Bannen

INTRODUCTION

THE PLAY *King Lear*, written between 1603 and 1606, is considered by many to be Shakespeare's magnum opus. It is an incredibly complex, harrowing and poignant drama. Shakespeare comes dangerously close to complete pessimism, but skilfully balances out the evil that humanity is capable of with the love that we are also capable of. Every human emotion is explored and analysed in this play, and that is why it is such an astonishing achievement.

The play follows Lear's emotional journey to self-knowledge, but Lear is by no means the only compelling character. His evil daughters Goneril and Regan are also fascinating, while Cordelia's goodness reminds us of a time when innocence was prized rather than discouraged. The Fool speaks the play's most hilarious, yet poignant words, while Kent's loyalty is quite heartbreaking.

The main plot was inspired by a variety of existing stories and plays, for example *King Leir and his Three Daughters*, an anonymous old play, and *The Faerie Queene* by Edmund Spenser. However, there are two plots in *King Lear*, and this is a key reason why the play is so gripping. The sub-plot involves Gloucester and his two sons, Edgar and Edmund, and it mirrors and exaggerates the events of the main plot. The two plots also collide at key points, and this, too, adds much drama to the play (the love triangle), as well as pathos (Lear and Gloucester's meeting in Act IV).

The sub-plot was taken from one primary source, *Arcadia* by Philip Sidney, but in the original source there was a happy ending between Gloucester, Edmund and Edgar. Shakespeare clearly wished the sub-plot to echo the tragic ending of the main plot, for throughout the play the two plots run in tandem with one another, enhancing and exaggerating all the main characters and events.

Many of the names in the play are taken from the legend of the ancient King Leir, who supposedly lived around the seventh or eighth century BC. Shakespeare does try to make this play seem pre-Christian, and the Fool mentions living before King Arthur's time, but it must be said that the play seems very much rooted in Shakespeare's own era. One cannot help being reminded of Christ in the description of Poor Tom, and Cordelia is clearly based on the Virgin Mary. It seems that Shakespeare got rough ideas from a variety of sources and used old English names such as Goneril, but otherwise this play is very much his own work, and no previous version bears comparison with it.

King Lear is a play that anyone who has ever made a mistake can identify with. Perhaps more of us can identify with Lear's rashness than Cordelia's integrity! It is also a play about family and about loyalty. It may sound a cliché, but the fundamental message of *King Lear* is to be the best version of yourself that you can possibly be, and to always do what you know in your heart is the right thing to do.

THE LIFE AND TIMES OF
WILLIAM SHAKESPEARE

*'He was not of an age,
but for all time!'*

— BEN JONSON

WILLIAM SHAKESPEARE was a brilliant and prolific poet and playwright. He was born in Stratford-upon-Avon in 1564, the third child in his family, but the first surviving child after two sisters died in infancy. His father, John, was a glove-maker and a wine merchant. The family's fortunes were mixed. They were wealthy at first, but later John lost much of his fortune and later still regained it again. This may be why Shakespeare is so egalitarian, and it is often the lower-ranking characters, like the Nurse in *Romeo and Juliet* or Nerissa in *The Merchant of Venice*, who steal the show. In *King Lear*, to give another example, the servants show more loyalty to the king than do his own daughters.

Shakespeare, unlike many of his characters (who tended to be rich or royal, or both) lived in the real world. His family endured their share of tragedy, as only five of their eight children survived into adulthood, and then

Shakespeare's beloved younger brother, Edmund, died in 1607, when he was just twenty-seven.

We presume that Shakespeare went to grammar school in Stratford, but he did not attend either Oxford or Cambridge, so he was obviously self-taught, which makes his achievements all the more astonishing. Books were not easily available in those days, but it is clear that Shakespeare was incredibly well read and that he went to a lot of effort to educate himself. It is obvious from the breadth and depth of his works that he had a voracious curiosity about the world around him.

Shakespeare married at the young age of eighteen. It is often presumed that, like Romeo and Juliet, everyone in Shakespeare's era married in their teens. In fact, the average marriage age was in the mid-twenties, and the age of consent for a man was twenty-one. Shakespeare, however, married for one of the most obvious of reasons: his bride, Anne Hathaway, was pregnant. She was twenty-six, eight years his senior, so there was quite a significant age gap between them, something that was particularly scandalous at that time. The couple's first daughter, Susanna, was born in 1583, followed by twins, Hamnet and Judith, two years later. Tragically, Shakespeare's son Hamnet died aged just eleven, and this had a profound effect on his writing. It became deeper and darker after his terrible loss. Macduff's moving speech when he learns of the death of his children in Act IV, Scene III of *Macbeth* was undoubtedly inspired by Shakespeare's own loss. 'I must feel it as a man,' he says, echoing the playwright's own experience.

Given that the couple had just three children and that Shakespeare spent most of his adult life in London, many biographers surmise that William and Anne's marriage was not a happy one. Much has been made of the fact that in his will Shakespeare bequeathed Anne his 'second-best bed' and nothing more! This sounds rather unchivalrous, but in fact it was common practice then to leave everything to your children rather than your spouse. And the second-best bed would have been the marital bed; the best one would have been kept for guests. While the evidence, as always, is scant, many would agree that the couple did separate, in deed if not in word. There have been many hypotheses put forward about Shakespeare's relationships with other women (and there have also been unsubstantiated rumours of dalliances with men), but in the end we simply do not know. What we do know is that Shakespeare did return to Stratford to retire, so whatever their changing circumstances, the couple were perhaps in truth happily married. The playwright certainly experienced great passion. His many sonnets often concern themselves with that most universal of themes, love.

Despite the fact that so much of Shakespeare's writing is still extant, we tend to feel we know very little about him, especially in comparison with what we know about more modern writers. He is sometimes viewed as an unreliable charlatan, who bluffed his way through an amazing dramatic career (many volumes have been devoted to the study of lacunae – gaps or missing parts – in his works). Other scholars are convinced that he was a man to whom honour meant everything. What we do know for sure is that Shakespeare was an astute observer of the human condition. His plays indicate that he was a detached spectator, someone on the periphery of society, well placed to judge those around him. He saw the misfortune and cruelty of life – this was an age when unfortunate criminals might be hanged on the street – but rather than losing his humanity, he became a compassionate recorder of what it means to be human. Shakespeare recognised that not many people are truly evil, and few are completely good. Morality is not black and white. There is a huge grey area between good and evil, and it is on this that *King Lear* and his other great tragedies, *Hamlet*, *Macbeth* and *Othello*, focus.

After leaving Stratford-upon-Avon in his early twenties, the life Shakespeare lived must have been colourful. He was drawn to the theatre – most biographers believe that he would have found settled family life no substitute for the dramatic world – and he began his career as an actor. Acting troupes regularly visited Stratford, and may have recruited him there, or he may have followed them to London. His experience as an actor helped him forge a real connection with the audience; he knew what made them laugh and what made them cry. Writing was a natural progression. Now he learned how to create brilliant stories to capture his audiences' attention.

Shakespeare began to make a name for himself as a poet, and, with some powerful personalities such as the Earl of Southampton numbered among his admirers, he quickly grew in stature. Shakespeare's success as a poet gave his name a certain cachet, and drew audiences to the point where his troupe of actors, the Lord Chamberlain's Men, later the King's Men, were easily the most successful of the day. After London's theatres had to shut for some years because of the plague, when they reopened in 1593 there was a void to be filled.

Shakespeare was just the playwright to fill it. Timing and circumstance played their part in contributing to his success, as they often do.

Shakespeare deals with many themes in his plays and poetry: love, hatred, kingship, ambition, mercy, greed, violence, war, filial duty and revenge. All these themes are universal, and so they are always relevant. He portrays his characters in all their human frailty; his heroes are not infallible, and that is why they engage our sympathy.

Shakespeare's plays are classed as the tragedies, the comedies and the histories. The tragedies are full of torment and suffering, whereas the comedies are full of humour and happy timing. Yet every tragedy has at least some comic elements (such as the Fool's jesting in *King Lear*), and every comedy has a little tragedy. All of Shakespeare's heroes have 'fatal flaws', human weaknesses that contribute to their downfall. This makes the characters so very believable, and their tragedy all the more tragic.

Shakespeare regularly presented plays for the enjoyment of Queen Elizabeth I. She was not easy to please and would often send specific instructions on the kind of play she wished to see. This would sometimes call for last-minute rewrites and a lot of improvising! Elizabeth ruled England, without ever marrying, for over forty years. For a woman to hold the highest position in the kingdom was an amazing accomplishment at a time when women had no social power and were considered mere possessions of men.

Shakespeare was clearly trying to please the queen when he wrote strong female characters, such as Portia,

who saves the day in *The Merchant of Venice*, even though she is obliged to disguise herself as a man. This is all the more remarkable when you remember that, in this period, women weren't actually allowed on stage, so their parts were played by men.

Shakespeare was ahead of his time in his treatment of female characters. While many of his contemporaries polarised women into angels or whores, Shakespeare's female characters are realistic human beings, in all their frailty. No doubt, the reign of such a strong woman as Elizabeth I in his lifetime influenced Shakespeare's view of women.

Elizabeth never married, and she left no heirs. When she died in 1603, England's 'Golden Age', a period when theatre and the arts flourished, ended with her. Her successor, King James I, was a more moderate ruler than Elizabeth, but he was also less devoted to the arts. Shakespeare was still favoured at court, however, and his plays continued to be performed to great acclaim.

Shakespeare wrote many of his greatest works – *King Lear, Othello, Hamlet* and *Macbeth* – between 1603 and 1606. They made Shakespeare famous in his own lifetime and he was able to retire to Stratford-upon-Avon a wealthy man. He continued writing almost to the end of his life, but the passion and ferocity of the great quartet of tragedies was notably absent from his later plays. While his writing continued to be as elegant and insightful as ever, Shakespeare mellowed in his later years, and as a result his later works tended to be more gentle and philosophical. *King Lear* can be viewed as the work of a playwright who was at the very height of his genius.

Lear was a particularly daring play in that it tackled some of the most sensitive political issues of the day. James I was not a popular king. Though he had great abilities, he was an extravagant and unpredictable leader, and his aim of uniting England and Scotland created great uncertainty for the future. Here, the playwright opens his play with a kingdom that is about to be divided …

It is not just as a writer that Shakespeare excels, but also as a man with the deepest level of human understanding. Shakespeare understood people. He understood the human condition, our triumphs and our failings, the fact that we are capable of the ridiculous, but also the sublime. *King Lear* is an exceptional play with a truly memorable hero. It takes a rare talent to introduce such a vain, arrogant man as Lear, and somehow make everyone in the audience identify with him and travel with him on his journey to enlightenment. Shakespeare's insight was an innate gift, the kind of transcendent knowing we find in a Van Gogh painting or a Beethoven concerto. Certainly many of the playwright's lines have passed down through the years as gems of wisdom, such as the expression 'be true to yourself', which comes from *Hamlet*: 'To thine own self be true, And it must follow, as the night the day, Thou can'st not then be false to any man.'

Much has been written about William Shakespeare, and if you want to find out more about his life, Bill Bryson's entertaining book, *Shakespeare: The World as Stage*, is well worth a read, as is *In Search of Shakespeare* by Michael Woods, which is very insightful and beautifully illustrated. The film *Elizabeth* (1998), starring Cate Blanchett, gives a great insight into the life and reign of Elizabeth I.

ELIZABETHAN THEATRE

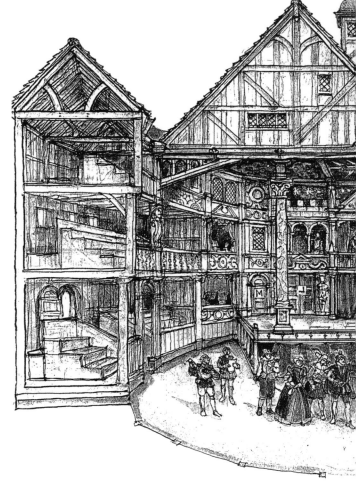

THE LAYOUT of the Elizabethan stage was very simple. There were few props, no scenery, and the actors were on view the entire time. The stage, which projected out into the theatre, had a rectangular shape. The theatre itself was a large semicircle. The pit immediately around the stage was not covered with a roof. This was where the groundlings, the poorer members of the audience, stood. Around the perimeter were tiered rows of seats, which were covered against the elements, for the merchant and noble classes, and in the centre, directly facing the stage, was the royal box for the monarch and the monarch's retinue.

Shakespeare's company put on their productions at the Globe Theatre, built in 1599, until 1608, when they leased the Blackfriar's Theatre, which had the advantage of a full roof. The Lord Chamberlain's Men, who later became the King's Men, included some of the most famous actors of the day. Acting was a hard existence for most, though. They were badly paid and often ill-treated by their audience.

The Elizabethans who came to the theatre were a very different audience from any we might find today. We are saturated with media in the twenty-first century. We have cinema, television, radio, iPads, computers, iPods, and as many books, magazines and newspapers as we could want. Imagine a time when none of these were available, when, if you were very wealthy, you might be lucky enough to own a few books. Most people, however, were illiterate, and they worked long, hard hours with very little respite or entertainment. Even a long church service lasting several hours was a welcome break in those dreary times. Indeed, touring companies brought 'Passion Plays' around the country, where they would act out scenes from the life of Christ on the village green. We would probably find these plays quite heavy going, but in those days people would eagerly queue for hours to see them.

When Shakespeare's audience came to the theatre, they wanted to be entertained with stories. They wanted to hear about the lives of the wealthy and the titled, to learn of exotic countries which they knew they would never see. They expected drama, intrigue and suspense. A tragedy had to be really tragic; a comedy had to make them laugh heartily. If the audience did not like the play, they would pelt the actors with eggs and rotten fruit in protest. Often, someone would start throwing missiles during the briefest lull in the play, so Shakespeare and other playwrights had to make sure to hold their interest. The audience were incredibly hardened in some respects

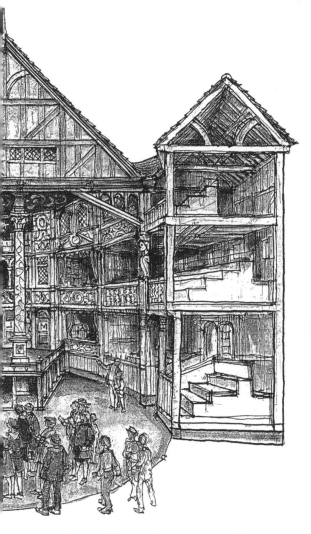

LEFT: *An artist's impression of London's Globe Theatre in Shakespeare's day, showing a cross-section of the building*

BELOW: *The Globe Theatre, reconstructed in 1997 and dedicated to the exploration of Shakespeare's work*

– they would often have seen dead bodies hanging from the gallows or people being tortured in the most inhumane way. But, in other respects, they were quite innocent. They believed in ghosts and witches, for example, and were terrified of them. Shakespeare used such fears to grab their attention.

Plays in the Elizabethan era were principally an entertainment, but they could also be vehicles for social or political criticism, just as they often are today. *King Lear* highlights the plight of the poor and the excesses of the rich. *The Merchant of Venice* seems anti-Semitic today, but in its time it was seen as pro-Christian. In *Macbeth*, Shakespeare clearly criticises those who would do anything for power, and there were many in his day.

As you read through *King Lear* in class and see it in performance on stage or in film, always think of the original audience for whom it was written. Think of how riveted they would have been by the love test, and how horrified they would have been by Goneril's and Regan's cruelty to the king. Imagine their astonishment at the love triangle, and their emotional response to the play's heart-breaking finale. This will help you to understand the brilliance of Shakespeare's drama and give you a unique insight into the play.

You might also like to note that the 1998 film *Shakespeare in Love,* although it is almost wholly fictional, gives a great view of Shakespeare's life in the theatre.

SHAKESPEARE'S ENGLISH

YOU MAY find the language used in Shakespeare's plays difficult at first, but as you grow more familiar with the play you will find that it becomes easier to understand. Language is always in a state of flux, always growing and changing. Ten years ago, for example, you might have said, 'I'll look that up on the Internet,' but now you might just say, 'I'll Google it.' Or someone might say, 'I have to do the hoovering,' when what they really mean to do is vacuum the carpet. 'Hoover' is a brand of vacuum cleaner, but, like Google, so many people had Hoovers that it became a common noun and a verb, as well as a product. Another example of how language is constantly changing is that the Oxford English Dictionary added the expression 'D'oh!' to the lexicon in 2002. Because *The Simpsons* is so popular, Homer's catchphrase has become known, and used, the world over.

You can tell a lot about a society from its language. The English spoken in Ireland is known as Hiberno-English, and it has a particular character and poetry. An Irish person might say, 'I'm after doing that already,' an expression that makes no sense to an English person (for whom 'after' means 'behind' or 'later than'), but we know what it means because it comes from the Irish *'tar éis'*. Ireland has traditionally been a very religious country, too, and our greetings make this apparent. We say *'Dia duit'* for hello, and the response is *'Dia is Muire duit.'* These characteristics give the works of writers like John B. Keane and Patrick Kavanagh a particular eloquence, which Irish people are naturally proud of. English was never formally taught in Ireland, until it eventually replaced Irish as our main language, and this accounts for the relative informality of Irish speech. 'I had a right mare of a day,'

we might say, to describe a particularly hard day, or a person from the country might be described as a 'culchie'.

If you consider that *King Lear* was written 400 years ago, it is no wonder that the language is so different from what we use today. What is not so different, however, are people themselves. We use language as a tool for communication. It expresses our practical needs, but also our deeper emotions and desires. Language is our most eloquent form of expression.

The Elizabethans had an incredibly colourful language. Some words are almost onomatopoeic. To 'beslubber' someone, for example, meant to say something bad about them. Even if we are not familiar with the word, 'beslubber' still sounds like an awful thing to do! They also had lots of words for partying and making merry, like 'carousing' and 'capering'. Some words and phrases considered rude then would not be considered at all offensive today. A 'worsted-stocking knave' was a terrible insult. It meant your stockings (men wore white knitted stockings under puffy shorts at one stage) were sagging, and someone could take deep offence at such a remark. Similarly, some words we consider impolite, like 'shit' were perfectly acceptable in Shakespeare's day!

With Shakespeare, it can be the 'thou's and 'thee's which put us off, as those terms are no longer in common usage. Also, there is a tendency to drop 'e's, as in 'quench'd', 'shriek'd' or 'drugg'd', so the word looks unfamiliar on the page. However, you soon get used to it, and to the characters' tendency to greet each other formally, with their 'Noble sir' and 'My Lord'.

The word order in sentences is often reversed in Shakespearean English, but this is not very complicated. ***Mean you his majesty?*** *Do you mean his majesty?* Or

What says our second daughter? *What does our second daughter say?* Here are some of the more commonly used words and phrases, and their modern equivalents.

Thou	*You*
Thee	*You*
Hath	*Has*
How now?	*How is everything going?*
Wherein	*In which* or *when*
Wouldst?	*Would you?*
Didst?	*Did/do you?*
Is't?	*Is it?*
O'	*Of*
Th'	*The*
I'	*In*

The trick to understanding the language is to just take it sentence by sentence. For example:

The jewels of our father, with wash'd eyes:

Our father's favourites, with tearful eyes

Cordelia leaves you: I know you what you are:

I [Cordelia] leave you. I know what you are

And like a sister am most loath to call:

And as your sister I am most reluctant to point out

Your faults as they are named. Use well our father

Your faults. Take care of our father

To your professed bosoms I commit him:

To your care I commit him

But yet, alas, stood I within his grace:

But if I had any control over his fate

I would prefer him to a better place:

I would prefer him to be in a better place

There are also numerous cultural references, which might not be immediately obvious to us, but which we can understand in the context of the time. **Therefore to horse** means to start a journey, whereas we might say, *Let's get on the road.*

There are many times in *King Lear* when the English used is really not so different from the English we use today. For example:

> **Howl, howl, howl, howl! O, you are men**
>   **of stones:**
> **Had I your tongues and eyes, I'd use them so**
> **That heaven's vault should crack. She's gone**
>   **for ever!**
> **I know when one is dead, and when one lives;**
> **She's dead as earth. Lend me a looking-glass;**
> **If that her breath will mist or stain the stone,**
> **Why, then she lives.**

> *Howl, howl, howl, howl! Oh, you are men of stone*
> *If I had your mouths and eyes, I'd howl and cry so*
> *That Heaven's roof would crack. She is gone*
>   *for ever!*
> *I know when someone is dead, and when someone*
>   *is alive.*
> *She is as dead as earth. Lend me a mirror*
> *If her breath mists or stains the glass*
> *Then she is still alive.*

In conclusion, Shakespeare's language is certainly different from ours, but it is also eloquent, poignant and historically interesting, teaching us so much about the way of life four centuries ago, as well as telling us stories which are simply timeless.

TRAGEDY AS A GENRE

I ″66N GREEK, the word tragedy – *tragoidia* – means 'goat song'. In the ancient dramatic festivals of classical Greece, a goat would have formed part of the prize. 'Tragedy' is a word used daily in our society, and used in popular speech it means that something terribly sad has occurred. The genre of tragedy is very different, however, in that you cannot just have a play where there are sad events and call it a tragedy; you must adhere to the conventions of the genre. Put simply, this means that there are certain rules that a tragedian must follow, and this is what Shakespeare did in his plays.

- A tragic hero generally passes from good fortune to bad fortune. (King Lear goes from being a beloved king with great wealth and power to being homeless and destitute.)

- A tragic hero generally possesses a *hamartia* or fatal flaw, which causes his downfall. He brings disaster upon himself. In Lear's case it is his rashness and his lack of self-knowledge, while in *Romeo and Juliet* it is Romeo's temper.

- When a tragic hero's actions produce opposite results from those he had anticipated (for example, when Lear's daughters do not respond to the love test as he thought they would), they are said to be 'ironic'.

- When the audience knows what is going to happen to a character before he or she does, it is called 'dramatic irony'. For example, when Edmund tricks Gloucester and Edgar, while we know the truth.

- Essentially, all tragedies portray suffering and cause a catharsis in their audience; that is, a purging of negative emotions (or a good cry, which actually does cause the expulsion from the body of negative chemicals which make you feel sad).

- The 'fickleness of fortune', fate, predestination, etc. all play a role in the hero's downfall. In the end, certain things in life cannot be avoided, no matter how hard we may try to do so.

The Shakespearean hero is nearly always a man of exceptional character, a man of exaggerated consciousness and overflowing emotions. He feels everything to an extreme pitch. But despite his excellent characteristics, events and fate – and his own fallibility – combine to create a force he cannot defeat. Nonetheless, the action of the play relies on the audience's empathy with the hero and their hope that he will in fact overcome the terrible obstacles he faces.

King Lear, however, perhaps because of his age, is arguably the greatest tragic hero of them all. Lear's journey is not physical, but spiritual. During the course of the play, he is transformed from a narcissistic, arrogant, blind man, to a kind, considerate and enlightened one. He learns through suffering, showing us that the hard times we have to endure have value and that what doesn't kill us makes us stronger.

– THE TRAGEDY OF –
KING LEAR

BY WILLIAM SHAKESPEARE

DRAMATIS PERSONAE (CHARACTERS)

Lear	*King of Britain*
Goneril	
Regan	*daughters to Lear*
Cordelia	
King of France	*husband to Cordelia*
Duke of Burgundy	
Duke of Cornwall	*husband to Regan*
Duke of Albany	*husband to Goneril*
Earl of Kent	
Earl of Gloucester	
Edgar	*son to Gloucester*
Edmund	*bastard son to Gloucester*
Curan	*a courtier*
Oswald	*steward to Goneril*
Old Man	*tenant to Gloucester*
Doctor	
Fool	
An Officer	*employed by Edmund*
A Gentleman	*attendant on Cordelia*
A Herald	
Servants to Cornwall	

*Knights of Lear's train, Officers, Messengers,
Soldiers, and Attendants*

KING LEAR'S PALACE

Enter Kent, Gloucester, and Edmund

Kent   I thought the King had more affected[1] the Duke of
Albany than Cornwall.

[1] Preferred

Gloucester   It did always seem so to us: but now, in the division of
the kingdom, it appears not which of the Dukes he
values most; for qualities are so weigh'd, that curiosity   5
in neither can make choice of either's moiety.[2]

[2] Half (so they are both equal in Lear's estimation)

Kent   Is not this your son, my lord?

Gloucester   His breeding, sir, hath been at my charge: I have so often
blush'd to acknowledge him, that now I am braz'd[3] to it.

Edmund is illegitimate, and so has been hidden away from public life so far

[3] Brazen, indifferent

Kent   I cannot conceive[4] you.   10

[4] This is a pun – Kent is using it in the sense that he can't understand Gloucester

Gloucester   Sir, this young fellow's mother could: whereupon she
grew round-wombed,[5] and had, indeed, sir, a son for
her cradle ere she had a husband for her bed.
Do you smell a fault?

[5] Pregnant

Kent   I cannot wish the fault undone, the issue[6] of it being   15
so proper.

[6] Result

Gloucester   But I have, sir, a son by order of law,[7] some year elder than
this, who yet is no dearer in my account. Though this
knave came something saucily into the world before
he was sent for, yet was his mother fair; there was good   20
sport at his making, and the whoreson[8] must be
acknowledged. Do you know this noble gentleman,
Edmund?

[7] Legitimate

Gloucester loves both his sons equally

[8] Son of a 'whore' (prostitute)

Edmund   No, my lord.

Gloucester   My lord of Kent: remember him hereafter as my   25
honourable friend.

Edmund   My services to your lordship.

Kent   I must love you, and sue to know you better.

| | Edmund | Sir, I shall study deserving. |

Gloucester He hath been out nine years, and away he shall again.[9] 30
The King is coming.

Sennet.[10] Enter Lear, Cornwall, Albany, Goneril, Regan, Cordelia, and Attendants

Lear Attend the lords of France and Burgundy, Gloucester.

Gloucester I shall, my liege.[11]

Exit Gloucester and Edmund

Lear Meantime we shall express our darker purpose.[12]
Give me the map there. Know that we have divided 35
In three our kingdom; and 'tis our fast intent
To shake all cares and business from our age;
Conferring them on younger strengths, while we
Unburden'd crawl toward death. Our son of Cornwall,
And you, our no less loving son of Albany, 40
We have this hour a constant will to publish

Our daughters' several dowers,[13] that future strife[14]
May be prevented now. The princes, France and
    Burgundy,
Great rivals in our youngest daughter's love,

Long in our court have made their amorous sojourn,[15] 45
And here are to be answer'd. Tell me, my daughters, –
Since now we will divest us both of rule,
Interest of territory, cares of state, –
Which of you shall we say doth love us most?

That we our largest bounty may extend 50
Where nature doth with merit challenge? Goneril,
Our eldest-born, speak first.

Goneril Sir, I love you more than words can wield[16] the matter;
Dearer than eye-sight, space, and liberty;[17]
Beyond what can be valued, rich or rare; 55
No less than life, with grace, health, beauty, honour;
As much as child e'er loved, or father found;
A love that makes breath poor, and speech unable:
Beyond all manner of so much I love you.

Cordelia *[Aside]* What shall Cordelia speak? Love, and be silent. 60

Lear

Of all these bounds,[18] even from this line to this,
With shadowy forests and with champains rich'd,[19]
With plenteous rivers and wide-skirted meads,[20]
We make thee lady. To thine and Albany's issue[21]
Be this perpetual.[22] What says our second daughter,   65
Our dearest Regan, wife to Cornwall? Speak.

Regan

Sir, I am made of the self-same metal as my sister,
And prize me at her worth. In my true heart
I find she names my very deed of love;
Only she comes too short: that I profess   70
Myself an enemy to all other joys,
Which the most precious square of sense possesses,
And find I am alone felicitate[23]
In your dear Highness' love.

Cordelia

[Aside] Then poor Cordelia!   75
And yet not so; since, I am sure, my love's
More ponderous than my tongue.[24]

Lear

To thee and thine hereditary ever
Remain this ample third of our fair kingdom;
No less in space, validity, and pleasure,   80
Than that conferr'd on Goneril. Now, our joy,
Although the last, not least; to whose young love
The vines of France and milk of Burgundy
Strive to be interess'd,[25] what can you say to draw
A third more opulent[26] than your sisters? Speak.   85

Cordelia

Nothing, my lord.

Lear

Nothing!

Cordelia

Nothing.

Lear

Nothing will come of nothing: speak again.

Cordelia

Unhappy that I am, I cannot heave   90
My heart into my mouth: I love your Majesty
According to my bond; nor more nor less.

Lear

How, how, Cordelia! Mend[27] your speech a little,
Lest it may mar[28] your fortunes.[29]

---

[18] Boundaries
[19] Rich plains
[20] Big meadows
[21] Children
[22] Forever

An aside is a very short soliloquy. Like a soliloquy, it is a character's private thoughts revealed to the audience. It is an important dramatic device as it tells us what is going on, and we can always trust its sincerity

Regan claims to love Lear just a little more than her sister

[23] Happy

[24] Her love is too deep to articulate

[25] To have interest in – meaning they want Cordelia's love
[26] Lavish

[27] Adjust
[28] Ruin [29] Inheritance

[30] Brought about her existence

Cordelia	Good my lord,	95
	You have begot me,[30] bred me, lov'd me: I	
	Return those duties back as are right fit,	
	Obey you, love you, and most honour you.	
	Why have my sisters husbands, if they say	
	They love you all? Haply, when I shall wed,	100
	That lord whose hand must take my plight shall carry	
	Half my love with him, half my care and duty:	
	Sure, I shall never marry like my sisters,	
	To love my father all.	

| Lear | But goes thy heart with this? | 105 |

| Cordelia | Ay, my good lord. |

| Lear | So young, and so untender? |

| Cordelia | So young, my lord, and true. |

[31] Goddess of witchcraft

[32] Planets

Lear is saying he will not be Cordelia's father any more

[33] Renounce (give up)

[34] Proximity [35] Blood ties

[36] Scythia was an ancient kingdom whose residents were considered savage

[37] Someone who eats his own children

Lear	Let it be so; thy truth, then, be thy dower:	
	For, by the sacred radiance of the sun,	110
	The mysteries of Hecate,[31] and the night;	
	By all the operation of the orbs[32]	
	From whom we do exist, and cease to be;	
	Here I disclaim[33] all my paternal care,	
	Propinquity[34] and property of blood,[35]	115
	And as a stranger to my heart and me	
	Hold thee, from this, for ever. The barbarous Scythian,[36]	
	Or he that makes his generation messes[37]	
	To gorge his appetite, shall to my bosom	
	Be as well neighbour'd, piti'd, and reliev'd,	120
	As thou my sometime daughter.	

| Kent | Good my liege, – |

[38] Anger

Lear admits Cordelia was his favourite, and that he had hoped she would nurse him in his old age

Lear	Peace, Kent!	
	Come not between the dragon and his wrath.[38]	
	I lov'd her most, and thought to set my rest	125
	On her kind nursery. [To Cordelia] Hence, and	
	avoid my sight!	
	So be my grave my peace, as here I give	
	Her father's heart from her! Call France. – Who stirs?	
	Call Burgundy. Cornwall and Albany,	
	With my two daughters' dowers digest this third:	130

Let pride, which she calls plainness,[39] marry her.
I do invest you jointly with my power,
Pre-eminence, and all the large effects[40]
That troop with majesty. Ourself, by monthly course,
With reservation of an hundred knights,   135
By you to be sustain'd, shall our abode
Make with you by due turns. Only we still retain
The name, and all th' additions to a king;
The sway, revenue, execution of the rest,
Beloved sons, be yours: which to confirm,   140
This coronet[41] part betwixt you.

Kent Royal Lear,
Whom I have ever honour'd as my king,
Lov'd as my father, as my master follow'd,
As my great patron thought on in my prayers, –   145

Lear The bow is bent and drawn; make from the shaft.[42]

Kent Let it fall rather, though the fork invade[43]
The region of my heart: be Kent unmannerly,
When Lear is mad. What wouldst thou do, old man?
Think'st thou that duty shall have dread to speak,   150
When power to flattery bows? To plainness honour's
    bound,
When majesty falls to folly. Reverse thy state;
And in thy best consideration check
This hideous rashness: answer my life my judgement,
Thy youngest daughter does not love thee least;   155
Nor are those empty-hearted whose low sound
Reverbs[44] no hollowness.

Lear Kent, on thy life,[45] no more.

Kent My life I never held but as a pawn[46]
To wage against thy enemies; nor fear to lose it,   160
Thy safety being the motive.

Lear Out of my sight!

Kent See better, Lear; and let me still remain
The true blank[47] of thine eye.

Lear Now, by Apollo, –   165

[39] Honesty

[40] The material goods that come with such a kingdom

Lear intends to spend alternate months with each daughter. He only wishes to keep his title and 100 knights to attend him. All the land and power is to be handed over

[41] Crown

[42] The arrow has been shot from the bow, meaning it is too late to turn back now

[43] Pierces

Kent says he is not afraid to tell Lear that he is making a huge mistake. He is letting his temper and pride prevent him from seeing that Cordelia does love him. She is just being honest, unlike Goneril and Regan

[44] Amplify

[45] Lear is threatening Kent with death

[46] A chess piece that is often sacrificed to save more valuable pieces; in chess, the king is the most valuable piece

Kent speaks up for Cordelia, even though he must realise the consequences for himself. This establishes him as a character we can trust. His dramatic function is to provide a link between the action of the play and the audience

[47] Centre

| | Kent | Now, by Apollo, king, |
| | | Thou swear'st thy gods in vain. |

48 Slave 49 Traitor **Lear** O, vassal!48 miscreant!49 *[Laying his hand on his sword]*

Albany/Cornwall Dear sir, forbear.

50 Doctor **Kent** Kill thy physician,50 and the fee bestow 170
51 Lear's disease is his rashness Upon thy foul disease.51 Revoke thy gift;
52 While he can speak Or, whilst I can vent clamour from my throat,52
I'll tell thee thou dost evil.

53 Coward **Lear** Hear me, recreant!53
On thine allegiance, hear me! 175
That thou hast sought to make us break our vows,
Which we durst never yet, and with strain'd pride
A furious Lear sentences To come betwixt our sentence and our power,
Kent to permanent exile for Which nor our nature nor our place can bear,
questioning his judgement Our potency made good, take thy reward. 180
Five days we do allot thee, for provision
To shield thee from disasters of the world;
And on the sixth to turn thy hated back
Upon our kingdom. If, on the tenth day following,
54 Body 55 In Lear's lands Thy banish'd trunk54 be found in our dominions,55 185
The moment is thy death. Away! by Jupiter,
This shall not be revok'd.

56 Since **Kent** Fare thee well, king! Sith56 thus thou wilt appear,
Freedom lives hence, and banishment is here.
[To Cordelia]
Kent is firmly established The gods to their dear shelter take thee, maid, 190
as a character we can That justly think'st, and hast most rightly said!
trust, no matter what *[To Regan and Goneril]*
And your large speeches may your deeds approve,
That good effects may spring from words of love.
Thus Kent, O princes, bids you all adieu;
He'll shape his old course in a country new. 195

Exit

Flourish. Re-enter Gloucester, with King of France,
Burgundy, and Attendants

Gloucester Here's France and Burgundy, my noble lord.

Lear	My Lord of Burgundy.
	We first address towards you, who with this king
	Hath rivall'd for our daughter: what, in the least,
	Will you require in present dower with her,
	Or cease your quest of love?
Burgundy	Most royal Majesty,
	I crave[57] no more than what your Highness offer'd,
	Nor will you tender less.
Lear	Right noble Burgundy,
	When she was dear to us, we did hold her so;
	But now her price is fall'n. Sir, there she stands:
	If aught[58] within that little seeming substance,
	Or all of it, with our displeasure piec'd,
	And nothing more, may fitly like your Grace,
	She's there, and she is yours.
Burgundy	I know no answer.
Lear	Will you, with those infirmities[59] she owes,
	Unfriended, new-adopted to our hate,
	Dower'd with our curse, and stranger'd with our oath,
	Take her, or leave her?
Burgundy	Pardon me, royal sir;
	Election makes not up on such conditions.[60]
Lear	Then leave her, sir; for, by the power that made me,
	I tell you all her wealth. *[To King of France]*
	For you, great king,
	I would not from your love make such a stray,
	To match you where I hate; therefore beseech[61] you
	To avert your liking a more worthier way
	Than on a wretch whom nature is asham'd
	Almost to acknowledge hers.
King of France	This is most strange,
	That she, whom even but now was your best object,
	The argument of your praise, balm[62] of your age,
	Most best, most dearest, should in this trice[63] of time
	Commit a thing so monstrous, to dismantle
	So many folds of favour. Sure, her offence
	Must be of such unnatural degree,

200

205

210

215

220

225

230

[57] *Want*

Lear is refusing to give Cordelia a dowry, and doesn't care who marries her

[58] *Anything*

[59] *Drawbacks*

Lear's harsh words seem to be an attempt to dissuade the suitors from marrying Cordelia

[60] *Burgundy claims Lear is leaving him no real choice*

[61] *Beg*

France questions what Cordelia possibly could have done to have fallen out of favour in this manner. He says that only a monstrous action could explain her fall from grace. He also says that the Cordelia he knows is not capable of such acts. In other words, he is saying that Lear is wrong

[62] *Comfort*

[63] *Moment*

That monsters it, or your fore-vouch'd affection
Fall'n into taint: which to believe of her, 235
Must be a faith that reason without miracle
Could never plant in me.

Cordelia   I yet beseech your Majesty, –
If for I want that glib⁶⁴ and oily⁶⁵ art,
To speak and purpose not; since what I well intend, 240
I'll do't before I speak, – that you make known
It is no vicious blot, murder, or foulness,
No unchaste action, or dishonour'd step,
That hath deprived me of your grace and favour;
But even for want of that for which I am richer, 245
A still-soliciting eye, and such a tongue
As I am glad I have not, though not to have it
Hath lost me in your liking.

Cordelia wants Lear to tell France that the reason he is cutting off all ties with her is because she didn't flatter him falsely. And she adds for good measure that she is still not sorry that she spoke honestly, even if it has lost her Lear's favour

Lear   Better thou
Hadst not been born than not to have pleas'd me better. 250

⁶⁶ Quirk

France   Is it but this, – a tardiness⁶⁶ in nature
Which often leaves the history unspoke
That it intends to do? My Lord of Burgundy,
What say you to the lady? Love's not love

⁶⁷ Mixed

When it is mingled⁶⁷ with regards that stand 255
Aloof from the entire point. Will you have her?
She is herself a dowry.

Burgundy   Royal king,
Give but that portion which yourself propos'd,
And here I take Cordelia by the hand, 260
Duchess of Burgundy.

Lear   Nothing. I have sworn; I am firm.

Burgundy   I am sorry, then, you have so lost a father
That you must lose a husband.

Cordelia   Peace be with Burgundy! 265
Since that respects and fortune are his love,
I shall not be his wife.

France   Fairest Cordelia, that art most rich, being poor,
Most choice forsaken; and most lov'd despis'd!

Thee and thy virtues here I seize upon: 270
Be it lawful I take up what's cast away.
Gods, gods! 'tis strange that from their cold'st neglect
My love should kindle to inflam'd respect.
Thy dowerless daughter, king, thrown to my chance,
Is queen of us, of ours, and our fair France: 275
Not all the dukes of waterish Burgundy
Can buy this unpriz'd precious maid of me.
Bid them farewell, Cordelia, though unkind:
Thou losest here, a better where to find.

France sees that it is a person's capacity for love, and not material wealth, which proves their worth. His understanding of the value of true love shows him to be a worthy husband for Cordelia

Lear   Thou hast her, France. Let her be thine; for we 280
Have no such daughter, nor shall ever see
That face of hers again. Therefore be gone
Without our grace, our love, our benison.
Come, noble Burgundy.

Flourish. Exit all but France, Goneril, Regan, and Cordelia

France   Bid farewell to your sisters. 285

Cordelia The jewels[68] of our father, with wash'd[69] eyes
Cordelia leaves you: I know you what you are;
And like a sister am most loath[70] to call
Your faults as they are nam'd. Use well our father:
To your professed bosoms I commit him; 290
But yet, alas, stood I within his grace,
I would prefer him to a better place.
So, farewell to you both.

[68] *Prized possession*   [69] *Tearful*

[70] *Reluctant*

Cordelia shows great spirit in standing up to her sisters. She sees them for what they really are

Regan   Prescribe not us our duties.[71]

[71] *Don't tell us what to do*

Goneril   Let your study 295
Be to content your lord, who hath receiv'd you
At fortune's alms. You have obedience scanted,[72]
And well are worth the want that you have wanted.

[72] *Neglected*

Cordelia Time shall unfold what plighted[73] cunning hides:
Who cover faults, at last shame them derides.[74] 300
Well may you prosper!

[73] *Hidden*

[74] *The truth will eventually be revealed*

Cordelia wisely predicts that time will reveal the truth. 'Plighted cunning' might refer to the garments Goneril and Regan wear, which hide the ugliness of their true characters

France   Come, my fair Cordelia.

Exit France and Cordelia

Goneril	Sister, it is not a little I have to say of what most nearly appertains to us both. I think our father will hence to-night.
Regan	That's most certain, and with you; next month with us. 305
Goneril	You see how full of changes his age is; the observation we have made of it hath not been little. He always loved our sister most; and with what poor judgement he hath now cast her off appears too grossly.[75]
Regan	'Tis the infirmity[76] of his age: yet he hath ever but 310 slenderly known himself.
Goneril	The best and soundest of his time hath been but rash; then must we look to receive from his age, not alone the imperfections of long-engraffed[77] condition, but therewithal the unruly waywardness that infirm and 315 choleric years bring with them.
Regan	Such unconstant starts are we like to have from him as this of Kent's banishment.
Goneril	There is further compliment of leavetaking between France and him. Pray you, let's hit together: if our father 320 carry authority with such dispositions as he bears, this last surrender of his will but offend us.
Regan	We shall further think of it.
Goneril	We must do something, and i' th' heat.

Exit

Regan astutely points out that Lear is devoid of any self-knowledge

[75] *Clearly*

[76] *Weakness*

Goneril says that Lear has always been rash and difficult, and this is only going to get worse as he gets older

[77] *Ingrained*

Goneril and Regan now see their father as a burden, despite their eloquent words of love just moments earlier

WHEN THE PLAY opens, Gloucester is introducing

Kent to his illegitimate son, Edmund. Edmund had been sent away because of the stigma surrounding his birth. King Lear, King of Britain, is to abdicate and will divide his kingdom between his three daughters, Goneril, Regan and Cordelia. The fact that the play begins with the sub-plot will later prove significant.

Lear has devised a 'love test' to see which of his daughters loves him best and thus will get the choicest piece of the kingdom. Goneril, who speaks first, speaks effusively about her love for the king. She duly receives a third of the kingdom. Regan is next. She pronounces herself to feel about Lear as Goneril does, only more so. (There is clearly a degree of competition between the sisters.) However, Cordelia angers Lear by not being able to put into words how she feels about her father. Though she says she loves him according to her 'bond' – that is, she loves him as a proper daughter ought – that is not good enough for him. He banishes her immediately in a hasty and impetuous manner that he will later deeply regret.

He tells Cordelia's two suitors, France and Burgundy, that either of them may have her, but that it will be without a dowry. He has given her share of the kingdom to Goneril and Regan instead. France is still happy to marry her, so, unwittingly, Lear ensures that she ends up with her true love.

Cordelia shows spirit when she admonishes her sisters for their duplicity, and tells them to look after Lear properly.

Lear also banishes Kent, his loyal servant of long standing, because he tries to defend Cordelia. As the first, dramatic scene of the play closes, Goneril and Regan, having secured their inheritance, plan to join forces against Lear. This shows their filial ingratitude.

KEY **POINTS**

- *King Lear's love test does not work out as he had expected.*

- *Goneril and Regan receive half the kingdom each.*

- *Cordelia is banished, but France opts to marry her even without a dowry.*

- *Kent is also banished.*

Which of you shall we say doth love us most?
That we our largest bounty may extend
Where nature doth with merit challenge?

— LEAR

THE EARL OF GLOUCESTER'S CASTLE

Enter Edmund, with a letter

Edmund declares nature to be his ruler. It is the laws of the time that prevent him from having the same rights as his brother, so he is going to ignore the law and do what comes naturally to him

[1] Edmund is pointing out that he is just as good as his brother. He is of no less value than Edgar, just because his mother wasn't married to Gloucester

[2] Base means lowest of the low

[3] In the passion of the moment

Edmund says that at least he was conceived in passion, whereas Edgar was conceived in the marital bed, which Edmund considers dull, stale and tired

[4] Dandies (effeminate men)

[5] Legitimate literally means lawful, right, correct

[6] His lie about Edgar

Edmund	Thou, nature, art my goddess; to thy law
	My services are bound. Wherefore should I
	Stand in the plague of custom, and permit
	The curiosity of nations to deprive me,
	For that I am some twelve or fourteen moonshines 5
	Lag of a brother? Why bastard? Wherefore base?
	When my dimensions are as well compact,
	My mind as generous, and my shape as true,
	As honest madam's issue?[1] Why brand they us
	With base?[2] with baseness? bastardy? base, base? 10
	Who, in the lusty stealth of nature,[3] take
	More composition and fierce quality
	Than doth, within a dull, stale, tired bed,
	Go to creating a whole tribe of fops,[4]
	Got 'tween asleep and wake? Well, then, 15
	Legitimate Edgar, I must have your land:
	Our father's love is to the bastard Edmund
	As to the legitimate: fine word, – legitimate![5]
	Well, my legitimate, if this letter speed,
	And my invention[6] thrive, Edmund the base 20
	Shall top the legitimate. I grow; I prosper:
	Now, gods, stand up for bastards!

Enter Gloucester

[7] On bad terms

[8] Abdicated

[9] Lear only retains the outward trappings of kingship (crown and knights)

[10] On a whim – meaning Lear hasn't thought it through

Gloucester	Kent banish'd thus! and France in choler[7] parted!
	And the King gone to-night! Subscrib'd[8] his power!
	Confin'd to exhibition![9] All this done 25
	Upon the gad![10] Edmund, how now! what news?

| Edmund | So please your lordship, none. |

Putting up the letter

| Gloucester | Why so earnestly seek you to put up that letter? |

| Edmund | I know no news, my lord. |

| Gloucester | What paper were you reading? 30 |

| Edmund | Nothing, my lord. |

Gloucester	No? What needed, then, that terrible dispatch of it into your pocket? The quality of nothing hath not such need to hide itself. Let's see: come, if it be nothing, I shall not need spectacles.

35

Edmund	I beseech you, sir, pardon me. It is a letter from my brother, that I have not all o'er-read;¹¹ and for so much as I have perused, I find it not fit for your o'er-looking.

¹¹ *He has not studied it in detail*

Gloucester   Give me the letter, sir.

Edmund   I shall offend, either to detain or give it. The contents, as in part I understand them, are to blame.

40

Edmund cleverly feigns reluctance to show his father the letter. Gloucester is already shaken by recent events, so is vulnerable to Edmund's clever manipulation

Gloucester   Let's see, let's see.

Edmund   I hope, for my brother's justification, he wrote this but as an essay¹² or taste of my virtue.

¹² *Test*

Gloucester   *[Reads]* 'This policy and reverence of age makes the world bitter to the best of our times; keeps our fortunes from us till our oldness cannot relish them. I begin to find an idle and fond bondage in the oppression of aged tyranny;¹³ who sways, not as it hath power, but as it is suffer'd. Come to me, that of this I may speak more. If our father would sleep till I wak'd him, you should enjoy half his revenue¹⁴ for ever, and live the beloved of your brother, Edgar.'
Hum – conspiracy! – 'Sleep till I waked him, – you should enjoy half his revenue,' – My son Edgar!
Had he a hand to write this? a heart and brain to breed it in? – When came this to you? who brought it?

45

50

55

¹³ *Cruel and oppressive rule*

¹⁴ *Wordly goods*

Edmund   It was not brought me, my lord; there's the cunning¹⁵ of it; I found it thrown in at the casement¹⁶ of my closet.

¹⁵ *Sneaky brilliance*
¹⁶ *Window-sill*

Gloucester   You know the character¹⁷ to be your brother's?

60

¹⁷ *Handwriting*

Edmund   If the matter were good, my lord, I durst¹⁸ swear it were his; but, in respect of that, I would fain¹⁹ think it were not.

¹⁸ *Would*
¹⁹ *Prefer*

Gloucester   It is his.

Edmund   It is his hand, my lord; but I hope his heart is not in the contents.

65

*Edmund appears to be calming the
situation, and he also appears to be
loyal to his brother. This all helps
to win Gloucester's trust*

Gloucester   Hath he never heretofore[20] sounded you in this
business?

Edmund   Never, my lord: but I have heard him oft maintain it to be
fit that, sons at perfect age,[21] and fathers declin'd,[22] the
father should be as ward[23] to the son, and the son   70
manage his revenue.

Gloucester   O villain, villain! His very opinion in the letter!
Abhorred[24] villain! Unnatural, detested, brutish villain!
worse than brutish! Go, sirrah, seek him; I'll apprehend
him. Abominable villain! Where is he?   75

Edmund   I do not well know, my lord. If it shall please you to
suspend your indignation[25] against my brother till you
can derive from him better testimony of his intent, you
shall run a certain course; where, if you violently
proceed against him, mistaking his purpose, it would   80
make a great gap in your own honour, and shake in
pieces the heart of his obedience. I dare pawn down my
life for him, that he hath wrote this to feel my affection to
your honour, and to no further pretence of danger.

Gloucester   Think you so?   85

Edmund   If your honour judge it meet, I will place you where you
shall hear us confer[26] of this, and by an auricular
assurance[27] have your satisfaction; and that without any
further delay than this very evening.

Gloucester   He cannot be such a monster –   90

Edmund   Nor is not, sure.

Gloucester   To his father, that so tenderly and entirely loves him.
Heaven and earth! Edmund, seek him out: wind me
into him, I pray you: frame the business after your
own wisdom. I would unstate myself, to be in a due   95
resolution.[28]

Edmund   I will seek him, sir, presently: convey the business as I
shall find means, and acquaint you withal.[29]

Gloucester   These late eclipses in the sun and moon portend[30] no

O villain, villain! His very opinion in the letter!
Abhorred villain! Unnatural, detested, brutish villain!

– GLOUCESTER

good to us: though the wisdom of nature can reason it 100
thus and thus, yet nature finds itself scourg'd by the
sequent effects: love cools, friendship falls off, brothers
divide: in cities, mutinies; in countries, discord;[31] in
palaces, treason; and the bond cracked 'twixt son and
father. This villain of mine comes under the prediction; 105
there's son against father: the King falls from bias[32] of
nature; there's father against child. We have seen the
best of our time: machinations,[33] hollowness, treachery,
and all ruinous disorders, follow us disquietly to our
graves. Find out this villain, Edmund; it shall lose thee 110
nothing; do it carefully. And the noble and true-hearted
Kent banished! his offence, honesty! 'Tis strange.

Exit

Edmund   This is the excellent foppery[34] of the world, that, when
we are sick in fortune, – often the surfeit[35] of our own
behaviour, – we make guilty of our disasters the sun, the 115
moon, and the stars, as if we were villains by necessity,
fools by heavenly compulsion, knaves, thieves, and
treachers, by spherical predominance,[36] drunkards,
liars, and adulterers, by an enforced obedience of
planetary influence, and all that we are evil in, by a 120
divine thrusting on. An admirable evasion of
whoremaster man, to lay his goatish[37] disposition to the
charge of a star! My father compounded with my mother
under the dragon's tail,[38] and my nativity was under
Ursa Major;[39] so that it follows, I am rough and 125
lecherous. Fut, I should have been that I am, had the
maidenliest[40] star in the firmament[41] twinkled on my
bastardizing. Edgar –

Enter Edgar

And pat he comes like the catastrophe[42] of the old
comedy: my cue is villanous melancholy, with a sigh 130
like Tom o' Bedlam. O, these eclipses do portend these
divisions! fa, sol, la, mi.

Edgar   How now, brother Edmund! what serious contemplation
are you in?

Edmund   I am thinking, brother, of a prediction I read this other 135

---

[31] *Disagreement, conflict*

Gloucester is superstitious, which was common in Shakespeare's day. He is more likely to think ill of Edgar because of the recent eclipses, which were believed to be bad omens. Considering the events of the previous scene, it is unsurprising that Gloucester is rattled

[32] *Favour*

[33] *Scheming*

[34] *Stupidity*

[35] *Consequence*

The banishment of his friend and fellow earl, Kent, bothers Gloucester, and makes him feel insecure

[36] *The influence of the planets (spheres)*

[37] *Lusty*

[38] *Constellation of Draco*

[39] *The Great Bear*

Edmund mocks the general belief in the significance of astronomy, claiming that his character has nothing to do with the time of his conception and birth. He would be the same no matter when he was born

[40] *Purest*

[41] *The heavens*

[42] *Climax*

day, what should follow these eclipses.

Edgar   Do you busy yourself about that?

Edmund   I promise you, the effects he writes of succeed
              unhappily; as of unnaturalness between the child
              and the parent; death, dearth,[43] dissolutions of   140
              ancient amities;[44] divisions in state, menaces and
              maledictions[45] against king and nobles; needless
              diffidences,[46] banishment of friends, dissipation
              of cohorts,[47] nuptial breaches,[48] and I know not what.

Edgar   How long have you been a sectary astronomical?   145

Edmund   Come, come; when saw you my father last?

Edgar   Why, the night gone by.

Edmund   Spake you with him?

Edgar   Ay, two hours together.

Edmund   Parted you in good terms? Found you no displeasure in   150
              him by word or countenance?

Edgar   None at all.

Edmund   Bethink yourself wherein you may have offended him:
              and at my entreaty forbear his presence till some little
              time hath qualified the heat of his displeasure; which at   155
              this instant so rageth in him, that with the mischief of
              your person it would scarcely allay.

Edgar   Some villain hath done me wrong.

Edmund   That's my fear. I pray you, have a continent forbearance
              till the speed of his rage goes slower; and, as I say, retire   160
              with me to my lodging, from whence I will fitly bring you
              to hear my lord speak: pray ye, go; there's my key: if you
              do stir abroad, go arm'd.

Edgar   Arm'd, brother!

Edmund   Brother, I advise you to the best; go armed. I am no   165

---

[43] *Lack (such as a lack of food)*

[44] *Allegiances/friendships*

[45] *Speaking evilly against*

[46] *Arguments*

[47] *Bands or teams*   [48] *Marriage break-ups*

Edmund advises Edgar to avoid their father. This makes Edgar trust his brother, and will also make Gloucester even more convinced of his guilt

An example of dramatic irony

honest man if there be any good meaning towards you:
I have told you what I have seen and heard; but faintly,
nothing like the image and horror of it: pray you, away.

Edgar Shall I hear from you anon?

Edmund I do serve you in this business.   170

Exit Edgar

A credulous father! and a brother noble,
Whose nature is so far from doing harms
That he suspects none: on whose foolish honesty
My practices ride easy. I see the business.
Let me, if not by birth, have lands by wit: 175
All with me's meet that I can fashion fit.

Exit

MODERN ENGLISH VERSION

THE EARL OF GLOUCESTER'S CASTLE

Enter Edmund, with a letter

Edmund It's not fair that I am treated so differently from my brother. He's only a year older but he'll inherit everything and I'll get nothing. It's so stupid that he gets it all just because he is 'legitimate' and I'll get nothing because I'm 'illegitimate'. I'm just as natural as he is. Nature created me, and I'm going to make sure I get everything I naturally deserve. If the only way I can get what I want is to take it from my brother, then so be it. It's not my fault. I didn't create this system. I've faked a letter from Edgar. All I have to do is get Father to believe it.

Enter Gloucester

Gloucester The world's gone crazy! Kent has been banished. France has left with Cordelia, never to return. Lear has voluntarily given away all his worldly goods – what the hell is happening? Oh Edmund, there you are. Any news?

Edmund Not really …

*Thou, nature, art my goddess; to thy law
My services are bound*

– EDMUND (ACT I SCENE II)

Quickly hiding the letter

Gloucester   What letter do you have there?

Edmund   Ah, it's nothing really …

Gloucester   I said what are you reading?

Edmund   Nothing, my lord.

Gloucester   Nothing? Then why did you stuff it into your pocket the minute you saw me coming? Let me see it now! If it is nothing, then I won't need my glasses.

Edmund   Sorry, Father. It's just a letter from my brother. I've only glanced at it, but I can already see it's not fit for your eyes.

Gloucester   Give me the letter, now!

Edmund   I'll upset you if I don't give it to you, but I'll also upset you if I do. I can't win!

Gloucester	I want to see it.
Edmund	In Edgar's defence, maybe he wrote it to test my loyalty. I just can't believe he means the awful things that he says.
Gloucester	[Reads] *'It's ridiculous that we have to wait until our father dies in order to get our inheritance. But that's the law, I suppose. Although, if our father were to die sooner (if you get my drift), I'd be willing to split his fortune with you fifty-fifty. From Edgar.'* Oh my God! My own son is conspiring against me. He's planning to kill me? I don't believe this. Who delivered this letter?
Edmund	That's the sneaky thing about it. I just found it in my room.
Gloucester	Is it Edgar's handwriting, though?
Edmund	If it said good things, I would swear it's his writing; but with what is in it, I'd rather think it isn't.
Gloucester	It is his handwriting then.
Edmund	Well, yes. But I hope his heart isn't in it. I hope he was just testing me, rather than plotting to kill you.
Gloucester	Has he ever said anything about getting rid of me before?
Edmund	Well, no. But he has often commented that it is ridiculous for old people to hold on to their money as they age, and that they should give it to their children when their children are young enough to enjoy it.
Gloucester	Oh my God, what an ungrateful … I am going to kill him! Where is he?
Edmund	I can't believe it. My beloved brother … there must be some explanation. Would you give me some time to investigate the matter further?
Gloucester	Hmmm, all right then.
Edmund	I'll talk to him later. You can hide somewhere near by and listen in. Then you'll know for sure.
Gloucester	Maybe you're right. There must be some explanation.
Edmund	There must be. I agree totally.

Gloucester	I've been a good father to him. I don't deserve this. Thanks for taking care of this matter. I'm too upset to do it myself.
Edmund	Leave it to me, Father.
Gloucester	I don't know what on earth is going on. The world is going mad! Sons turning against their fathers, children taking their parents' wealth. I fear the recent eclipse of the moon was a bad omen. Kent banished! I'm frightened by all these bizarre events.

Exit

Edmund	My father is so superstitious. He blames everything on the sun and the stars. How pathetic. My father slept with my mother because he fancied her, and then he blames it on astrology. What a dope! Here comes Edgar!

Enter Edgar

	This is like a bad comedy. He is the fool and I am the villain!
Edgar	Hi, Edmund, you look as if you're miles away.
Edmund	I was just thinking about a prediction I read about things that are going to happen. All these eclipses show something bad is going on in the world today.
Edgar	You don't believe that, do you?
Edmund	Well, some of it has come true already! Tension between parent and child, death, the dissolving of old friendships, countries being divided, plots against the king …
Edgar	How long have you been an astronomer?
Edmund	I can see you don't believe me, but when did you last speak to our father?
Edgar	Last night.
Edmund	Did you chat to him?
Edgar	Yes, for two hours.
Edmund	Did you argue? Did he seem annoyed with you about something?
Edgar	Not at all.

Edmund   You need to think about it because he is really angry with you. You'd better avoid him until he calms down.

Edgar   Someone must have been plotting against me. I haven't done anything wrong.

Edmund   That's my worry. Just stay out of his way and come to my bedroom later. We'll try and find out what's going on. Carry a weapon to protect yourself. Here's my key.

Edgar   A weapon?

Edmund   I'm telling you, Edgar, he's furious. Trust me. Make sure you're armed.

Edgar   Will I hear from you soon?

Edmund   You will. I'm on your side, don't forget that.

Exit Edgar

A gullible father and an innocent brother! This is going to be easier than I thought. If I can't have wealth by birth then I'll get rich by using my brains.

THE DUKE OF ALBANY'S PALACE

Enter Goneril, and Oswald, her steward

Goneril   Did my father strike my gentleman for chiding[1] of
his Fool?

Oswald   Ay, madam.

Goneril

By day and night he wrongs me; every hour
He flashes into one gross[2] crime or other,   5
That sets us all at odds: I'll not endure it.
His knights grow riotous, and himself upbraids[3] us
On every trifle.[4] When he returns from hunting,
I will not speak with him; say I am sick:
If you come slack of former services,   10
You shall do well; the fault of it I'll answer.

Oswald   He's coming, madam; I hear him.

Horns within

Goneril

Put on what weary negligence you please,
You and your fellows; I'll have it come to question:
If he distate it, let him to my sister,   15
Whose mind and mine, I know, in that are one,
Not to be over-ruled. Idle old man,
That still would manage those authorities
That he hath given away! Now, by my life,
Old fools are babes again;[5] and must be us'd   20
With checks[6] as flatteries, – when they are seen abus'd.
Remember what I tell you.

Oswald   Well, madam.

Goneril

And let his knights have colder looks among you;
What grows of it, no matter. Advise your fellows so: 25
I would breed from hence occasions, and I shall,
That I may speak: I'll write straight to my sister
To hold my very course. Prepare for dinner.

Exit

[1] *Disciplining*

[2] *Terrible*

[3] *Criticises*

[4] *Every little thing*

*Goneril is deliberately trying to
antagonise her father by telling
Oswald to neglect him*

[5] *The elderly are like children*

[6] *Reprimands*

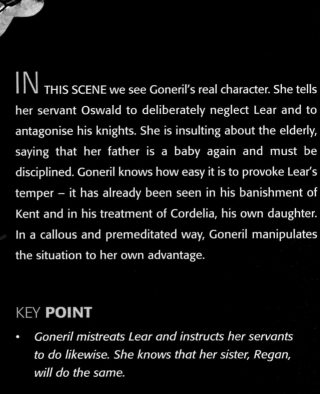

IN THIS SCENE we see Goneril's real character. She tells her servant Oswald to deliberately neglect Lear and to antagonise his knights. She is insulting about the elderly, saying that her father is a baby again and must be disciplined. Goneril knows how easy it is to provoke Lear's temper – it has already been seen in his banishment of Kent and in his treatment of Cordelia, his own daughter. In a callous and premeditated way, Goneril manipulates the situation to her own advantage.

KEY **POINT**

- *Goneril mistreats Lear and instructs her servants to do likewise. She knows that her sister, Regan, will do the same.*

Put on what weary negligence you please, You and your fellows

– GONERIL

A HALL IN THE SAME

Enter Kent, disguised

Kent

If but as well I other accents borrow,
That can my speech defuse, my good intent
May carry through itself to that full issue
For which I raz'd my likeness. Now, banish'd Kent,
If thou canst serve where thou dost stand condemn'd,
So may it come, thy master, whom thou lov'st,
Shall find thee full of labours.

Instead of fleeing, Kent has shaved off his beard and hair, changed his clothing and put on a different accent. His intent is to continue to protect and serve Lear, whom he still loves, despite Lear having banished him. His loyalty is in stark contrast to Goneril's disloyalty

Horns within. Enter Lear, Knights, and Attendants

Lear Let me not stay a jot for dinner; go get it ready.[1] *[Exit an Attendant]* How now! what art thou?

Kent A man, sir.

Lear What dost thou profess? What wouldst thou with us?

Kent I do profess to be no less than I seem; to serve him truly that will put me in trust: to love him that is honest; to converse with him that is wise and says little; to fear judgement; to fight when I cannot choose; and to eat no fish.

Lear What art thou?

Kent A very honest-hearted fellow, and as poor as the King.

Lear If thou be as poor for a subject as he is for a king, thou art poor enough. What wouldst thou?

Kent Service.

Lear Who wouldst thou serve?

Kent You.

Lear Dost thou know me, fellow?

Kent No, sir; but you have that in your countenance which I would fain call master.

[1] Lear is impatiently waiting for his dinner

Lear	What's that?
Kent	Authority.
Lear	What services canst thou do?

2 Good advice 3 Ruin 3 Interesting

Kent I can keep honest counsel,[2] ride, run, mar[3] a curious[4]   30
tale in telling it, and deliver a plain message bluntly.
That which ordinary men are fit for, I am qualified in;
and the best of me is diligence.[5]

5 His best quality is that he is hardworking

Lear How old art thou?

Kent Not so young, sir, to love a woman for singing, nor so   35
old to dote on her for any thing. I have years on my
back forty-eight.

Lear Follow me; thou shalt serve me: if I like thee no worse
after dinner, I will not part from thee yet. Dinner, ho,
dinner! Where's my knave? my Fool? Go you, and call   40
my Fool hither.

Exit an Attendant. Enter Oswald

You, you, sirrah, where's my daughter?

Oswald So please you, –

Exit

6 Idiot

Lear What says the fellow there? Call the clotpoll[6] back.

[Exit a Knight] Where's my Fool, ho? I think the world's   45
asleep.

Re-enter Knight

How now! where's that mongrel?

Knight He says, my lord, your daughter is not well.

Lear Why came not the slave back to me when I call'd him?

Knight Sir, he answered me in the roundest manner, he would not. 50

Lear   He would not!

Knight   My lord, I know not what the matter is; but, to my
             judgement, your Highness is not entertained with that
             ceremonious affection as you were wont. There's a
             great abatement[7] of kindness appears as well in the   55
             general dependants as in the Duke himself also and
             your daughter.

Lear   Ha! Say'st thou so?

Knight   I beseech you, pardon me, my lord, if I be mistaken;
             for my duty cannot be silent when I think your   60
             Highness wrong'd.

Lear   Thou but rememb'rest[8] me of mine own conception.
             I have perceived a most faint neglect of late; which I
             have rather blamed as mine own jealous curiosity
             than as a very pretence and purpose of unkindness.   65
             I will look further into't. But where's my Fool? I
             have not seen him this two days.

Knight   Since my young lady's going into France, sir, the
             Fool hath much pined away.

Lear   No more of that; I have noted it well. Go you, and   70
             tell my daughter I would speak with her.

             Exit an Attendant
             Go you, call hither my Fool.

             Re-enter Oswald

             O, you sir, you, come you hither, sir: who am I, sir?

Oswald   My lady's father.

Lear   'My lady's father'! My lord's knave! You whoreson dog!   75
             you slave! you cur![9]

Oswald   I am none of these, my lord; I beseech your pardon.

Lear   Do you bandy looks with me, you rascal?[10]
             [Striking him]

The knight points out that Goneril's household is not treating Lear with anything like the respect they should

[7] Lessening

[8] Reminded

Lear is already learning not to be so quick to judge. Is he regretting his treatment of Cordelia and Kent?

[9] Mongrel

[10] Do you look at me in a disrespectful way?

Oswald	I'll not be struck, my lord.	
Kent	Nor tripp'd neither, you base foot-ball player. *[Tripping up his heels]*	
Lear	I thank thee, fellow; thou serv'st me, and I'll love thee.	80
Kent	Come, sir, arise, away! I'll teach you differences. Away, away! if you will measure your lubber's[11] length again, tarry: but away! go to. Have you wisdom? So. *[Pushes Oswald out]*	
Lear	Now, my friendly knave, I thank thee: there's earnest of thy service. *[Giving Kent money]*	85

11 Clumsy body's

Enter Fool

Fool	Let me hire him too: here's my coxcomb.[12] *[Offering Kent his cap]*	
Lear	How now, my pretty knave! how dost thou?	
Fool	Sirrah, you were best take my coxcomb.	
Kent	Why, Fool?	
Fool	Why, for taking one's part that's out of favour: nay, an thou can'st not smile as the wind sits, thou'lt catch cold shortly. There, take my coxcomb. Why, this fellow has banish'd two on's daughters, and did the third a blessing against his will; if thou follow him, thou must needs wear my coxcomb. – How now, nuncle! Would I had two coxcombs and two daughters!	90 95
Lear	Why, my boy?	
Fool	If I gave them all my living, I'd keep my coxcombs myself. There's mine; beg another of thy daughters.	
Lear	Take heed, sirrah; the whip.	100
Fool	Truth's a dog must to kennel; he must be whipped out, when Lady the brach[13] may stand by the fire and stink.	

12 Jester's hat

Immediately, we can see that the Fool is one of the cleverest and most perceptive characters in the play

13 Dog (Lady must be one of Lear's pet dogs)

Lear A pestilent gall[14] to me!

Fool Sirrah, I'll teach thee a speech.

Lear Do.   105

Fool Mark it, nuncle: –
    Have more than thou showest,
    Speak less than thou knowest,
    Lend less than thou owest,
    Ride more than thou goest,   110
    Learn more than thou trowest,[15]
    Set less than thou throwest;
    Leave thy drink and thy whore,
    And keep in-a-door,
    And thou shalt have more   115
    Than two tens to a score.[16]

Kent This is nothing, Fool.

Fool Then 'tis like the breath of an unfee'd lawyer; you gave me nothing for't. Can you make no use of nothing, nuncle?   120

Lear Why, no, boy; nothing can be made out of nothing.

Fool *[To Kent]* Prithee, tell him, so much the rent of his land comes to: he will not believe a Fool.

Lear A bitter fool!

Fool Dost thou know the difference, my boy, between a bitter 125
fool and a sweet fool?

Lear No, lad; teach me.

Fool *That lord that counsell'd*[17] *thee*
    To give away thy land,
    Come place him here by me,   130
    Do thou for him stand:
    The sweet and bitter fool
    Will presently appear;
    The one in motley[18] *here,*
    The other found out there.   135

[14] *Bitter annoyance*

[15] *Think*

[16] *A score is 20*

[17] *Advised*

[18] *The multicoloured clothing a jester or clown would wear*

Lear   Dost thou call me fool, boy?

Fool   All thy other titles thou hast given away; that thou wast born with.

Kent   This is not altogether fool, my lord.

Fool   No, faith, lords and great men will not let me; if I had a   140
monopoly out, they would have part on't: and ladies too,
they will not let me have all fool to myself; they'll be
snatching. Give me an egg, nuncle, and I'll give thee
two crowns.

The Fool is astutely commenting on society by saying that he does not have the monopoly on foolishness. Many people – Lear, for example – are fools in some ways

Lear   What two crowns shall they be?   145

Fool   Why, after I have cut the egg i' th' middle, and eat up the
meat, the two crowns of the egg. When thou clovest thy
crown i' th' middle, and gavest away both parts, thou
borest thine ass[19] on thy back o'er the dirt. Thou hadst
little wit in thy bald crown, when thou gav'st thy golden   150
one away. If I speak like myself in this, let him be
whipped that first finds it so. *[Singing]*
   Fools had ne'er less wit in a year;
   For wise men are grown foppish,[20]
   And know not how their wits to wear,   155
   Their manners are so apish.[21]

[19] *Donkey*

[20] *Foolish, silly*

[21] *Silly*

Lear   When were you wont[22] to be so full of songs, sirrah?

[22] *Inclined*

Fool   I have used it, nuncle, ever since thou mad'st thy
daughters thy mothers: for when thou gav'st them
the rod, and putest down thine own breeches, *[Singing]*   160
   Then they for sudden joy did weep,
   And I for sorrow sung,
   That such a king should play bo-peep,
   And go the fools among.
Prithee, nuncle, keep a schoolmaster that can teach   165
thy Fool to lie. I would fain[23] learn to lie.

The Fool tends to speak in rich imagery – such as this vivid picture of Lear handing Goneril and Regan a rod and pulling down his own trousers to have his bottom smacked

[23] *Like to*

Lear   An you lie, sirrah, we'll have you whipped.

Fool   I marvel what kin thou and thy daughters are: they'll
have me whipped for speaking true, thou'lt have me
whipped for lying; and sometimes I am whipped for   170

holding my peace. I had rather be any kind o' thing than
a Fool: and yet I would not be thee, nuncle; thou hast
pared thy wit o' both sides, and left nothing i' th'
middle. Here comes one o' the parings.

Enter Goneril

Lear	How now, daughter! what makes that frontlet[24] on?	175
	Methinks you are too much of late i' th' frown.	

[24] *Goneril has a sour expression on her face*

Fool   Thou wast a pretty fellow when thou had'st no need to
care for her frowning; now thou art an O without a
figure:[25] I am better than thou art now; I am a Fool, thou
art nothing. *[To Goneril]* Yes, forsooth, I will hold my   180
tongue; so your face bids me, though you say nothing.
[Singing]
    Mum, mum
    He that keeps nor crust nor crumb,
    Weary of all, shall want some.
[Pointing to Lear] That's a shealed peascod.[26]   185

[25] *He has nothing*

[26] *Pod without peas*

Goneril   Not only, sir, this your all-licens'd Fool,
But other of your insolent[27] retinue
Do hourly carp[28] and quarrel; breaking forth
In rank and not-to-be endured riots. Sir,
I had thought, by making this well known unto you,   190
To have found a safe redress;[29] but now grow fearful,
By what yourself too late have spoke and done,
That you protect this course, and put it on
By your allowance; which if you should, the fault
Would not scape censure,[30] nor the redresses sleep,   195
Which, in the tender of a wholesome weal,[31]
Might in their working do you that offence,
Which else were shame, that then necessity
Will call discreet proceeding.

[27] *Cheeky, rude, disrespectful*

[28] *Argue*

[29] *Remedy*

[30] *Disapproval*

[31] *A red mark left by a slap or a blow*

Fool   For, you trow, nuncle,   200
    'The hedge-sparrow fed the cuckoo so long,
    That it had it head bit off by it young.'
So, out went the candle, and we were left darkling.

The Fool uses simple images every member of the audience could easily understand. The sparrow being eaten by the cuckoo it has fed is a particularly apt image

Lear   Are you our daughter?

Goneril   Come, sir,   205

I would you would make use of that good wisdom,
Whereof I know you are fraught,[32] and put away
These dispositions,[33] that of late transform you
From what you rightly are.

Fool   May not an ass know when the cart draws the horse?   210
'Whoop, Jug! I love thee.'[34]

Lear   Doth any here know me? This is not Lear:
Doth Lear walk thus? speak thus? Where are his eyes?
Either his notion weakens, his discernings[35]
Are lethargied[36] – Ha! waking? 'Tis not so.   215
Who is it that can tell me who I am?

Fool   Lear's shadow.

Lear   I would learn that; for, by the marks of sovereignty,[37]
knowledge, and reason, I should be false persuaded
I had daughters.   220

Fool   Which they will make an obedient father.

Lear   Your name, fair gentlewoman?

Goneril   This admiration, sir, is much o' the savour[38]
Of other your pranks. I do beseech you
To understand my purposes aright: 225
As you are old and reverend, should be wise.
Here do you keep a hundred knights and squires;
Men so disorder'd, so debosh'd[39] and bold,
That this our court, infected with their manners,
Shows like a riotous inn. Epicurism[40] and lust   230
Make it more like a tavern or a brothel
Than a graced palace. The shame itself doth speak
For instant remedy. Be then desired
By her, that else will take the thing she begs,
A little to disquantity[41] your train;   235
And the remainder, that shall still depend,
To be such men as may besort[42] your age,
And know themselves and you.

Lear   Darkness and devils!
Saddle my horses; call my train together: 240
Degenerate[43] bastard! I'll not trouble thee.

32 Filled

Goneril is deviously trying to make Lear feel that he is the one who is at fault

33 Moods

34 The chorus from a song which was popular in Shakespeare's day

35 Judgements

36 Tired

37 Supreme power

38 Is similar to

39 Debauched

40 Pleasure

41 Reduce the number of

42 Fit

An affronted Lear walks straight into Goneril's trap – by losing his temper, and announcing his departure *43 Immoral*

Yet have I left a daughter.

Goneril You strike my people; and your disorder'd rabble[44]
Make servants of their betters.

Enter Albany

Lear Woe, that too late repents, –   245
[To Albany] O, sir, are you come?
Is it your will? Speak, sir. Prepare my horses.
Ingratitude, thou marble-hearted fiend,[45]
More hideous when thou show'st thee in a child
Than the sea-monster!   250

Albany Pray, sir, be patient.

Lear *[To Goneril]* Detested kite![46] thou liest.
My train are men of choice and rarest parts,
That all particulars of duty know,
And in the most exact regard support   255
The worships of their name. O most small fault,
How ugly didst thou in Cordelia show!
Which, like an engine, wrench'd my frame of nature
From the fix'd place; drew from heart all love,
And added to the gall.[47] O Lear, Lear, Lear!   260
Beat at this gate, that let thy folly in, *[Striking his head]*
And thy dear judgement out! Go, go, my people.

Albany My lord, I am guiltless,[48] as I am ignorant
Of what hath moved you.

Lear It may be so, my lord.   265
Hear, Nature, hear; dear Goddess, hear!
Suspend thy purpose, if thou did'st intend
To make this creature fruitful!
Into her womb convey sterility!
Dry up in her the organs of increase,[49]   270
And from her derogate[50] body never spring
A babe to honour her! If she must teem,[51]
Create her child of spleen;[52] that it may live,
And be a thwart disnatur'd torment to her!
Let it stamp wrinkles in her brow of youth;   275
With cadent[53] tears fret channels in her cheeks;
Turn all her mother's pains and benefits

[44] *Mob (the knights)*
[45] *Devil*
[46] *Bird of prey*
[47] *Bitter anger*
[48] *Innocent*
[49] *Her reproductive organs*
[50] *Debased*
[51] *Breed*
[52] *Spite and bad temper*
[53] *Tears from both eyes*

⁵⁴ *Character*

⁵⁵ *Old age*

⁵⁶ *Inevitably*

⁵⁷ *Cry over*

⁵⁸ *Soften*

A good example of dramatic irony: the audience knows that Regan is the same as Goneril, but Lear does not yet know this

⁵⁹ *Scrape*   ⁶⁰ *Face*

⁶¹ *He'll become king again*

	To laughter and contempt; that she may feel	
	How sharper than a serpent's tooth it is	
	To have a thankless child! – Away, away!	280

Exit

Albany   Now, gods that we adore, whereof comes this?

Goneril   Never afflict yourself to know more of it,
But let his disposition⁵⁴ have that scope
That dotage⁵⁵ gives it.

Re-enter Lear

Lear   What, fifty of my followers at a clap!   285
Within a fortnight!

Albany   What's the matter, sir?

Lear   I'll tell thee: *[To Goneril]* Life and death! I am asham'd
That thou hast power to shake my manhood thus
That these hot tears, which break from me perforce,⁵⁶   290
Should make thee worth them. Blasts and fogs upon thee!
Th' untented woundings of a father's curse
Pierce every sense about thee! Old fond eyes,
Beweep⁵⁷ this cause again, I'll pluck ye out,
And cast you, with the waters that you lose,   295
To temper⁵⁸ clay. Yea, it is come to this?
Let it be so: I have another daughter,
Who, I am sure, is kind and comfortable:
When she shall hear this of thee, with her nails
She'll flay⁵⁹ thy wolvish visage. ⁶⁰ Thou shalt find   300
That I'll resume the shape⁶¹ which thou dost think
I have cast off for ever: thou shalt,
I warrant thee.

Exit Lear, Kent, and Attendants

Goneril   Do you mark that, my lord?

Albany   I cannot be so partial, Goneril,   305
To the great love I bear you, –

Goneril   Pray you, content. – What, Oswald, ho!

[To the Fool] You, sir, more knave than fool, after your
master.

Fool Nuncle Lear, nuncle Lear, tarry and take the Fool   310
with thee.

> *A fox, when one has caught her,*
> *And such a daughter,*
> *Should sure to the slaughter,*
> *If my cap would buy a halter:*   315
> *So the Fool follows after.*

Exit

Goneril This man hath had good counsel:[62] – a hundred knights!

’Tis politic[63] and safe to let him keep

At point a hundred knights: yes, that, on every dream,

Each buzz,[64] each fancy, each complaint, dislike,   320

He may enguard his dotage with their powers,

And hold our lives in mercy. Oswald, I say!

Albany Well, you may fear too far.

Goneril Safer than trust too far:

Let me still take away the harms I fear,   325

Not fear still to be taken: I know his heart.

What he hath utter’d I have writ my sister.

If she sustain him and his hundred knights

When I have show’d the unfitness, –

Re-enter Oswald

How now, Oswald!   330

What, have you writ that letter to my sister?

Oswald Yes, madam.

Goneril Take you some company, and away to horse:

Inform her full of my particular fear;

And thereto add such reasons of your own   340

As may compact[65] it more. Get you gone;

And hasten your return.

Exit Oswald
No, no, my lord,

[62] *Advice*

[63] *Sensible*

[64] *Whisper*

**Goneril pretends to Albany
that Lear is going senile and
that she is afraid of him**

[65] *Make more of an impact*

	This milky gentleness and course of yours	
	Though I condemn not, yet, under pardon,	345
[66] Attacked	You are much more attask'd[66] for want of wisdom	
	Than praised for harmful mildness.	
Albany	How far your eyes may pierce I cannot tell:	
	Striving to better, oft we mar what's well.	
Goneril	Nay, then –	350
Albany	Well, well; th' event.	
	Exit	

KENT RETURNS TO Lear's service in disguise, and remains as his loyal, if unappreciated, companion. Meanwhile, Goneril wastes no time putting her plan into action. When one of the knights points out that Lear is not being treated well in her home, she accuses the knights of bad behaviour, saying that they have turned her house into a brothel. Knights of that age were impeccably behaved, and it is obvious to Lear that Goneril is lying. She makes him feel so unwelcome that he curses her viciously and leaves to stay with Regan, whom he is sure will treat him better. This plays right into Goneril's hands.

Lear goes too far when he loses his temper, wishing terrible things upon his daughter. This helps to convince Albany (who seems wholly unaware of his wife's real

Detested kite! thou liest

— LEAR

plans) that there is some justification for Goneril's resentment towards her father.

Goneril sends her servant Oswald to Regan to warn her not to be at home to receive Lear. Lear's reversal of fortune has begun in earnest.

The Fool joins the play and is a source of both comic relief and shrewd wisdom. Interestingly, the Fool only appears after Cordelia has left. Some suggest he is Cordelia in disguise.

Lear is starting to have an inkling that he has made a terrible mistake:

> *O most small fault,*
> *How ugly didst thou in Cordelia show!...*
> *O Lear, Lear, Lear!*
> *Beat at this gate, that let thy folly in,*
> *And thy dear judgement out!*

KEY **POINTS**

- *An emotional Lear leaves Goneril's home in disgust at his mistreatment.*

- *Kent and the Fool become Lear's loyal companions.*

- *Lear starts to realise how imprudent he has been.*

COURT BEFORE THE SAME

Enter Lear, Kent, and Fool

Lear Go you before to Gloucester with these letters.
Acquaint my daughter no further with anything you
know than comes from her demand out of the letter.
If your diligence be not speedy, I shall be there afore you.[1]

Kent I will not sleep, my lord, till I have delivered your letter. 5

Exit

Fool If a man's brains were in's heels, were't not in danger
of kibes?[2]

Lear Ay, boy.

Fool Then, I prithee, be merry; thy wit shall ne'er go slip-shod.[3]

Lear Ha, ha, ha! 10

Fool Shalt see thy other daughter will use thee kindly; for
though she's as like this as a crab's like an apple,[4] yet
I can tell what I can tell.

Lear Why, what canst thou tell, my boy?

Fool She will taste as like this as a crab does to a crab. Thou 15
canst tell why one's nose stands i' the middle on's face?

Lear No.

Fool Why, to keep one's eyes of either side 's nose, that what
a man cannot smell out, he may spy into.

Lear I did her wrong – 20

Fool Canst tell how an oyster makes his shell?

Lear No.

Fool Nor I neither; but I can tell why a snail has a house.

1 If Kent isn't quick enough, Lear will be there before him

2 Chilblains

3 In slippers

4 Crab apple – the Fool has deduced that Goneril and Regan are the same

Lear	Why?
Fool	Why, to put his head in; not to give it away to his daughters and leave his horns without a case.	25
Lear	I will forget my nature. So kind a father! Be my horses ready?
Fool	Thy asses are gone about 'em. The reason why the seven stars are no more than seven is a pretty reason.
Lear	Because they are not eight?	30
Fool	Yes, indeed: thou wouldst make a good fool.
Lear	To take it again perforce! Monster ingratitude!
Fool	If thou wert my fool, nuncle, I'd have thee beaten for being old before thy time.
Lear	How's that?	35
Fool	Thou shouldst not have been old till thou had'st been wise.
Lear	O, let me not be mad, not mad, sweet heaven! Keep me in temper: I would not be mad!

Enter Gentleman

How now! are the horses ready?

Gentleman	Ready, my lord.	40
Lear	Come, boy.
Fool	She that's a maid now, and laughs at my departure, Shall not be a maid long, unless things be cut shorter.

Exit

Using simple, natural imagery, the Fool constantly reminds Lear of the mistake that he has made, saying that a snail would never give away his shell because it would leave him vulnerable. Lear's wealth and status were his 'shell', but he gave them away

Despite his great age, Lear has never learned to be wise. He has never suffered and so has never learned to know himself

Thou shouldst not have been old till thou had'st been wise

– THE FOOL

ACT 1 SCENE V

IN THIS SCENE we see Lear already starting to change and become more independent. He sends Kent ahead with a letter for Gloucester. The significance of this will be revealed later in the play.

The Fool continues to remind Lear of the huge mistake he has made. If Lear cannot face up to the truth of who he is, he will never reach his full potential. The Fool is also a source of comic relief for the audience. This is important in such a heavy-going psychological play. As a visual spectacle, the Fool also serves an important function, dancing and prancing about the stage in his jester's clothing and belled hat (coxcomb).

Although Lear is convinced that he will find a warmer welome at Regan's house, he is also starting to realise his cruelty towards Cordelia: *I did her wrong.*

KEY **POINTS**

- *Lear is slowly evolving into a better version of himself.*

- *The dramatic function of the Fool is to be the voice of truth and reason.*

- *Lear knows he wronged Cordelia.*

FOCUS ON ACT 1

'Cordelia won't play the game. She loves her father too much to insult their relationship by being insincere'

THE FIRST act of *King Lear* is full of drama. The first part of a play is the 'exposition', in which we are introduced to all the characters. As in real life, we form our impressions quickly. With Lear, we are shocked at first by his unconventional approach in dividing up his kingdom. Yet it seems to be working when his two elder daughters articulate their love in poetic and seemingly heartfelt ways. But Cordelia won't play the game. She loves her father too much to insult their relationship by being insincere. It seems strange that Lear did not anticipate this, but it becomes clear to us that Lear lacks any insight into his daughters' personalities.

A king was surrounded by flatterers and yes-men. His every whim was indulged to the extent that he might never have to deal with reality. In a way, a king might never grow up. Lear is certainly childish and immature. He throws a raging tantrum and sulks when things don't go his way, and in doing so he hurts the two people who love him most. He refuses Cordelia a dowry and humiliates her in front of the royal court. Luckily, France is a man of integrity; otherwise Cordelia's fate would have been much worse. Lear also banishes Kent, his trusted friend and adviser. But Kent returns to Lear's service in disguise, a display of loyalty that contrasts sharply with Goneril's treachery.

Goneril wastes no time in putting her and Regan's plan into action. She understands her father's character, and his inclination to lose his temper at the least provocation. So she gives the servants sly orders to neglect him, and then attacks the integrity of his royal knights. Lear's outburst is exactly what she had anticipated: he takes his knights and storms out, saving her the trouble of kicking him out herself. What's more, because of Lear's violent temper, she still appears innocent in the eyes of her husband, Albany.

O, let me not be mad, not mad, sweet heaven!
Keep me in temper: I would not be mad!

– LEAR (ACT I SCENE V)

The Fool, a court jester, quickly emerges as one of the most astute, intelligent and fearless characters in the play. Lear is very fond of the Fool. The fact that he allows the Fool to poke fun at his foibles is a sign that there is more depth to Lear than we might expect after his behaviour in Scene I. Significantly, the Fool and Cordelia are never on stage at the same time. Symbolically, at least, their roles are the same. They both speak the truth regardless of the consequences.

The sub-plot also engages our attention. Gloucester's illegitimate son Edmund has been nursing a grudge against his elder brother Edgar. Edmund is bitter about the fact that, because Edgar is legitimate, he will inherit his father's wealth, while Edmund, being illegitimate, will get nothing. Edgar has in fact done nothing wrong, and is innocent of Edmund's resentment. Yet, to a certain extent, we can understand Edmund's jealously too.

Edmund forges a letter, supposedly in Edgar's hand, saying that they should kill Gloucester so as to get their inheritance early, just as Lear's children did. When he shows it to his father, Gloucester believes this far-fetched plot immediately and threatens to punish Edgar severely.

Edmund then tells Edgar that Gloucester is angry with him and that his very life is in danger. Edgar flees and in Act II will disguise himself as Poor Tom, a beggar. Edmund cannot believe how readily his brother and father have fallen for his plan.

The role of the sub-plot is to echo what happens in the main plot. The sub-plot in *King Lear*, however, is also interesting in and of itself. A lot of this is due to the intriguing character of Edmund.

By the end of Act I, the characters have been initially established, and a sense of suspense has been created.

IMPORTANT THEMES IN ACT I

- The theme of self-knowledge is, conversely, seen in the fact that Lear clearly has none.

- The theme of truth is seen in Cordelia's insistence on speaking the truth no matter what the personal cost to her. It forces us to question our own capacity to tell the truth even if we lose something or someone in the process.

CHARACTER DEVELOPMENT IN ACT I

- At this stage, we are still getting to know the characters, but it is clear that Cordelia and Kent are both exemplary. Lear is rash and heedless, as is Gloucester, albeit to a lesser degree. Edgar is noble yet gullible, while Edmund is a cynical opportunist. Goneril and Regan are giving strong indications of their villainous natures, while Cornwall and Albany are as yet quite inscrutable.

QUESTIONS ON ACT 1

1. If you were a director, how do you think you would stage the love test in a twenty-first-century production? You could refer in your answer to set, costumes, props, soundtrack and movement.

2. Do you think Cordelia should have played the game in order to keep the peace?

3. What was your impression of Lear's character after studying Scene I?

4. Write a diary entry for Kent after Lear has banished him from court, explaining his decision to return to Lear's service in disguise.

5. Why does Burgundy decide he does not want to marry Cordelia? Do you agree with his reasons?

6. What did you think of the final words between the three sisters? What sort of a relationship did it reveal?

7. Imagine King Lear as a novel instead of a play and rewrite Scene II in that style. You could start off: 'Edmund stood by the window, a look of cunning on his handsome face …'

8. Write the text of a dialogue between two of Lear's knights, in which they give their views on Lear and his daughters.

9. What did you think of Albany's and Goneril's relationship? Are they happily married?

10. What is the Fool's dramatic function in the play?

11. Write out the conversation you think France and Cordelia might have had after they left Lear's castle.

12. Pick ten quotations across a range of characters and themes that you think best sum up this act and say, in each case, why you have chosen it.

GLOUCESTER'S CASTLE

Enter Edmund, and Curan meets him

Edmund	Save thee, Curan.
Curan	And you, sir. I have been with your father, and given him notice that the Duke of Cornwall and Regan his duchess will be here with him this night.
Edmund	How comes that? 5
Curan	Nay, I know not. You have heard of the news abroad; I mean the whispered ones, for they are yet but ear-kissing arguments?[1]
Edmund	Not I; pray you, what are they?
Curan	Have you heard of no likely wars toward, 'twixt the 10 Dukes of Cornwall and Albany?
Edmund	Not a word.
Curan	You may do, then, in time. Fare you well, sir.

Exit

Edmund	The Duke be here to-night? The better! best! This weaves itself perforce into my business. 15 My father hath set guard to take my brother; And I have one thing, of a queasy question,[2] Which I must act. Briefness and fortune, work! Brother, a word; descend, Brother, I say!

Enter Edgar

	My father watches: O sir, fly this place; 20 Intelligence is given where you are hid; You have now the good advantage of the night. Have you not spoken 'gainst the Duke of Cornwall? He's coming hither: now, i' th' night, i' th' haste, And Regan with him. Have you nothing said 25 Upon his party 'gainst the Duke of Albany? Advise yourself.

[1] *Gossip and rumours*

Edmund realises that he may be able to take advantage of the unsettled situation and turn it to his own benefit

[2] *Of a difficult nature*

Edgar	I am sure on't, not a word.

| Edmund | I hear my father coming: pardon me,
In cunning I must draw my sword upon you.   30
Draw; seem to defend yourself; now quit you well.
Yield! Come before my father. Light, ho, here! –
Fly, brother. – Torches, torches! – So, farewell. |

Exit Edgar

³ Edmund wounds himself to convince
his father of Edgar's treachery

| | [*Aside*] Some blood drawn on me would beget opinion,³
[*Wounds his arm*]
Of my more fierce endeavour: I have seen drunkards   35
Do more than this in sport. – Father, father! –
Stop, stop! – No help? |

Enter Gloucester, and Servants with torches

Gloucester	Now, Edmund, where's the villain?

Edmund is an incredibly convincing liar, which somewhat explains Gloucester's gullibility

| Edmund | Here stood he in the dark, his sharp sword out,
Mumbling of wicked charms, conjuring the moon   40
To stand auspicious mistress, – |

Gloucester	But where is he?

| Edmund | Look, sir, I bleed. |

| Gloucester | Where is the villain, Edmund? |

| Edmund | Fled this way, sir. When by no means he could –   45 |

| Gloucester | Pursue him, ho! Go after. [*Exit some Servants*]
By no means what? |

⁴ Patricide (to murder one's father)

⁵ Many diverse ways

⁶ Completely

⁷ Defenceless (no armour or weapon)

| Edmund | Persuade me to the murder of your lordship;
But that I told him, the revenging gods
'Gainst parricides⁴ did all their thunders bend;   50
Spoke, with how manifold⁵ and strong a bond
The child was bound to the father; sir, in fine,
Seeing how loathly⁶ opposite I stood
To his unnatural purpose, in fell motion,
With his prepared sword, he charges home   55
My unprovided⁷ body, lanc'd mine arm: |

But when he saw my best alarum'd spirits,
Bold in the quarrel's right, rous'd to the encounter,
Or whether gasted[8] by the noise I made,
Full suddenly he fled.   60

Gloucester Let him fly far:
Not in this land shall he remain uncaught;
And found, – dispatch. The noble Duke my master,
My worthy arch[9] and patron, comes to-night:
By his authority I will proclaim it,   65
That he which finds him shall deserve our thanks,
Bringing the murderous coward to the stake;
He that conceals him, death.

Edmund When I dissuaded[10] him from his intent,
And found him pight[11] to do it, with curst speech   70
I threaten'd to discover him: he replied,
'Thou unpossessing bastard! dost thou think,
If I would stand against thee, would the reposal[12]
Of any trust, virtue, or worth in thee
Make thy words faith'd?[13] No: what I should deny, –   75
As this I would: ay, though thou did'st produce
My very character, – I'd turn it all
To thy suggestion, plot, and damned practice:
And thou must make a dullard[14] of the world,
If they not thought the profits of my death   80
Were very pregnant and potential spurs
To make thee seek it.'

Gloucester Strong and fast'ned villain!
Would he deny his letter? I never got him.
[Tucket[15] within]
Hark, the Duke's trumpets! I know not why he comes.   85
All ports I'll bar; the villain shall not scape;
The Duke must grant me that. Besides, his picture
I will send far and near, that all the kingdom
May have the due note of him; and of my land,
Loyal and natural boy, I'll work the means   90
To make thee capable.

Enter Cornwall, Regan, and Attendants

Cornwall How now, my noble friend! since I came hither,
Which I can call but now, I have heard strange news.

---

[8] Appalled

Edmund paints himself as the innocent victim. He claims that Edgar realised he could not be corrupted and fled

[9] Superior

[10] Discouraged
[11] Determined

[12] Existence

[13] Believed

Edmund continues to make Edgar the villain, cleverly attributing his own characteristics to his brother

[14] Idiot

[15] Trumpets

The use of the word 'natural' is significant here. Edmund's plotting against his father is unnatural Also, Gloucester claims he will change the law to allow Edmund to inherit

Regan	If it be true, all vengeance comes too short Which can pursue th' offender. How dost, my lord?

[16] Broken

Gloucester   O, madam, my old heart is crack'd,[16] it's crack'd!

Regan tries to draw a clear association between Lear and Edgar, i.e. that they are both villains

Regan   What, did my father's godson seek your life?
He whom my father named? your Edgar?

Gloucester   O, lady, lady, shame would have it hid!

Regan   Was he not companion with the riotous knights
That tend upon my father?

Gloucester   I know not, madam: 'tis too bad, too bad.

[17] Group

Edmund   Yes, madam, he was of that consort.[17]

Regan now affects to blame the knights for Edgar's 'plot'

Regan   No marvel, then, though he were ill affected:
'Tis they have put him on the old man's death,
To have the expense and waste of his revenues.
I have this present evening from my sister
Been well inform'd of them; and with such cautions,
That if they come to sojourn[18] at my house,
I'll not be there.

[18] Stay

Cornwall   Nor I, assure thee, Regan.
Edmund, I hear that you have shown your father
A child-like office.[19]

[19] The loyalty you would expect from a child

Edmund   'Twas my duty, sir.

[20] Reveal

Gloucester   He did bewray[20] his practice; and received
This hurt you see, striving to apprehend him.

Cornwall   Is he pursued?

Gloucester   Ay, my good lord.

Cornwall   If he be taken, he shall never more
Be fear'd of doing harm. Make your own purpose,
How in my strength you please. For you, Edmund,
Whose virtue and obedience doth this instant
So much commend itself, you shall be ours.
Natures of such deep trust we shall much need;
You we first seize on.

95 · 100 · 105 · 110 · 115 · 120 · 125

Edmund   I shall serve you, sir,
Truly, however else.

Gloucester   For him I thank your Grace.

Cornwall   You know not why we came to visit you, –

Regan   Thus out of season, threading dark-eyed night: 130
Occasions, noble Gloucester, of some poise,
Wherein we must have use of your advice:
Our father he hath writ, so hath our sister,
Of differences, which I best thought it fit
To answer from our home; the several messengers   135
From hence attend dispatch. Our good old friend,
Lay comforts to your bosom; and bestow
Your needful counsel²¹ to our business,
Which craves the instant use.

Gloucester   I serve you, madam: 140
Your Graces are right welcome.

Exit

Regan is trying to make Gloucester complicit in her scheming

²¹ *Advice*

... if they come to sojourn at my house,
I'll not be there

– REGAN

WE WITNESS THE completion of Edmund's plot against his brother in this scene. He first convinces Edgar that the reason for Cornwall's visit is to confront Edgar for plotting against him. As Cornwall is their superior, Edgar could be held guilty of treason.

Edgar quickly flees. A modern audience might consider him gullible, which perhaps he is, but, to his credit, he also trusts his brother completely. This is one of the cruel ironies of Edmund's behaviour: he is hurting a person who loves him enough to believe everything he says.

Gloucester reacts to Edgar's deceitfulness with what can only be called zero tolerance. Edgar, if found, is to be put to death immediately. Like Lear, Gloucester is impulsive and impetuous, but unlike Lear, there is at least some justification (Edmund's lies) for his fury.

Regan and Cornwall's arrival allows us to get to know Regan better. She is clearly just as cunning as her sister and even claims that Edgar was probably led astray by Lear's knights, which is a complete fabrication. In this scene, all, aside from Gloucester, are serving their own agendas, no one more so than Edmund.

KEY **POINTS**

- *Edmund betrays Edgar and turns Gloucester against his own son.*

- *Regan is perhaps even more treacherous than her sister.*

BEFORE GLOUCESTER'S CASTLE

Enter Kent and Oswald, severally

Oswald	Good dawning to thee, friend: art of this house?
Kent	Ay.
Oswald	Where may we set our horses?
Kent	I' the mire.[1]
Oswald	Prithee,[2] if thou lov'st me, tell me.
Kent	I love thee not.
Oswald	Why, then, I care not for thee.
Kent	If I had thee in Lipsbury pinfold,[3] I would make thee care for me.
Oswald	Why dost thou use me thus? I know thee not.
Kent	Fellow, I know thee.
Oswald	What dost thou know me for?
Kent	A knave; a rascal; an eater of broken meats;[4] a base, proud, shallow, beggarly, three-suited,[5] hundred-pound,[6] filthy, worsted-stocking[7] knave; a lily-livered,[8] action-taking, whoreson, glass-gazing,[9] super-serviceable[10] finical[11] rogue; one-trunk-inheriting[12] slave; one that would'st be a bawd,[13] in way of good service, and art nothing but the composition of a knave, beggar, coward, pandar, and the son and heir of a mongrel bitch; one whom I will beat into clamorous whining, if thou deni'st the least syllable of thy addition.
Oswald	Why, what a monstrous fellow art thou, thus to rail on one that is neither known of thee nor knows thee!
Kent	What a brazen-fac'd varlet art thou, to deny thou knowest me! Is it two days ago since I tripp'd up thy heels, and beat thee before the King? Draw, you rogue:

5

10

15

20

25

1 *Swamp*

2 *Please*

3 *This was a pound for stray dogs; it can also mean pinned between teeth*

4 *Scraps*
5 *Servants were only allowed three suits*
6 *Skinny – an insult in Shakespeare's day*
7 *His stockings are sagging*
8 *Cowardly*
9 *Vain – always looking in the mirror*
10 *Too eager to serve others for his own gain*
11 *Vain*
12 *All his belongings would fit into one trunk*
13 *Pimp*

Kent is calling Oswald every insult under the sun. This demonstrates his loyalty to Lear, but also provides comic relief. The audience would really have enjoyed seeing Oswald abused in this way

for, though it be night, yet the moon shines; I'll make a
sop o' the moonshine[14] of you: *[Drawing his sword]*
draw, you whoreson cullionly[15] barber-monger![16] Draw! 30

Oswald   Away! I have nothing to do with thee.

Kent   Draw, you rascal! You come with letters against the King;
and take Vanity the puppet's part against the royalty of
her father: draw, you rogue, or I'll so carbonado[17] your
shanks, – draw, you rascal! Come your ways! 35

Oswald   Help, ho! murder! help!

Kent   Strike, you slave; stand, rogue, stand; you neat slave,
strike.

Beating him

Oswald   Help, ho! murder! murder!

*Enter Edmund, with his rapier[18] drawn, Cornwall, Regan,
Gloucester, and Servants*

Edmund   How now! What's the matter? 40

Kent   With you, goodman boy, an you please: come, I'll flesh
ye;[19] come on, young master.

Gloucester   Weapons! arms! What 's the matter here?

Cornwall   Keep peace, upon your lives!
He dies that strikes again. What is the matter? 45

Regan   The messengers from our sister and the King.

Cornwall   What is your difference? speak.

Oswald   I am scarce in breath, my lord.

Kent   No marvel, you have so bestirr'd your valour. You
cowardly rascal, Nature disclaims in thee: a tailor 50
made thee.

Cornwall   Thou art a strange fellow. A tailor make a man?

[14]He'll make mincemeat of him
*[15]Base, vile [16]Always at the hairdresser
– so his hair is always perfect*

[17]Chop up

[18]Sword

[19]I'll teach you to fight

Kent   Ay, a tailor, sir. A stone-cutter or painter could not have
                  made him so ill, though he had been but two hours at
                  the trade.   55

Cornwall   Speak yet, how grew your quarrel?

Oswald   This ancient ruffian, sir, whose life I have spared
                  at suit of his gray beard, –

Kent   Thou whoreson zed! thou unnecessary letter! My lord, if
                  you will give me leave, I will tread this unbolted villain   60
                  into mortar, and daub[20] the wall of a jakes[21] with him.
                  Spare my gray beard, you wagtail?[22]

[20] Paint [21] 'Jacks', i.e. an outhouse
[22] Rude person

Cornwall   Peace, sirrah!
                  You beastly knave, know you no reverence?

Kent   Yes, sir; but anger hath a privilege.   65

Cornwall   Why art thou angry?

Kent   That such a slave as this should wear a sword,
                  Who wears no honesty. Such smiling rogues as these,
                  Like rats, oft bite the holy cords[23] a-twain
                  Which are too intrinse[24] t' unloose; smooth every passion 70
                  That in the natures of their lords rebel;
                  Bring oil to fire, snow to their colder moods;
                  Renege, affirm, and turn their halcyon beaks
                  With every gale and vary of their masters,
                  Knowing nought, like dogs, but following.   75
                  A plague upon your epileptic visage!
                  Smile you my speeches, as I were a fool?
                  Goose, if I had you upon Sarum[25] plain,
                  I'd drive ye cackling home to Camelot.

[23] Bonds

[24] Tight

*Kent says he hates servants who follow
their master's every whim and are like
lapdogs without any personality or
spirit of their own. Clearly he despises
Oswald for neglecting Lear even though
he knew it was wrong. So Kent, and
Shakespeare, are saying that everyone
has to do the right thing, regardless of
their position in life*

[25] Salisbury

Cornwall   Why, art thou mad, old fellow?   80

Gloucester   How fell you out? Say that.

Kent   No contraries[26] hold more antipathy[27]
                  Than I and such a knave.

[26] Opposites [27] Hatred, ill-feeling

Cornwall   Why dost thou call him a knave? What's his offence?

| Kent | His countenance likes me not. | 85 |

| Cornwall | No more, perchance, does mine, nor his, nor hers. | |

Kent	Sir, 'tis my occupation to be plain:	
	I have seen better faces in my time	
	Than stands on any shoulder that I see	
	Before me at this instant.	90

28 Goes too far

Cornwall	This is some fellow,	
	Who, having been praised for bluntness, doth affect	
	A saucy roughness, and constrains the garb[28]	
	Quite from his nature. He cannot flatter, he,	
	An honest mind and plain, he must speak truth!	95
	An they will take it, so; if not, he's plain.	
	These kind of knaves I know, which in this plainness	
	Harbour more craft and more corrupter ends	
	Than twenty silly ducking observants[29]	
	That stretch their duties nicely.	100

29 Bowing obsequiously

Kent mocks Cornwall by mimicking Oswald's obsequious manner

30 Truth

Kent	Sir, in good sooth, in sincere verity,[30]	
	Under the allowance of your great aspect,	
	Whose influence, like the wreath of radiant fire	
	On flickering Phoebus'[31] front, –	

31 God of the sun

| Cornwall | What mean'st by this? | 105 |

32 Dislike

Kent	To go out of my dialect, which you discommend[32] so	
	much. I know, sir, I am no flatterer: he that beguiled	
	you in a plain accent was a plain knave; which for my	
	part I will not be, though I should win your displeasure	
	to entreat me to 't.	110

| Cornwall | What was the offence you gave him? | |

Oswald	I never gave him any:	
	It pleased the King his master very late	
	To strike at me, upon his misconstruction;	
	When he, compact, and flattering his displeasure,	115
	Tripp'd me behind; being down, insulted, rail'd,	
	And put upon him such a deal of man,	
	That 't worthied him, got praises of the King	
	For him attempting who was self-subdued;[33]	

33 Didn't put up a fight

34 Bloodthirstiness

| | And, in the fleshment[34] of this dread exploit, | 120 |

Kent	Drew on me here again.

Kent
None of these rogues and cowards
But Ajax[35] is their fool.

Cornwall
Fetch forth the stocks![36]
You stubborn ancient knave, you reverend braggart,[37]   125
We'll teach you –

Kent
Sir, I am too old to learn:
Call not your stocks for me: I serve the King,
On whose employment I was sent to you.
You shall do small respect, show too bold malice   130
Against the grace and person of my master,
Stocking his messenger.

Cornwall
Fetch forth the stocks! As I have life and honour,
There shall he sit till noon.

Regan
Till noon! Till night, my lord; and all night too.   135

Kent
Why, madam, if I were your father's dog,
You should not use me so.

Regan
Sir, being his knave, I will.

Cornwall
This is a fellow of the self-same colour
Our sister speaks of. Come, bring away the stocks!   140

Stocks brought out

Gloucester
Let me beseech your Grace not to do so:
His fault is much, and the good King his master
Will check him for 't: your purpos'd low correction
Is such as basest and contemned'st[38] wretches
For pilferings[39] and most common trespasses   145
Are punish'd with. The King must take it ill,
That he's so slightly valued in his messenger,
Should have him thus restrain'd.

Cornwall
I'll answer that.

Regan
My sister may receive it much more worse,   150
To have her gentleman abus'd, assaulted,

---

[35] Oswald brags even more than the Greek hero Ajax, who was famous for his boasting

[36] Instrument of humiliation and punishment where wooden structures were used to secure a person's hands and feet. They were then exposed to public ridicule or assault. See image on page 68

[37] Boaster

Kent points out that putting him in the stocks would be a grave insult to King Lear because this punishment was normally reserved for common criminals, and is highly inappropriate for a servant of a former king

[38] Most despised

[39] Petty theft

Gloucester attempts to stand up for Lear and Kent by pointing out that the stocks are not a fit punishment for a servant of the king

Regan shows where her loyalties lie

For following her affairs. Put in his legs.

Kent is put in the stocks

Come, my good lord, away.

Exit all but Gloucester and Kent

Gloucester doesn't think much of Cornwall, who seems to be a bully

Gloucester   I am sorry for thee, friend; 'tis the Duke's pleasure,
Whose disposition, all the world well knows,   155
Will not be rubb'd nor stopp'd: I'll entreat for thee.

Kent   Pray, do not, sir: I have watch'd and travell'd hard;
Some time I shall sleep out, the rest I'll whistle.
A good man's fortune may grow out at heels.
Give you good morrow!   160

Gloucester   The Duke's to blame in this; 'twill be ill taken.

Exit

40 Blessing

Kent   Good King, that must approve the common saw,
Thou out of heaven's benediction[40] com'st
To the warm sun!
Approach, thou beacon to this under globe,   165
That by thy comfortable beams I may
Peruse this letter! Nothing almost sees miracles
But misery: I know 'tis from Cordelia,
Who hath most fortunately been inform'd

41 Disguised

A note of hope is provided by the fact that Cordelia is still in contact. No matter how bad things get, there is someone on Lear's side

Of my obscured[41] course; '– and shall find time   170
From this enormous state – seeking to give
Losses their remedies.' – All weary and o'erwatch'd,
Take vantage, heavy eyes, not to behold
This shameful lodging.
Fortune, good night: smile once more: turn thy wheel!   175

Sleeps

MODERN ENGLISH VERSION

IN FRONT OF GLOUCESTER'S CASTLE

Enter Kent and Oswald, separately

Oswald   Hello, do you work here?

Kent   Yeah.

Oswald   Where will we leave our horses?

Kent   In the swamp!

Oswald   No, seriously, where do we put them?

Kent   I'm not helping you. I can't stand you!

Oswald   Well then, I don't like you either!

Kent   I have my reasons … we've already met.

Oswald   When?

Kent   That doesn't matter, but I know you are a creep, a brown-noser, you only eat scraps, and you're proud, arrogant, fake and untrustworthy. You only have three sets of clothes! All your belongings would fit in one suitcase. You'd do anything your boss asked you to, but you're weak, and you're always looking to get ahead, no matter what the cost. I can't stand people like you. Don't even deny it. Try, and I'll beat the crap out of you.

Oswald   How dare you call me those names! You don't even know me!

Kent   Are you stupid or what? It wasn't even two days ago that I tripped you up and you fell on the floor. Have you forgotten already? How dare you treat the king the way you did? I am going to kill you!

Oswald   Stay away from me. I don't know what you're talking about.

Kent   Take out your sword. Fight me, you coward, and stop pretending to be innocent. We both know you have letters from Goneril which detail how she intends to hurt Lear. Well, I'll slice you to pieces before I let that happen.

Oswald   Help me! Someone's trying to kill me!

Kent	Not trying!
Oswald	Help! Help!
	Enter Edmund, with his sword drawn, Cornwall, Regan, Gloucester, and Servants
Edmund	What the hell is going on here?
Kent	None of your business, boy. Come any closer and I'll show you my fists.
Gloucester	What's the matter?
Cornwall	I'll kill the next person who throws a punch. What on earth are you arguing over?
Oswald	We … I … can't talk … out of breath!
Kent	Surprise, surprise. You're pathetic.
Cornwall	I want to know what's going on.
Oswald	This old fogey, whom I could easily have beaten except I didn't want to kill an elderly man …
Kent	The cheek of you! I'm going to rip you to shreds, mash you into a paste and smear the walls of the toilet with you.
Cornwall	Take it easy, man!
Kent	I'm too angry to speak anything other than angry words.
Cornwall	Why are you so angry?
Kent	I can't stand men like him. They're weak and they follow their masters blindly. I can't respect someone who follows orders they know to be cruel and wrong. Nothing angers me more than a spineless, toadying, flattering, grovelling idiot like Oswald.
Cornwall	Are you mad?
Gloucester	Tell us how you first fell out with one another.
Kent	I just hate him and people like him. And I'm the kind of person who says exactly what he thinks, unlike Oswald.
Cornwall	Oh, you're one of those people who pride themselves on being

honest when really they are just rude. Well, I'd much prefer a servant who did what he was told than an uncouth, rough, insulting man like you.

Kent	You're so wonderful, you're like a Greek god. I respect you so much … Ha!
Cornwall	What do you mean?
Kent	Oh, I thought that was what you wanted, for me to grovel at your feet like your smarmy servant.
Cornwall	What did you do to upset him, Oswald?
Oswald	I never did anything to him, but he beat me up and the king not only allowed him, he encouraged him.
Kent	That is total rubbish!
Cornwall	Get the stocks, and let's teach this dope a lesson.
Kent	I'm too old to learn anything and, what's more, I'm the king's messenger. If you put me in the stocks you're insulting him, and that is just not on.
Cornwall	Get the stocks! He can stay in them until noon.
Regan	Until noon? No, he can stay until midnight. Actually, he can stay there until noon tomorrow!
Kent	What? You wouldn't treat a dog belonging to your father as badly as that.
Regan	You're worth less than a dog!
Cornwall	He seems to be as bad as the knights Goneril told us about.
Gloucester	I have to intervene and ask you not to do this. He is the king's servant. Let the king deal with him. And besides, the stocks are for petty criminals. It's really not an appropriate punishment in this circumstance. I think it'll really upset the king.
Cornwall	I'll deal with the king.
Regan	What about Goneril? Imagine how upset she'll be when she hears how her servant has been treated.

Kent is put in the stocks

Come on, love, let's go.

Exit all but Gloucester and Kent

Gloucester   I'm really sorry about this, friend. Cornwall is a bully, but I'll try and sort it out.

Kent   Not at all. I'm tired after all the travel, so I'll just have a bit of a sleep. Don't worry about me. Thanks for your concern.

Gloucester   This is all Cornwall's fault.

Exit

Kent   Blessings on my king. I hope he is all right. I hope the sun comes up soon so I can read this letter. It's from Cordelia. She knows what has happened so far, and I know she'll do all she can to help me. Now I'll try to get some sleep. I'll just have to ignore this shameful 'bed'!

Sleeps

A WOOD

Enter Edgar

Edgar   I heard myself proclaim'd;[1]
And by the happy hollow of a tree
Escap'd the hunt. No port is free; no place,
That guard, and most unusual vigilance,
Does not attend my taking. Whiles I may scape,   5
I will preserve myself, and am bethought
To take the basest and most poorest shape
That ever penury, in contempt of man,
Brought near to beast. My face I'll grime with filth,
Blanket my loins, elf[2] all my hair in knots,   10
And with presented nakedness out-face
The winds and persecutions of the sky.
The country gives me proof and precedent
Of Bedlam beggars, who, with roaring voices,
Strike in their numb'd and mortified arms   15
Pins, wooden pricks, nails, sprigs of rosemary;
And with this horrible object, from low farms,
Poor pelting villages, sheep-cotes,[3] and mills,
Sometime with lunatic bans, sometime with prayers,
Enforce their charity. Poor Turlygod! poor Tom!   20
That's something yet: Edgar I nothing am.

Exit

[1] Outlawed

Edgar knows his life is in danger. He hid inside a hollow tree to evade his hunters. To protect himself, he has adopted an extreme disguise and has become Tom of Bedlam. Bedlam refers to Bethlem Royal Hospital, which was a notorious lunatic asylum in Shakespeare's day. Edgar wears only a loincloth, his hair is matted, and his face is filthy. He has scratched his body all over. No one would ever think such a pathetic-looking creature is really the son of the Earl of Gloucester. So Edgar's disguise, extreme as it seems, will keep him safe, as people tended to keep their distance from 'madmen'

[2] Tangle

[3] Sheep-folds

I heard myself proclaim'd;
And by the happy hollow of a tree
Escap'd the hunt

– EDGAR

THIS IS A very short scene with just one character, Edgar. He has, in fear for his life, disguised himself just as Kent did. It may seem strange to a modern audience that the mere act of changing your hair and clothes could be a successful disguise but, in Shakespeare's day, clothing was very expensive. Kent mocked Oswald for owning only three suits, which was actually quite good for the time. Wealthy people dressed in extravagant costumes, and were perfectly groomed, with elaborate hairstyles. For Edgar, an aristocrat's son, to be dressed only in a loincloth, his body covered in mud, bruises and scrapes, and his hair a tangled mass, would have been inconceivable. Also, Edgar is pretending to be a lunatic from Bedlam asylum (think of how we now use the word 'bedlam' to describe chaos), and people kept as much distance as possible from such a person.

We also learn of how the vulnerable were treated at this time. There are many instances in the play where Shakespeare seems to be making social comments, and this is certainly one of them.

Though there was a great fear of madness in Shakespeare's day, there was often a certain fascination with it too, and having Edgar speak as a madman would have been another source of entertainment for the audience.

The madness in this scene is feigned but still distressing. Soon we will see real madness and how much a person suffers when they are truly mad, and this time it will be Lear himself.

KEY **POINT**

- *Edgar disguises himself as Poor Tom, a madman from Bedlam.*

BEFORE GLOUCESTER'S CASTLE. KENT IN THE STOCKS

Enter Lear, Fool, and Gentleman

Lear 'Tis strange that they should so depart from home,
And not send back my messenger.

Gentleman As I learn'd,
The night before there was no purpose in them
Of this remove.   5

Kent Hail to thee, noble master!

Lear Ha!
Mak'st thou this shame thy pastime?

Kent No, my lord.

Fool Ha, ha! he wears cruel garters.[1] Horses are tied by the   10
heads, dogs and bears by th' neck, monkeys by th' loins,
and men by th' legs: when a man's over-lusty at legs,
then he wears wooden nether-stocks.[2]

Lear What's he that hath so much thy place mistook
To set thee here?   15

Kent It is both he and she;
Your son and daughter.

Lear No.

Kent Yes.

Lear No, I say.   20

Kent I say, yea.

Lear No, no, they would not.

Kent Yes, they have.

Lear By Jupiter,[3] I swear, no.

Kent By Juno,[4] I swear, ay.   25

[1] *A band worn around the thigh to keep the stocking up*

[2] *Knitted stockings*

[3] *The Roman god of gods*

[4] *Jupiter's wife*

Lear is horrified at the disrespect
Cornwall and Regan have shown
his servant. He must also have an
inkling that things are going to
go badly with Regan

Lear   They durst not do't;
They could not, would not do't; 'tis worse than murder,
To do upon respect such violent outrage.
Resolve me, with all modest haste, which way
Thou mightst deserve, or they impose, this usage,   30
Coming from us.

Kent   My lord, when at their home
I did commend your Highness' letters to them,
Ere I was risen from the place that show'd
My duty kneeling, came there a reeking post,   35
Stew'd[5] in his haste, half breathless, panting forth
From Goneril his mistress salutations;
Deliver'd letters, spite of intermission,
Which presently they read: on whose contents,
They summon'd up their meiny,[6] straight took horse;   40
Commanded me to follow, and attend
The leisure of their answer; gave me cold looks:
And meeting here the other messenger,
Whose welcome, I perceiv'd, had poison'd mine, –
Being the very fellow that of late   45
Display'd so saucily[7] against your Highness, –
Having more man than wit about me, drew.
He raised the house with loud and coward cries.
Your son and daughter found this trespass worth
The shame which here it suffers.   50

⁵ Sweating

⁶ Servants

⁷ Cheekily

Fool   Winter's not gone yet, if the wild-geese fly that way.
> *Fathers that wear rags*
> *Do make their children blind;*
> *But fathers that bear bags*
> *Shall see their children kind.*   55
> *Fortune, that arrant[8] whore,*
> *Ne'er turns the key to th' poor.*
But, for all this, thou shalt have as many dolours
for thy daughters as thou canst tell in a year.

A cynical view of family. The
Fool says that children love rich
parents, but ignore poor ones

⁸ Complete

Lear   O, how this mother swells up toward my heart!   60
Hysterica passio?[9] down, thou climbing sorrow,
Thy element's below! – Where is this daughter?

*⁹ A hysterical ailment – like
a panic attack*

Kent   With the Earl, sir, here within.

Lear   Follow me not;

Stay here.   65

Exit

Gentleman   Made you no more offence but what you speak of?

Kent   None.
How chance the King comes with so small a train?

Fool   An thou hadst been set i' th' stocks for that question,
thou hadst well deserved it.   70

Kent   Why, Fool?

Fool   We'll set thee to school to an ant, to teach thee there's
no labouring i' th' winter. All that follow their noses are
led by their eyes but blind men; and there's not a nose
among twenty but can smell him that's stinking. Let go   75
thy hold when a great wheel runs down a hill, lest it break
thy neck with following it; but the great one that goes up
the hill, let him draw thee after. When a wise man gives
thee better counsel, give me mine again; I would have
none but knaves follow it, since a fool gives it. *[Singing]*   80
   That sir which serves and seeks for gain,
   And follows but for form,
   Will pack when it begins to rain,
   And leave thee in the storm,
   But I will tarry; the Fool will stay,   85
   And let the wise man fly.
   The knave turns fool that runs away;
   The Fool no knave, perdy.[10]

Kent   Where learned you this, Fool?

Fool   Not i' th' stocks, fool.   90

Re-enter Lear with Gloucester

Lear   Deny to speak with me? They are sick? They are weary?
They have travell'd all the night? Mere fetches;[11]
The images of revolt and flying off.[12]
Fetch me a better answer.

Gloucester   My dear lord,   95

The Fool's words describe a situation that is going to spiral out of control. Events are gaining momentum. The 'wheel' is a reference to the wheel of fortune, which belongs to the goddess Fortuna, and every time she spins it, your position changes. You can be at the top one moment, enjoying good fortune, but another spin might put you at the bottom, where your fortune will be bad. The wheel of fortune symbolises the randomness of fate

Fair-weather friends (or daughters) are no kind of friend

[10] *Short for 'par Dieu', which means 'by God'*

[11] *Excuses*
[12] *Rebellion*

Cornwall is depicted as a tyrant

You know the fiery quality of the Duke;
How unremovable and fix'd he is
In his own course.

Lear   Vengeance! plague! death! confusion!
Fiery? What quality? Why, Gloucester, Gloucester, 100
I'd speak with the Duke of Cornwall and his wife.

Gloucester   Well, my good lord, I have inform'd them so.

Lear   Inform'd them! Dost thou understand me, man?

Gloucester   Ay, my good lord.

This speech is significant because it shows Lear is changing. He is learning from his mistakes. He starts to get angry and makes threats, but then makes excuses for Cornwall, saying he might be ill

Lear   The King would speak with Cornwall; the dear father 105
Would with his daughter speak, commands her service.
Are they inform'd of this? My breath and blood!
Fiery? the fiery Duke? Tell the hot Duke that –
No, but not yet: may be he is not well.
Infirmity doth still neglect all office 110
Whereto our health is bound; we are not ourselves
When nature, being oppress'd,[13] commands the mind
To suffer with the body: I'll forbear;[14]
And am fall'n out with my more headier will,
To take the indispos'd[15] and sickly fit 115
For the sound man. – Death on my state! Wherefore
[Looking on Kent] Should he sit here? This act persuades me
That this remotion[16] of the Duke and her
Is practice only. Give me my servant forth.
Go tell the Duke and his wife I'd speak with them, 120
Now, presently. Bid them come forth and hear me,
Or at their chamber-door I'll beat the drum
Till it cry sleep to death.[17]

13 Sick

14 Be patient

15 Unwell

16 Departure

17 Until it wakes them up

Gloucester   I would have all well betwixt you.

Exit

Lear   O me, my heart, my rising heart! But, down! 125

Eel pie was a speciality in these times. Live eels were covered with pastry, and the cook had to keep banging them on the head to stop them bursting out before they were put in the oven

Fool   Cry to it, nuncle, as the cockney did to the eels when
she put 'em i' th' paste alive; she knapped 'em o' th'
coxcombs with a stick, and cried 'Down, wantons,

down!' 'Twas her brother that, in pure kindness to his
horse, buttered his hay.   130

Enter Cornwall, Regan, Gloucester, and Servants

Lear   Good morrow to you both.

Cornwall Hail to your Grace!

Kent is set at liberty

Regan   I am glad to see your Highness.

Lear   Regan, I think you are; I know what reason
I have to think so: if thou shouldst not be glad,   135
I would divorce me from thy mother's tomb,
Sepulchring an adultress.[18] *[To Kent]* O, are you free?
Some other time for that. Beloved Regan,
Thy sister's naught. O Regan, she hath tied
Sharp-tooth'd unkindness, like a vulture,[19] here: 140
[Points to his heart] I can scarce speak to thee;
        thou'lt not believe
With how depraved a quality – O Regan!

Regan   I pray you, sir, take patience: I have hope
You less know how to value her desert
Than she to scant her duty.   145

Lear   Say, how is that?

Regan   I cannot think my sister in the least
Would fail her obligation. If, sir, perchance
She have restrain'd the riots of your followers,
'Tis on such ground, and to such wholesome end,   150
As clears her from all blame.

Lear   My curses on her!

Regan   O, sir, you are old.
Nature in you stands on the very verge
Of her confine: you should be rul'd and led
By some discretion, that discerns your state   155
Better than you yourself. Therefore, I pray you,
That to our sister you do make return;

[18] *If Regan were not glad to see Lear, it could only mean that her mother was an adulteress, i.e. that Regan is not his real daughter*

[19] *Bird of prey*

Regan is basically telling Lear that he is too old to make a fit judgement. She also tells him to return to Goneril and apologise. Like her sister, she is deliberately antagonising Lear. This way, he'll leave of his own accord

Say you have wrong'd her, sir.

Lear Ask her forgiveness? 160
Do you but mark how this becomes the house:
'Dear daughter, I confess that I am old; *[Kneeling]*
Age is unnecessary: on my knees I beg

[20] *It is not a crime to be old* That you'll vouchsafe me raiment, bed, and food.'[20]

Regan Good sir, no more; these are unsightly tricks: 165
Return you to my sister.

Lear *[Rising]* Never, Regan:

[21] *Deprived* She hath abated[21] me of half my train;
Look'd black upon me; struck me with her tongue,
Most serpent-like, upon the very heart: 170

[22] *Punishment* All the stored vengeances[22] of heaven fall
On her ingrateful top! Strike her young bones,

[23] *Infections* You taking airs,[23] with lameness!

Cornwall Fie, sir, fie!

Lear You nimble lightnings, dart your blinding flames 175
Into her scornful eyes! Infect her beauty,

[24] *Marsh fogs* You fen-suck'd[24] fogs, drawn by the powerful sun,
To fall and blast her pride!

Regan O the blest gods! so will you wish on me,
When the rash mood is on. 180

Lear No, Regan, thou shalt never have my curse:
Thy tender-hefted nature shall not give
Thee o'er to harshness: her eyes are fierce; but thine
Do comfort and not burn. 'Tis not in thee
To grudge my pleasures, to cut off my train, 185

[25] *Reduce* To bandy hasty words, to scant[25] my sizes,
And in conclusion to oppose the bolt
Against my coming in. Thou better know'st

[26] *Duties* The offices[26] of nature, bond of childhood,
Effects of courtesy, dues of gratitude; 190
Thy half o' th' kingdom hast thou not forgot,
Wherein I thee endow'd.

Regan Good sir, to th' purpose.

Thy half o' th' kingdom hast thou not forgot,
Wherein I thee endow'd

— LEAR

Lear	Who put my man i' th' stocks?	
	Tucket within	
Cornwall	What trumpet's that?	195
Regan	I know't, my sister's: this approves her letter, That she would soon be here. *Enter Oswald*	
	Is your lady come?	
Lear	This is a slave, whose easy-borrow'd pride Dwells in the fickle grace[27] of her he follows. Out, varlet,[28] from my sight!	200
Cornwall	What means your Grace?	
Lear	Who stock'd my servant? Regan, I have good hope Thou didst not know on't. Who comes here? O heavens,	205
	Enter Goneril	
	If you do love old men, if your sweet sway[29] Allow obedience, if yourselves are old, Make it your cause; send down, and take my part! *[To Goneril]* Art not ashamed to look upon this beard?[30] O Regan, wilt thou take her by the hand?	210
Goneril	Why not by th' hand, sir? How have I offended? All's not offence that indiscretion finds And dotage[31] terms so.	
Lear	O sides, you are too tough; Will you yet hold? How came my man i' th' stocks?	215
Cornwall	I set him there, sir; but his own disorders Deserv'd much less advancement.	
Lear	You! did you?	
Regan	I pray you, father, being weak, seem so. If, till the expiration of your month,	220

[27] *Goneril's loyalty is not to be trusted*

[28] *Rascal*

[29] *Power*

[30] *A beard was a symbol of age and wisdom*

[31] *Old age*

	You will return and sojourn[32] with my sister,	
	Dismissing half your train, come then to me:	
	I am now from home, and out of that provision	
	Which shall be needful for your entertainment.	

³² *Stay* → [32] *Stay*

Lear   Return to her, and fifty men dismiss'd?   225
No, rather I abjure[33] all roofs, and choose
To wage against the enmity[34] o' th' air;
To be a comrade with the wolf and owl, –
Necessity's sharp pinch! Return with her?
Why, the hot-blooded France, that dowerless took   230
Our youngest born, I could as well be brought
To knee his throne, and, squire-like, pension beg
To keep base life afoot. Return with her?
Persuade me rather to be slave and sumpter[35]
To this detested groom. *[Pointing at Oswald]*   235

[33] *Reject*
[34] *Hostilities*

Lear says he would choose to live outdoors, rather than with Goneril. Little does he know how prophetic his words are

[35] *Pack-horse*

Goneril   At your choice, sir.

Lear   I prithee, daughter, do not make me mad:
I will not trouble thee, my child; farewell!
We'll no more meet, no more see one another:
But yet thou art my flesh, my blood, my daughter;   240
Or rather a disease that's in my flesh,
Which I must needs call mine; thou art a boil,
A plague-sore, an embossed carbuncle,[36]
In my corrupted blood. But I'll not chide[37] thee;
Let shame come when it will, I do not call it.   245
I do not bid the thunder-bearer shoot,
Nor tell tales of thee to high-judging Jove:[38]
Mend when thou canst; be better at thy leisure:
I can be patient; I can stay with Regan,
I and my hundred knights.   250

[36] *An infected cluster of boils*
[37] *Chastise*

[38] *The god Jupiter*

Regan   Not altogether so:
I look'd not for you yet, nor am provided
For your fit welcome. Give ear, sir, to my sister;
For those that mingle reason with your passion[39]
Must be content to think you old, and so –   255
But she knows what she does.

[39] *Those who try to reason with Lear*

Lear   Is this well spoken?

Regan   I dare avouch it, sir: what, fifty followers?

ACT 2 SCENE IV

Is it not well? What should you need of more?
Yea, or so many, sith that both charge and danger   260
Speak 'gainst so great a number? How, in one house,
Should many people, under two commands,
Hold amity? [40] 'Tis hard; almost impossible.

[40] Get along

Goneril and Regan are baiting their father. It is uncomfortable and distressing to witness their manipulation

Goneril
Why might not you, my lord, receive attendance
From those that she calls servants or from mine?   265

Regan
Why not, my lord? If then they chanc'd to slack you,
We could control them. If you will come to me, –
For now I spy a danger, – I entreat you
To bring but five and twenty: to no more
Will I give place or notice.   270

Lear didn't, in fact, need to give them anything. He could have let them wait until his death

Lear
I gave you all –

Regan
And in good time you gave it.

Lear
Made you my guardians, my depositaries;
But kept a reservation to be follow'd
With such a number. What, must I come to you   275
With five and twenty, Regan? Said you so?

Regan
And speak 't again, my lord; no more with me.

[41] Beautiful

Lear
Those wicked creatures yet do look well-favour'd, [41]
When others are more wicked: not being the worst
Stands in some rank of praise. *[To Goneril]*   280
I'll go with thee:
Thy fifty yet doth double five and twenty,
And thou art twice her love.

Goneril
Hear me, my lord:
What need you five and twenty, ten, or five,   285
To follow in a house where twice so many
Have a command to tend you?

Regan
What need one?

Lear points out that even a poor beggar has things he does not really need. He wanted the knights because he wanted to retain some of his previous status as king. He points out that Goneril's and Regan's beautiful clothes do not even keep them warm

Lear
O, reason not the need! our basest beggars
Are in the poorest thing superfluous: 290
Allow not nature more than nature needs,
Man's life's as cheap as beast's. Thou art a lady;

96 KING LEAR

ACT 2 SCENE IV

If only to go warm were gorgeous,
Why, nature needs not what thou gorgeous wear'st,
Which scarcely keeps thee warm. But, for true need, –   295
You heavens, give me that patience, patience I need!
You see me here, you gods, a poor old man,
As full of grief as age; wretched in both!
If it be you that stir these daughters' hearts
Against their father, fool me not so much   300
To bear it tamely; touch me with noble anger,
And let not women's weapons, water-drops,[42]
Stain my man's cheeks! No, you unnatural hags,
I will have such revenges on you both,
That all the world shall – I will do such things, –   305
What they are, yet I know not: but they shall be
The terrors of the earth. You think I'll weep
No, I'll not weep:
I have full cause of weeping; but this heart
Shall break into a hundred thousand flaws,[43]   310
Or ere I'll weep. O Fool, I shall go mad!

Exit Lear, Gloucester, Kent, and Fool
Storm and tempest

Cornwall   Let us withdraw; 'twill be a storm.

Regan   This house is little: the old man and his people
Cannot be well bestow'd.

Goneril   'Tis his own blame; hath put himself from rest,   315
And must needs taste his folly.

Regan   For his particular, I'll receive him gladly,
But not one follower.

Goneril   So am I purpos'd.
Where is my Lord of Gloucester?   320

Cornwall   Follow'd the old man forth: he is return'd.

Re-enter Gloucester

Gloucester   The King is in high rage.

Cornwall   Whither is he going?

[42] *Tears*

One of the most important and powerful speeches in the play

[43] *Pieces*

Regan is justifying herself. Perhaps she feels some guilt?

Gloucester	He calls to horse; but will I know not whither.
Cornwall	'Tis best to give him way; he leads himself. 325
Goneril	My lord, entreat him by no means to stay.
Gloucester	Alack, the night comes on, and the high winds
	Do sorely ruffle; for many miles about
	There's scarce a bush.
Regan	O, sir, to wilful men, 230
	The injuries that they themselves procure
	Must be their schoolmasters.[44] Shut up your doors:
	He is attended with a desperate train;[45]
	And what they may incense him to, being apt
	To have his ear abus'd, wisdom bids fear. 235
Cornwall	Shut up your doors, my lord; 'tis a wild night:
	My Regan counsels well. Come out o' th' storm.

Exit

Gloucester's words paint a bleak picture of a stormy night, and acres of exposed moors

[44] *Lear must learn from his own mistakes*

[45] *Regan is slandering the knights again*

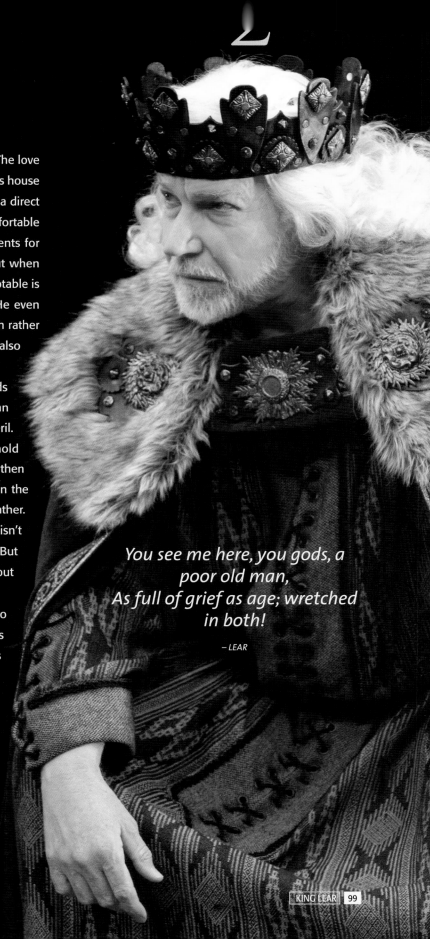

THIS SCENE MARKS the climax of the play. The love test was the catalyst. Lear has journeyed to Regan's house and is shocked to find his servant in the stocks – a direct insult to him. The Fool continues to speak uncomfortable truths, such as that children only love their parents for what they can get out of them. This is borne out when Regan and Cornwall refuse to see Lear. What is notable is that Lear is not as impetuous as he has been. He even suggests they might be ill, looking to excuse them rather than lose his temper with them. Of course, he is also running out of options.

When Lear eventually speaks to Regan, he finds little sympathy for his predicament. Regan repeatedly insists that he should return to Goneril. When Goneril herself arrives, she and Regan hold hands, showing where Regan's allegiances lie. We then witness one of the most uncomfortable scenes in the play as both daughters verbally bait their aged father. All Lear asked for was his retinue of knights. This isn't much to ask for, considering what he gave away. But the dispute is not about the knights: it is all about the two sisters completely breaking Lear's spirit.

Lear leaves, battling tears, and goes out into the storm. The storm is a metaphor for Lear's emotional turmoil. It signals that his world has utterly fallen apart.

KEY POINTS

- *Lear rejects Goneril and Regan and their treatment of him.*

- *Lear's departure from the 'civilised' world marks the beginning of his personal journey to redemption.*

> *You see me here, you gods, a poor old man,*
> *As full of grief as age; wretched in both!*
>
> – LEAR

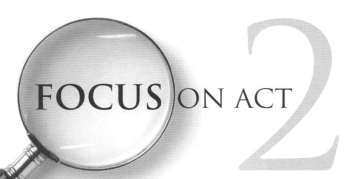

FOCUS ON ACT 2

'Lear may have a temper, but there is something sickening about how his daughters ensnare him'

ACT II is eventful. This is when things really start to unravel for Lear. At the end of Act I, Lear had burned his bridges with Goneril but was still confident that he had the love of at least one daughter. But we soon see how conniving Regan is, ensuring she will not even be at home to receive her father. Meanwhile, Edmund, the great opportunist, sees a chance for his own advancement by befriending Regan and Cornwall, and the sub-plot adds extra interest to an already action-packed act.

Significantly, we learn that Kent has received a communication from Cordelia, and this gives us hope that their relationship has not been irreparably damaged by Lear's reprehensible conduct during the love test:

> *I may*
> *Peruse this letter! Nothing almost sees miracles*
> *But misery: I know 'tis from Cordelia,*
> *Who hath most fortunately been inform'd*
> *Of my obscured course; and shall find time*
> *From this enormous state, seeking to give*
> *Losses their remedies*.

In the midst of this tension, we also have moments of comic relief, particularly in the fights between Oswald and Kent. The simpering, sycophantic Oswald is the type of character audiences love to hate, so they would have really enjoyed seeing the pair scrapping. We also learn a lot about Shakespeare's time from the insults Kent throws at Oswald. It is strange to hear that one of the worst things a man could say to another man was that he had saggy stockings! So it is as enjoyable for us, a modern audience, as it would have been to Shakespeare's audience, albeit for different reasons.

Cornwall is revealed to be just as treacherous, covetous and greedy as his wife when he sentences Kent to the humiliating punishment of the stocks, even though

*The injuries that they themselves procure
Must be their schoolmasters*

– REGAN (ACT 2 SCENE IV)

he is aware that this is a real insult to Lear. In a way he is even worse than Regan; she, at least, has a mind of her own, whereas Cornwall just seems to ape his wife's behaviour.

Edgar becomes Poor Tom in this act. In the naked, wretched figure of a madman, he knows that people will keep their distance. The sad thing is, there were many such lost souls in Shakespeare's day: ***The country gives me proof and precedent / Of Bedlam beggars*** …

Poor Tom is another character in disguise, but he may also be Shakespeare's comment on the vulnerable and dispossessed in society, and on how lonely these people must be. Shakespeare's audiences were both frightened and fascinated by madness, and that is why it is such a prominent theme.

What this act is really notable for is the bullying team of Goneril and Regan. The one thing their father has asked for is his retinue of knights. They know this is a sensitive issue with him. Most of the knights would have served him loyally for many years, so he wants to keep them in employment too. Regan and Goneril use this to cynically manipulate him. Lear may have a temper, but there is something sickening about how his daughters ensnare him. The altercation results in Lear resolving to battle the elements rather than put up with his daughters' duplicity. Many people say that Lear brought this on himself, but it is Cordelia whom he hurt, not Goneril and Regan. He did not do anything to deserve the ill treatment he receives at their hands. Regan's condescending justification at the end of this act is enough to make the audience pity Lear:

> ***O, sir, to wilful men,***
> ***The injuries that they themselves procure***
> ***Must be their schoolmasters.***

IMPORTANT THEMES IN ACT II

- The theme of filial ingratitude is most notable in this act. Goneril's and Regan's sly and cruel manipulation is quite disgusting to behold, as is Edmund's disloyalty to his father.

- The theme of madness is becoming prominent in Lear's struggle not to lose his mind.

CHARACTER DEVELOPMENT IN ACT II

- As Lear grows in character, so do Goneril and Regan degenerate. We did not realise their capacity for evil in Act I, just as we did not realise Lear's capacity for goodness. This is a prime example of Shakespeare's realistic and wholly believable characterisation.

- Gloucester seemed a rather insubstantial character in Act I, but in Act II he develops into an admirable counterpart to Lear. Gloucester is deceived by Edmund's lies, but elsewhere we see what a good and loyal man he is. He tries to talk Cornwall out of placing Kent in the stocks, and to make Goneril and Regan see how cruel it is to cast Lear into the storm: ***Alack, the night comes on, and the bleak winds / Do sorely ruffle; for many miles about / There's scarce a bush.***

QUESTIONS ON ACT 2

1. What is your favourite quotation from the Fool in this act? Give reasons for your choice.

2. List ten of the abusive names which Kent hurls at Oswald and explain why they would have been offensive at that time.

3. Write an account of what Kent might have been thinking during his time in the stocks.

4. Which sister do you think behaved worse in this act, Goneril or Regan?

5. Write a diary entry from the perspective of the Fool in this act.

6. Did your opinion of Gloucester change in this act?

7. Is it reasonable of Lear to want a retinue of a hundred knights, in your opinion?

8. Write a concise report of the altercation in the final scene of Act II.

9. Pick one scene (which hasn't already been translated) and render it into modern English, i.e. the type of language that you would use yourself.

10. Pick ten quotations across a range of characters and themes that you think best sum up Act II. Explain in each case why you have chosen it.

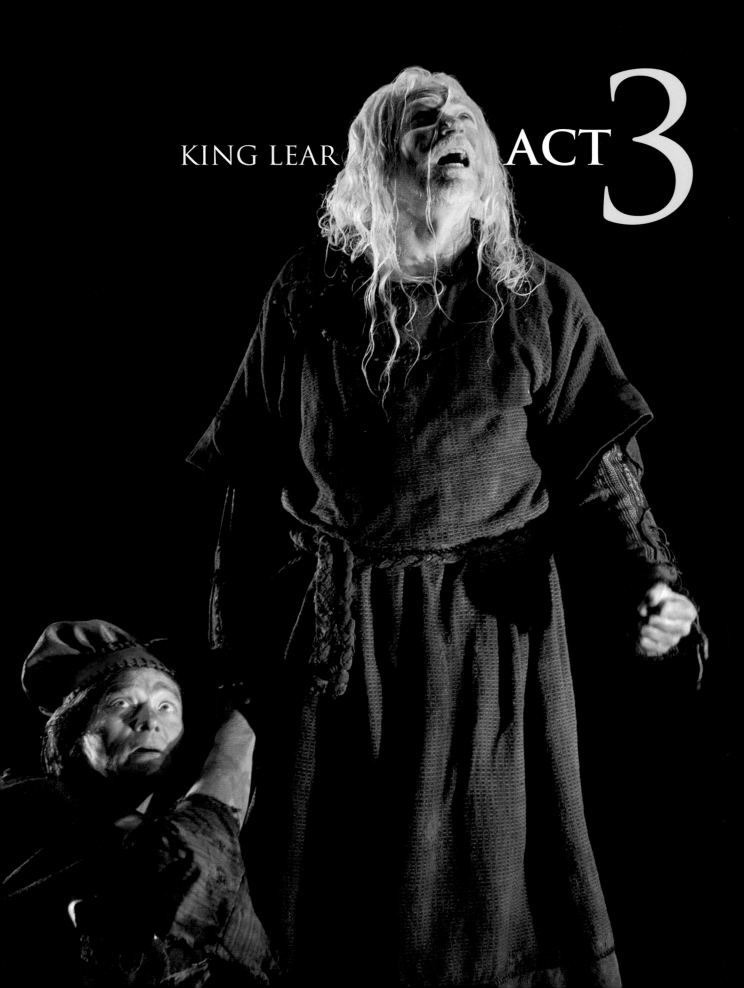

KING LEAR ACT 3

A HEATH

Storm still. Enter Kent and a Gentleman, meeting

Kent Who's there, besides foul weather?

Gentleman One minded like the weather, most unquietly.[1]

Kent I know you. Where's the King?

Gentleman Contending with the fretful elements:[2]
Bids the winds blow the earth into the sea,   5
Or swell the curled water 'bove the main,[3]
That things might change or cease; tears his white hair,
Which the impetuous[4] blasts, with eyeless rage,
Catch in their fury, and make nothing of;
Strives in his little world of man to out-scorn   10
The to-and-fro-conflicting wind and rain.
This night, wherein the cub-drawn bear would couch,
The lion and the belly-pinched wolf
Keep their fur dry, unbonneted[5] he runs,
And bids what will take all.   15

Kent But who is with him?

Gentleman None but the Fool; who labours[6] to out-jest[7]
His heart-struck[8] injuries.

Kent Sir, I do know you;
And dare, upon the warrant of my note,   20
Commend a dear thing to you. There is division,
Although as yet the face of it be cover'd
With mutual cunning,[9] 'twixt Albany and Cornwall;
Who have – as who have not, that their great stars
Thron'd and set high? – servants, who seem no less,   25
Which are to France the spies and speculations
Intelligent of our state. What hath been seen,
Either in snuffs[10] and packings[11] of the Dukes,
Or the hard rein which both of them have borne
Against the old kind king; or something deeper,   30
Whereof perchance these are but furnishings;
But, true it is, from France there comes a power
Into this scatter'd kingdom; who already,
Wise in our negligence, have secret feet

[1] Upset

[2] The weather

[3] The waves drown the mainland

[4] Unpredictable

The Gentleman paints a vivid picture of Lear railing at the storm. The vulnerable old man screaming at the rain, wind and cold is a poignant image, but also a metaphor for his powerlessness

[5] Without a hat

[6] Tries
[7] Joke about
[8] Heartfelt

[9] Deceit

Kent reports that France has spies in place (and wryly notes that all powerful families have spies in their midst), and they are reporting tensions between Albany and Cornwall. France is also poised to help Lear. This shows that Cordelia has not forgotten her father and is working to help him. This also increases suspense and tension, because we are waiting for help to arrive at any moment

[10] Quarrels
[11] Plots

In some of our best ports, and are at point   35
To show their open banner. Now to you:
If on my credit you dare build so far
To make your speed to Dover, you shall find
Some that will thank you, making just report
Of how unnatural and bemadding[12] sorrow   40
The King hath cause to plain.[13]
I am a gentleman of blood and breeding;
And, from some knowledge and assurance, offer
This office to you.

Gentleman   I will talk further with you.   45

Kent   No, do not.
For confirmation that I am much more
Than my out-wall,[14] open this purse, and take
What it contains. If you shall see Cordelia, –
As fear not but you shall, – show her this ring;   50
And she will tell you who your fellow is
That yet you do not know. Fie on this storm!
I will go seek the King.

Gentleman   Give me your hand: have you no more to say?

Kent   Few words, but, to effect, more than all yet;   55
That, when we have found the King, – in which your pain
That way, I'll this, – he that first lights on him
Holla the other.

Exit severally

12 *Maddening*

13 *Complain*

14 *Appearance*

THIS SCENE ESTABLISHES the mood of the entire act. Lear is absent, but we learn that he is reaching breaking point. Kent reports to the Gentleman that help is on its way. Cordelia and her husband are trying to intervene on Lear's behalf. They have spies placed in Goneril's and Regan's households, and French soldiers have secretly landed at English ports, awaiting the order to declare war on England. The ultimate aim is to restore Lear as full monarch.

Kent is impressive in this scene. He is clearly intelligent and an excellent strategist as well as being completely loyal.

This scene reminds the audience that hope is not lost. This is another example of how Shakespeare balances our emotional responses, because the rest of this act will grow more distressing for the audience.

KEY POINTS

- *Lear is going mad.*
- *Tensions are brewing between Albany and Cornwall.*
- *Cordelia is working on Lear's behalf.*

ANOTHER PART OF THE HEATH. STORM STILL

Enter Lear and Fool

Lear
Blow, winds, and crack your cheeks! rage! blow!
You cataracts[1] and hurricanoes, spout
Till you have drench'd our steeples, drown'd the cocks!
You sulph'rous and thought-executing fires,
Vaunt-couriers[2] to oak-cleaving thunderbolts,   5
Singe my white head! And thou, all-shaking thunder,
Smite flat the thick rotundity o' th' world!
Crack nature's moulds, an germens[3] spill at once,
That make ingrateful man!

Fool
O nuncle, court holy-water in a dry house is better   10
than this rain-water out o' door.[4]
Good nuncle, in, and ask thy daughters' blessing:
here's a night pities neither wise man nor fool.

Lear
Rumble thy bellyful! Spit, fire! Spout, rain!
Nor rain, wind, thunder, fire are my daughters: 15
I tax not you, you elements, with unkindness;
I never gave you kingdom, call'd you children,
You owe me no subscription: then let fall
Your horrible pleasure: here I stand, your slave,
A poor, infirm, weak, and despis'd old man: 20
But yet I call you servile[5] ministers,
That have with two pernicious[6] daughters join'd
Your high engender'd[7] battles 'gainst a head
So old and white as this. O! O! 'tis foul!

Fool
He that has a house to put his head in has a good   25
head-piece.
        The cod-piece[8] that will house
        Before the head has any,
        The head and he shall louse;[9]
        So beggars marry many.   30
        The man that makes his toe
        What he his heart should make
        Shall of a corn[10] cry woe,
        And turn his sleep to wake.
For there was never yet fair woman but she made   35
mouths in a glass.[11]

Side notes:

A powerful speech from Lear, basically saying, 'Bring it on!' He wants the rain to fall until the waters are higher than the weather vanes on the tops of roofs. He wants thunder and lightning to flatten the whole world

[1] Waterfalls

[2] Precursors

[3] Seeds

[4] Anything would be better than being out in the storm

[5] Eager to serve

[6] Destructive, treacherous

[7] Dangerous

[8] A decorative pouch worn over the crotch of a man's trousers

[9] Infest with lice

Quite a ribald song from the Fool. Shakespeare's audience would have enjoyed this humour. This comic relief helps to balance out the tragedy

[10] A callous on the foot

[11] Pouted while looking into a mirror

Lear	No, I will be the pattern of all patience; I will say nothing.
	Enter Kent
Kent	Who's there?
Fool	Marry, here's grace and a cod-piece; that's a wise man and a fool.
Kent	Alas, sir, are you here? Things that love night Love not such nights as these; the wrathful[12] skies Gallow[13] the very wanderers of the dark, And make them keep their caves. Since I was man, Such sheets of fire, such bursts of horrid thunder, Such groans of roaring wind and rain, I never Remember to have heard: man's nature cannot carry The affliction nor the fear.
Lear	Let the great gods, That keep this dreadful pudder[14] o'er our heads, Find out their enemies now. Tremble, thou wretch, That hast within thee undivulged[15] crimes, Unwhipp'd[16] of justice: hide thee, thou bloody hand; Thou perjur'd, and thou simular[17] man of virtue That art incestuous! Caitiff,[18] to pieces shake, That under covert and convenient seeming Hast practis'd on man's life: close pent-up guilts, Rive[19] your concealing continents, and cry These dreadful summoners grace. I am a man More sinn'd against than sinning.
Kent	Alack, bare-headed! Gracious my lord, hard by here is a hovel; Some friendship will it lend you 'gainst the tempest: Repose you there; while I to this hard house – More harder than the stones whereof 'tis raised; Which even but now, demanding after you, Denied me to come in – return, and force Their scanted[20] courtesy.
Lear	My wits begin to turn. Come on, my boy: how dost, my boy? art cold? I am cold myself. Where is this straw, my fellow?

12 Angry, malicious
13 Frighten

Kent paints a vivid picture of the storm – emphasising that it's the worst storm he has seen in his many years (Kent is 48)

14 Bother
15 Hidden
16 Unpunished
17 Pretender
18 Captive, prisoner
19 Split, rip
20 Inadequate

Lear is showing kindness and humility – a significant change in his personality

The art of our necessities is strange,
That can make vile things precious.[21] Come, your hovel.
Poor Fool and knave, I have one part in my heart   75
That's sorry yet for thee.

Fool   *[Singing] He that has a little tiny wit –*
            With hey, ho, the wind and the rain, –
            Must make content with his fortunes fit,[22]
            Though the rain it raineth every day.   80

Lear   True, my good boy. Come, bring us to this hovel.

            Exit Lear and Kent

Fool   This is a brave night to cool a courtezan.[23]
            I'll speak a prophecy ere I go:
            When priests are more in word than matter;[24]
            When brewers mar their malt with water;[25]   85
            When nobles are their tailors' tutors;
            No heretics[26] burn'd, but wenches'[27] suitors;
            When every case in law is right;
            No squire in debt, nor no poor knight;
            When slanders do not live in tongues;   90
            Nor cutpurses[28] come not to throngs;
            When usurers[29] tell their gold i' th' field;
            And bawds[30] and whores do churches build;
            Then shall the realm of Albion[31]
            Come to great confusion: 95
            Then comes the time, who lives to see 't,
            That going shall be us'd with feet.
            This prophecy Merlin[32] shall make; for I live before
            his time.

            Exit

Margin notes:

[21] Once so surrounded by luxury, now the hovel is a welcome sight to Lear

[22] We all have to take responsibility for our own fate

[23] Prostitute

[24] All talk but no action

[25] Water down their beer

[26] Someone who doesn't follow the accepted religion of a society

[27] Prostitute

This song cleverly pokes fun at Shakespeare's society, because everything the Fool mentions, such as brothel-keepers building churches, is rooted in reality

[28] Pickpockets

[29] Moneylenders

[30] Brothel-keeper

[31] Ancient name for Britain

[32] King Arthur's magician

THE STORM RAGES in this scene, literally and metaphorically. Lear screams at the thunder and lightning. It is a cathartic experience for him as he is letting go of years of pent-up emotions. Lear's speech in this scene is frightening because we are witnessing someone teetering on the brink of insanity: ***You sulph'rous and thought-executing fires, / Vaunt-couriers of oak-cleaving thunderbolts, / Singe my white head!***

The storm is so bad that the Fool pleads with Lear to beg forgiveness, so that they can have some shelter. But Lear is not about to do this. The scene is utterly depressing, but the Fool's witty comments and songs help alleviate the tension.

Kent finds a hovel (a shack), but Lear seems more concerned for the Fool than for himself. This is the same man who so casually threw away his daughter, but now we see his concern for the Fool, the lowest of the low in court life: ***Poor Fool and knave, I have one part in my heart / That's sorry yet for thee.***

Notwithstanding the significance of Lear's changing character, the Fool's monologue at the end of the scene is also an important comment on the evils of society. It is obvious that Shakespeare is talking not about the ancient Lear's society but about his own.

There is also a huge amount of imagery in this scene, from images of the storm to the Fool's closing speech.

Blow, winds, and crack your cheeks! rage! blow!

– LEAR

KEY **POINT**

- *Lear is totally exposed, literally and metaphorically. The storm exposes his vulnerability but also his humanity.*

GLOUCESTER'S CASTLE

Enter Gloucester and Edmund

Gloucester
Alack, alack, Edmund, I like not this unnatural dealing.
When I desired their leave that I might pity him, they
took from me the use of mine own house; charged me,
on pain of their perpetual¹ displeasure, neither to speak
of him, entreat for him, nor any way sustain him.   5

Edmund
Most savage and unnatural!

Gloucester
Go to; say you nothing. There's a division betwixt the
Dukes; and a worse matter than that. I have received a
letter this night; 'tis dangerous to be spoken; I have
lock'd the letter in my closet. These injuries the King   10
now bears will be revenged home; there's part of a
power already footed. We must incline to the King. I will
seek him, and privily relieve² him. Go you and maintain
talk with the Duke, that my charity be not of him
perceived. If he ask for me, I am ill, and gone to bed.   15
If I die for it, as no less is threaten'd me, the King my old
master must be relieved. There is some strange thing
toward, Edmund; pray you, be careful.

Exit

Edmund
This courtesy, forbid thee, shall the Duke
Instantly know; and of that letter too: 20
This seems a fair deserving, and must draw me
That which my father loses; no less than all:
The younger rises when the old doth fall.

Exit

¹ *Never-ending*

² *Secretly help*

A DIFFERENT SIDE to Gloucester is revealed in this scene. Our first impression of him was that he is a gullible, weak man – perhaps even a bit of a cad. But now we see a man who is willing to risk the displeasure of his immediate superiors in order to protect the king. He confides his misgivings to Edmund, and Edmund puts on a very convincing show of agreement: *Most savage and unnatural!* Crucially, however, Gloucester tells Edmund that he has a letter detailing plans to avenge the mistreatment of Lear. Dramatic irony was a feature Shakespeare's audience enjoyed enthusiastically: they often interacted with the actors, shouting advice to the characters on stage. We have an excellent use of dramatic irony here, when the old man confides dangerous information to the son who has betrayed him.

> *These injuries the King now bears will be revenged*
>
> *– GLOUCESTER*

The scene ends with a soliloquy from Edmund, who intends using this information to advance his own position. Is he truly evil or merely opportunistic? Certainly, at this point, he doesn't appear to have any conscience at all: *That which my father loses; no less than all: / The younger rises when the old doth fall.*

KEY POINTS

- *Gloucester is fiercely loyal to Lear, and will risk everything to serve him.*

- *Gloucester trusts Edmund implicitly.*

- *Edmund is prepared to betray his father to advance himself.*

THE HEATH. BEFORE A HOVEL

Enter Lear, Kent, and Fool

Kent	Here is the place, my lord; good my lord, enter:
	The tyranny of the open night's too rough
	For nature to endure.

Storm still

| Lear | Let me alone. |

| Kent | Good my lord, enter here. | 5 |

| Lear | Wilt break my heart? |

| Kent | I had rather break mine own. Good my lord, enter. |

Lear	Thou think'st 'tis much that this contentious storm
	Invades us to the skin: so 'tis to thee;
	But where the greater malady[1] is fix'd,	10
	The lesser is scarce felt. Thou'dst shun a bear;
	But if thy flight lay toward the raging sea,
	Thou'dst meet the bear i' th' mouth. When the mind's free,
	The body's delicate; the tempest in my mind
	Doth from my senses take all feeling else	15
	Save what beats there. Filial ingratitude![2]
	Is it not as this mouth should tear this hand
	For lifting food to 't?[3] But I will punish home.
	No, I will weep no more. In such a night
	To shut me out! Pour on; I will endure.	20
	In such a night as this! O Regan, Goneril!
	Your old kind father, whose frank heart gave all, –
	O, that way madness lies; let me shun that;
	No more of that.

| Kent | Good my lord, enter here. | 25 |

Lear	Prithee, go in thyself: seek thine own ease:
	This tempest will not give me leave to ponder
	On things would hurt me more. But I'll go in.
	[To the Fool] In, boy; go first. You houseless poverty, –
	Nay, get thee in. I'll pray, and then I'll sleep.	30

Marginal notes:

Bad as the storm is, Lear would rather face the tempest than his daughters' filial ingratitude. Also, he explains that he is numb to the severity of the storm. His emotional distress means that he is numb to physical distress

[1] *Sickness*

[2] *Ingratitude from a son or daughter*

[3] *Another way of saying 'don't bite the hand that feeds you'*

Fool goes in

Poor naked wretches, whereso'er you are,
That bide the pelting of this pitiless storm,
How shall your houseless heads and unfed sides,
Your loop'd and window'd raggedness, defend you
From seasons such as these? O, I have ta'en   35
Too little care of this! Take physic, pomp;
Expose thyself to feel what wretches feel,
That thou mayst shake the superflux[4] to them,
And show the heavens more just.

Edgar   *[Within]* Fathom[5] and half, fathom and half! Poor Tom!   40

The Fool runs out from the hovel

Fool   Come not in here, nuncle, here's a spirit
Help me, help me!

Kent   Give me thy hand. Who's there?

Fool   A spirit, a spirit: he says his name's poor Tom.

Kent   What art thou that dost grumble there i' th' straw?   45
Come forth.

Enter Edgar disguised as a madman

Edgar   Away! the foul fiend[6] follows me!
Through the sharp hawthorn blows the cold wind.
Hum! go to thy cold bed, and warm thee.

Lear   Hast thou given all to thy two daughters?   50
And art thou come to this?

Edgar   Who gives any thing to Poor Tom? whom the foul fiend
hath led through fire and through flame, and through
ford and whirlpool, o'er bog and quagmire;[7] that hath
laid knives under his pillow, and halters in his pew; set   55
ratsbane[8] by his porridge; made him proud of heart, to
ride on a bay trotting-horse over four-inched bridges,
to course[9] his own shadow for a traitor. Bless thy five
wits! Tom's a-cold, – O, do de, do de, do de. Bless thee
from whirlwinds, star-blasting,[10] and taking![11] Do poor   60

For the first time, Lear realises that he has been very fortunate in his life. There are many poor people in his kingdom who never have the comfort of a roof over their heads. He is now conscious that he did not do enough as king to improve their lives. He understands what poverty is, and sees that he is fallible

[4] Excess

[5] A fathom is about six feet

[6] The devil

[7] Like quicksand

[8] Poison

[9] Curse or chase

[10] Fate   [11] Infection

Tom some charity, whom the foul fiend vexes. There
could I have him now, – and there, – and there again,
and there.

Storm still

Lear   What, have his daughters brought him to this pass?
            Couldst thou save nothing? Didst thou give them all?   65

Fool   Nay, he reserved a blanket, else we had been all sham'd.

[12] Heavy, infected with disease

Lear   Now, all the plagues that in the pendulous[12] air
            Hang fated o'er men's faults light on thy daughters!

Kent   He hath no daughters, sir.

*Lear can't imagine a worse fate than
what he himself has endured*

Lear   Death, traitor! nothing could have subdued nature   70
            To such a lowness but his unkind daughters.
            Is it the fashion, that discarded fathers
            Should have thus little mercy on their flesh?
            Judicious punishment! 'twas this flesh begot
            Those pelican[13] daughters.   75

*[13] Young pelicans were reputed to
feed on their parents' blood*

Edgar   'Pillicock sat on Pillicock-hill.'
            Halloo, halloo, loo, loo!

Fool   This cold night will turn us all to fools and madmen.

Edgar   Take heed o' th' foul fiend: obey thy parents; keep
            thy word justly; swear not; commit not with man's   80
            sworn spouse;[14] set not thy sweet heart on proud
            array.[15] Tom's a-cold.

[14] Don't commit adultery
[15] Display

Lear   What hast thou been?

Edgar   A serving-man, proud in heart and mind; that curled my
            hair; wore gloves in my cap; served the lust of my   85
            mistress' heart, and did the act of darkness[16] with her;
            swore as many oaths[17] as I spake words, and broke them
            in the sweet face of heaven: one that slept in the
            contriving of lust, and waked to do it. Wine loved I
            deeply, dice[18] dearly: and in woman out-paramoured the   90
            Turk:[19] false of heart, light of ear, bloody of hand; hog in
            sloth, fox in stealth, wolf in greediness, dog in madness,

[16] Slept
[17] Promises

[18] Gambling
[19] Out-did Turkish men with his lust

lion in prey. Let not the creaking of shoes nor the
rustling of silks betray thy poor heart to woman: keep
thy foot out of brothels, thy hand out of plackets,[20] thy   95
pen from lenders' books, and defy the foul fiend. 'Still
through the hawthorn blows the cold wind.' Says suum,
mun, ha, no, nonny. Dolphin[21] my boy, my boy, sessa!
let him trot by.

Storm still

Lear   Why, thou wert better in thy grave than to answer with   100
thy uncover'd body this extremity of the skies. Is man no
more than this? Consider him well. Thou ow'st the worm
no silk, the beast no hide, the sheep no wool, the cat no
perfume. Ha! here's three on 's are sophisticated! Thou
art the thing itself: unaccommodated man is no more   105
but such a poor bare, forked[22] animal as thou art. Off,
off, you lendings! Come, unbutton here.
[Tearing off his clothes]

Fool   Prithee, nuncle, be contented; 'tis a naughty night to
swim in. Now a little fire in a wild field were like an old
lecher's[23] heart; a small spark, all the rest on 's body   110
cold. Look, here comes a walking fire.

Enter Gloucester, with a torch

Edgar   This is the foul fiend Flibbertigibbet: he begins at
curfew, and walks till the first cock; he gives the web
and the pin, squints the eye, and makes the hare-lip;
mildews the white wheat, and hurts the poor creature   115
of earth.
    Swithold footed thrice the 'old;
    He met the night-mare, and her nine-fold;
    Bid her alight,
    And her troth plight,   120
    And, aroint thee, witch, aroint thee!

Kent   How fares your Grace?

Lear   What's he?

Kent   Who's there? What is't you seek?

Gloucester   What are you there? Your names?   125

---

[20] *An opening or a slit in a garment*

[21] *The devil*

Lear admires Tom's nakedness because it is honest. There can be no artifice or false appearances if you are naked. This is another example of the clothing imagery found throughout the play. Lear rips off his clothes at this point, which is highly emotive and distressing for the audience

[22] *Two-legged*

[23] *Pervert's*

Edgar pretends to think his father is the 'demon' by which he is possessed. Edgar blames 'Flibbertigibbet' for crop diseases and birth defects. Perhaps Shakespeare is poking fun at the superstitions of the time, when witches or the devil were thought to have caused such natural events

Edgar   Poor Tom; that eats the swimming frog, the toad, the
tadpole, the wall-newt, and the water; that in the fury of
his heart, when the foul fiend rages, eats cow-dung for
sallets;[24] swallows the old rat and the ditch-dog;[25] drinks
the green mantle[26] of the standing pool; who is whipped   130
from tithing to tithing,[27] and stock'd, punish'd, and
imprison'd; who hath three suits to his back, six shirts to
his body. Horse to ride, and weapon to wear;
  But mice and rats, and such small deer,
  Have been Tom's food for seven long year.   135
Beware my follower. Peace, Smulkin;[28] peace, thou fiend!

Gloucester   What, hath your Grace no better company?

Edgar   The prince of darkness is a gentleman:
Modo he's call'd, and Mahu.

Gloucester   Our flesh and blood is grown so vile, my lord,   140
That it doth hate what gets it.

Edgar   Poor Tom's a-cold.

Gloucester   Go in with me: my duty cannot suffer
To obey in all your daughters' hard commands:
Though their injunction[29] be to bar my doors,   145
And let this tyrannous night take hold upon you,
Yet have I ventured to come seek you out,
And bring you where both fire and food is ready.

Lear   First let me talk with this philosopher.
What is the cause of thunder?   150

Kent   Good my lord, take his offer; go into th' house.

Lear   I'll talk a word with this same learned Theban.
What is your study?

Edgar   How to prevent the fiend, and to kill vermin.

Lear   Let me ask you one word in private.   155

Kent   Importune[30] him once more to go, my lord;
His wits begin t' unsettle.

[24] Salads   [25] Hedgehog

[26] Algae

[27] Tithing referred to the collection
of taxes (10%) annually

*Edgar paints a vivid picture
of the life of a beggar. He
claims to have once been a
respectable servant, until he
lost his mind after an affair
with his mistress.*   [28] Devil

[29] Instructions

[30] Beg

Gloucester	Canst thou blame him?

Storm still

	His daughters seek his death: ah, that good Kent!
	He said it would be thus, poor banish'd man!	160
	Thou say'st the King grows mad; I'll tell thee, friend,
	I am almost mad myself: I had a son,
	Now outlaw'd from my blood; he sought my life,
	But lately, very late. I loved him, friend;
	No father his son dearer: truth to tell thee,	165
	The grief hath crazed my wits. What a night 's this!
	I do beseech your Grace, –

Lear	O, cry your mercy, sir.
	Noble philosopher, your company.

Edgar	Tom's a-cold.	170

Gloucester	In, fellow, there, into th' hovel: keep thee warm.

Lear	Come let's in all.

Kent	This way, my lord.

Lear	With him;
	I will keep still with my philosopher.	180

Kent	Good my lord, soothe him; let him take the fellow.

Gloucester	Take him you on.

Kent	Sirrah, come on; go along with us.

Lear	Come, good Athenian.[31]

Gloucester	No words, no words: hush.	185

Edgar	'Child Rowland to the dark tower came,[32]
	His word was still, "Fie, foh, and fum,
	I smell the blood of a British man."'

Exit

Gloucester's words show how closely the sub-plot is paralleled with the main plot. It is also a dramatic irony – the son whom Gloucester speaks of is right there in disguise

[31] *Philosopher*

[32] *A fairy tale from Shakespeare's day*

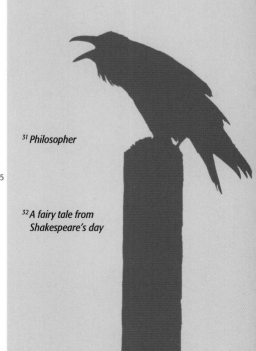

KENT TRIES TO make Lear go inside the hovel and take shelter from the raging storm. But Lear is in such a state of inner turmoil that he claims he does not even care about the outer turmoil of the storm. It does not affect him. What is tormenting him are the feelings and emotions that are swirling around in his head, threatening to envelop him completely. But Lear does make the Fool go in, showing that the compassion that became apparent earlier in this act is continuing to grow: *In, boy; go first. You houseless poverty, – / Nay, get thee in. I'll pray, and then I'll sleep.*

Lear also recognises that, for many, this is a way of life and not a temporary inconvenience. He sees that he did not do enough to help the poor when he was in power because he had no idea of how the poor lived. His dawning recognition of how fortunate he was to have been king is significant. It demonstrates the theme of learning through suffering. Here, too, Shakespeare acts as a social commentator, exposing the evils of his time:

> *Poor naked wretches, whereso'er you are,*
> *That bide the pelting of this pitiless storm,*
> *How shall your houseless heads and unfed sides,*
> *Your loop'd and window'd raggedness, defend you*
> *From seasons such as these? O, I have ta'en*
> *Too little care of this!*

The Fool runs out of the hovel in fright, exclaiming that there is a ghost inside. It is none other than Edgar, in his Tom o' Bedlam disguise, which he executes masterfully, claiming that he is being chased by the devil. Lear accepts Poor Tom into his little band of misfits, even asking if Poor Tom's daughters have driven him to madness.

A modern audience might find Edgar's crazy rants irrelevant and not very entertaining, but Shakespeare's audience found madness intriguing. Along with that, as nakedness was rarely witnessed, Poor Tom prancing about on stage in a loincloth was both riveting and hilarious. So, like the Fool, Poor Tom also provides comic relief and at other times he is a tragic figure. He claims that too much lust and partying drove him mad.

Gloucester arrives to bring Lear to shelter, no matter what the consequences. He is not impressed by Lear's companions, but Lear insists they will all take shelter together, once again showing how, on a very fundamental level, he has completely changed from the rash, impetuous man of the first act of the play.

KEY **POINTS**

- *Lear continues to plummet into madness, while at the same time coming to know himself.*

- *Poor Tom joins Lear's company.*

- *Gloucester risks all to help his king.*

GLOUCESTER'S CASTLE

Enter Cornwall and Edmund

Cornwall   I will have my revenge ere I depart his house.

Edmund   How, my lord, I may be censured, that nature thus gives
way to loyalty, something fears me to think of.

Cornwall   I now perceive, it was not altogether your brother's evil
disposition made him seek his death; but a provoking   5
merit, set a-work by a reprovable badness in himself.

Edmund   How malicious is my fortune, that I must repent to
be just! This is the letter which he spoke of, which
approves him an intelligent party to the advantages
of France: O heavens! that this treason were not,   10
or not I the detector!

Cornwall   Go with me to the Duchess.

Edmund   If the matter of this paper be certain, you have
mighty business in hand.

Cornwall   True or false, it hath made thee Earl of Gloucester.   15
Seek out where thy father is, that he may be ready
for our apprehension.

Edmund   *[Aside]* If I find him comforting the King, it will stuff
his suspicion more fully. – I will persevere in my
course of loyalty, though the conflict be sore between   20
that and my blood.

Cornwall   I will lay trust upon thee; and thou shalt find a dearer
father in my love.

Exit

This shows that Edmund does have a conscience of a sort

THIS IS A short scene but a disturbing one nonetheless. Edmund is making good on his promise to betray his father and has gone to Cornwall with news of the letter. Edmund is convincing in his reluctance to get his father into trouble, and Cornwall falls for his manipulation, promising rewards for Edmund's information.

Significantly, in an aside, Edmund reveals that he does feel bad about his decision. This is a very clever strategy by Shakespeare, because it makes Edmund more authentic and three-dimensional. This, in turn, is what keeps us interested in him. Straightforward villains are simply not as captivating.

KEY **POINTS**

- *Edmund betrays Gloucester to Cornwall.*
- *Edmund's conscience bothers him.*

I will persevere in my course of loyalty, though the conflict be sore between that and my blood

– EDMUND

A CHAMBER IN A FARMHOUSE ADJOINING THE CASTLE

Enter Gloucester, Lear, Kent, Fool, and Edgar

Gloucester	Here is better than the open air; take it thankfully. I will piece out the comfort with what addition[1] I can: I will not be long from you.
Kent	All the power of his wits have given way to his impatience: the gods reward your kindness!

Exit Gloucester

Edgar	Frateretto calls me; and tells me Nero[2] is an angler in the lake of darkness. Pray, innocent, and beware the foul fiend.
Fool	Prithee, nuncle, tell me whether a madman be a gentleman or a yeoman?[3]
Lear	A king, a king!
Fool	No, he's a yeoman that has a gentleman to his son; for he's a mad yeoman that sees his son a gentleman before him.
Lear	To have a thousand with red burning spits Come hissing in upon 'em, –
Edgar	The foul fiend bites my back.
Fool	He's mad that trusts in the tameness of a wolf, a horse's health, a boy's love, or a whore's oath.
Lear	It shall be done; I will arraign[4] them straight. *[To Edgar]* Come, sit thou here, most learned justicer; *[To the Fool]* Thou, sapient[5] sir, sit here. Now, you she foxes!
Edgar	Look, where he stands and glares! Wantest thou eyes at trial, madam? *'Come o'er the bourn,[6] Bessy, to me,'* –
Fool	*Her boat hath a leak, And she must not speak*

Line numbers: 5, 10, 15, 20, 25

Footnotes:
[1] *Extras*
[2] *Roman emperor noted for his cruelty*
[3] *Farmer or servant*
[4] *Try (as in a court of law)*
[5] *Wise*
[6] *River*

Why she dares not come over to thee.

Edgar The foul fiend haunts Poor Tom in the voice of a nightingale. Hopdance cries in Tom's belly for two 30
white herring. Croak not, black angel; I have no food for thee.

Kent How do you, sir? Stand you not so amaz'd:
Will you lie down and rest upon the cushions?

Lear I'll see their trial first. Bring in the evidence. 35
[To Edgar] Thou robed man of justice, take thy place;
[To the Fool] And thou, his yoke-fellow of equity,
Bench by his side: *[To Kent]* You are o' th' commission,
Sit you too.

Edgar Let us deal justly. 40
Sleepest or wakest thou, jolly shepherd?
Thy sheep be in the corn;
And for one blast of thy minikin[7] mouth,
Thy sheep shall take no harm.
Purr! the cat is gray. 45

The mock trial begins

Lear Arraign her first; 'tis Goneril. I here take my oath before this honourable assembly, she kicked the poor king her father.

Fool Come hither, mistress. Is your name Goneril?

Lear She cannot deny it. 50

Fool Cry you mercy, I took you for a joint-stool.

Lear And here's another, whose warp'd looks proclaim
What store her heart is made on. Stop her there!
Arms, arms, sword, fire! Corruption in the place!
False justicer, why hast thou let her scape? 55

Edgar Bless thy five wits!

Kent O pity! Sir, where is the patience now,
That thou so oft have boasted to retain?

Edgar *[Aside]* My tears begin to take his part so much,

The 'mock court' is a poignant scene. The battered old king assembles the farmhouse kitchen like a courtroom, and 'tries' his daughters. It shows both his madness and his difficulty in accepting or even understanding what they have done

[7] Shrill

The mock trial begins

	They'll mar my counterfeiting.[8]	60

[8] *Pretence or act*

Lear The little dogs and all,
Tray, Blanch, and Sweetheart, see, they bark at me.

Edgar Tom will throw his head at them. Avaunt, you curs!
    Be thy mouth or black or white,
    Tooth that poisons if it bite;   65
    Mastiff, grey-hound, mongrel grim,
    Hound or spaniel, brach or lym,
    Or bobtail tike or trundle-tail,
    Tom will make them weep and wail:
    For, with throwing thus my head,   70
    Dogs leap the hatch, and all are fled.
Do de, de, de. Sessa! Come, march to wakes and
fairs and market-towns. Poor Tom, thy horn is dry.

Lear Then let them anatomize Regan; see what breeds
about her heart. Is there any cause in nature that makes   75
these hard hearts? *[To Edgar]* You, sir, I entertain for one
of my hundred; only I do not like the fashion of your
garments. You will say they are Persian attire: but let
them be chang'd.

Kent Now, good my lord, lie here and rest awhile.   80

Lear Make no noise, make no noise; draw the curtains: so, so,
so. We'll go to supper i' th' morning. So, so, so.

Fool And I'll go to bed at noon.

Re-enter Gloucester

Gloucester Come hither, friend: where is the King my master?

Kent Here, sir; but trouble him not, his wits are gone.   85

Gloucester Good friend, I prithee, take him in thy arms;
I have o'erheard a plot of death upon him.
There is a litter[9] ready; lay him in 't,
And drive towards Dover, friend, where thou shalt meet
Both welcome and protection. Take up thy master.   90
If thou shouldst dally half an hour, his life,
With thine, and all that offer to defend him,

These are the last words spoken by the Fool in the play as he disappears after this scene. Presumably he means he will go to bed early, and by bed, he means death. It could be that the storm has worn him out

[9] *Like a stretcher, so that Lear can be carried*

Stand in assured loss: take up, take up;
And follow me, that will to some provision
Give thee quick conduct.   95

Kent Oppressed nature sleeps:

10 Soothed 11 Nerves

This rest might yet have balm'd[10] thy broken sinews,[11]
Which, if convenience will not allow,
Stand in hard cure. *[To the Fool]*
Come, help to bear thy master;   100
Thou must not stay behind.

Gloucester Come, come, away.

Exit all but Edgar

Edgar When we our betters see bearing our woes,
We scarcely think our miseries our foes.

*12 Emotional pain is worse
than physical pain*

Who alone suffers suffers most i' th' mind,[12]   105
Leaving free things and happy shows behind:
But then the mind much sufferance doth o'erskip,
When grief hath mates, and bearing fellowship.
How light and portable my pain seems now,
When that which makes me bend makes the King bow,   110

*13 Lear's children betrayed him, while
Edgar was betrayed by his father*

He childed as I fathered![13] Tom, away!
Mark the high noises; and thyself bewray,

14 Ruins

When false opinion, whose wrong thought defiles[14] thee,
In thy just proof, repeals and reconciles thee.
What will hap more to-night, safe scape the King!   115
Lurk, lurk.

Exit

A CHAMBER IN A FARMHOUSE ADJOINING THE CASTLE

Enter Gloucester, Lear, Kent, Fool, and Edgar

Gloucester   This is a bit better than being outside, anyway, so be grateful for it. I'll bring you more home comforts when I can. I'll be back soon.

Kent   I think Lear is losing his mind. Thank you so much for your kindness, though.

Exit Gloucester

Edgar   The devil tells me that the notorious Emperor Nero likes to go fishing in hell. Pray to the gods, Fool, and beware the devil!

Fool   Sir, is the madman a gentleman or a commoner?

Lear   A king, a king!

Fool   No, he's a commoner with a gentleman for a son, because you'd have to be crazy to let your children have more than you have.

Lear   There are a thousand hissing devils with pitchforks in hell, which is where I see my two daughters!

Edgar   The devil bites my back.

Fool   You'd have to be mad to trust in a tame wolf, a healthy horse, a teenager in love or a faithful prostitute.

Lear   I'm going to put my daughters on trial right now.
[*To Edgar*] Sit here, most esteemed judge!
[*To the Fool*] And you, wise sir, sit here. Now, you vixens …

Edgar   Look how he glares at me! [*Sings*] Hey Bessy, come over the river to me!

Fool   Her boat has a leak, so she can't go over to you.

Edgar   The devil torments me by singing like a nightingale. The demon in my belly is crying for some fish to eat. Shut up, devil! I've no food to give you!

Kent   Are you OK, Lear? Why don't you lie down and have a little rest? It would do you good.

Lear   I'll see their trial first. Bring in the evidence.

[To Edgar] Take your place, you robed man of justice.
[To Fool] And you, his fellow judge, sit beside him.
[To Kent] You too, another judge, sit alongside them.

Edgar   Let's give a fair verdict. Are you asleep or awake, happy shepherd? Your sheep are running about the cornfield, but if you blow your horn, everything will be fine. The devil's cat is grey!

Lear   Try Goneril first. I accuse her of kicking her father when he was down.

Fool   Come here, miss. Is your name Goneril?

Lear   She cannot deny it.

Fool   Oh, I thought you were a well-crafted chair, and not a crap stool!

Lear   And here's Regan, whose nasty expression reveals her evil heart. Guards, use your weapons, order in the courtroom! Order!

Edgar   Bless that poor man!

Kent   Oh sir, where is your self-control that you were always so proud of?

Edgar   *[Aside]* I'm crying out of compassion for him, but I have to stop or my disguise will be in jeopardy.

Lear   Even the dogs Tray, Blanch, and Sweetheart are barking at me.

Edgar   I'll scare them away no matter what kind of dog they are!

Lear   They should dissect Regan and find out what is wrong with her heart. Is there any natural cause that makes a heart hard, any illness? *[To Edgar]* You can be one of my hundred knights. But you'll have to change your outfit, it's very bizarre.

Kent   Please rest, you're exhausted.

Lear   Stay quiet, draw the curtains, we'll have supper in the morning.

Fool   And I'll go to bed at noon.

Re-enter Gloucester

Gloucester   Kent, where is the King my master?

All the power of his wits have given way to his impatience: the gods reward your kindness!

– KENT

Kent   He's here, but please don't disturb him. He's very overwrought and upset in himself.

Gloucester I'm sorry, but you're going to have to get him out of here; there is a plot to take his life, and if you delay even half an hour, he will die. Here is a carriage. Take him towards Dover and help will arrive. Quickly, there is no time to lose.

Kent   He's fast asleep. I hate disturbing him when a good sleep could have made all the difference to his tormented mind.
[To the Fool] Help me carry Lear. You can't stay here either.

Gloucester Come on!

                Exit all but Edgar

Edgar   When you see your betters having problems, it makes you forget your own. Suffering alone is the worst type of suffering. Companions in sorrow make it somewhat easier to bear. My problems seem bearable when I think of what Lear is going through. His children betrayed him just as my father betrayed me. I will have to wait until I'm proved innocent to reveal my true identity. But whatever else happens, I just hope the poor king escapes.

GLOUCESTER'S CASTLE.

Enter Cornwall, Regan, Goneril, Edmund, and Servants

Cornwall   Post speedily to my lord your husband; show him this
letter. The army of France is landed. – Seek out the
traitor Gloucester.

Exit some of the Servants

Regan   Hang him instantly.

Goneril   Pluck out his eyes.   5

Cornwall   Leave him to my displeasure. – Edmund, keep you our
sister company; the revenges we are bound to take
upon your traitorous father are not fit for your
beholding. Advise the Duke, where you are going, to
a most festinate¹ preparation: we are bound to the like.   10
Our posts shall be swift and intelligent betwixt² us.
Farewell, dear sister; farewell, my lord of Gloucester.

¹ *Happy*

² *Between*

Enter Oswald

How now! where's the King?

Goneril   My Lord of Gloucester hath convey'd him hence:
Some five or six and thirty of his knights,   15
Hot questrists³ after him, met him at gate;
Who, with some other of the lords' dependents,
Are gone with him towards Dover; where they boast
To have well-armed friends.

³ *The knights are searching for Lear*

*The knights' continuing loyalty
disproves the allegations
made against them*

Cornwall   Get horses for your mistress.   20

Goneril   Farewell, sweet lord, and sister.

Cornwall   Edmund, farewell.

Exit Goneril, Edmund, and Oswald

Go seek the traitor Gloucester,
Pinion⁴ him like a thief, bring him before us.

⁴ *Tie him up*

Exit other Servants

Though well we may not pass upon his life   25
Without the form of justice, yet our power
Shall do a courtesy to our wrath, which men
May blame, but not control. Who's there? The traitor?

Enter Gloucester, brought in by two or three servants

Regan   Ingrateful fox! 'tis he.

Cornwall   Bind fast his corky⁵ arms.   30

Gloucester   What means your Graces? Good my friends, consider
You are my guests. Do me no foul play, friends.

Cornwall   Bind him, I say.

Servants bind him

Regan   Hard, hard. O filthy traitor!

Gloucester   Unmerciful lady as you are, I'm none.   35

Cornwall   To this chair bind him. Villain, thou shalt find —

Regan plucks his beard

Gloucester   By the kind gods, 'tis most ignobly done
To pluck me by the beard.

Regan   So white, and such a traitor!

Gloucester   Naughty lady,   40
These hairs, which thou dost ravish from my chin,
Will quicken, and accuse thee. I am your host:
With robbers' hands my hospitable favours
You should not ruffle thus. What will you do?

Cornwall   Come, sir, what letters had you late from France?   45

Regan   Be simple-answer'd, for we know the truth.

Cornwall   And what confederacy⁶ have you with the traitors
Late footed in the kingdom?

Regan   To whose hands have you sent the lunatic king? Speak.

Cornwall means they may not kill Gloucester without a court's approval, but they can torture him. Torture was a common means of extracting information in Shakespeare's day

⁵ *Old, withered, frail*

Beards were a symbol of age, wisdom and dignity, so Regan is being incredibly disrespectful

A host was always to be treated well, so they are insulting Gloucester in every possible way

⁶ *Alliance*

Gloucester	I have a letter guessingly set down,	50
	Which came from one that's of a neutral heart,	
	And not from one oppos'd.	
Cornwall	Cunning.	
Regan	And false.	
Cornwall	Where hast thou sent the King?	55
Gloucester	To Dover.	
Regan	Wherefore to Dover? Wast thou not charged at peril –	
Cornwall	Wherefore to Dover? Let him first answer that.	
Gloucester	I am tied to th' stake, and I must stand the course.	
Regan	Wherefore to Dover, sir?	60
Gloucester	Because I would not see thy cruel nails	
	Pluck out his poor old eyes; nor thy fierce sister	
	In his anointed[7] flesh stick boarish fangs.	
	The sea, with such a storm as his bare head	
	In hell-black night endured, would have buoy'd up,	65
	And quench'd the stelled fires;	
	Yet, poor old heart, he holp the heavens to rain.	
	If wolves had at thy gate howl'd that dern[8] time,	
	Thou shouldst have said, 'Good porter, turn the key.'	
	All cruels else subscribed:[9] but I shall see	70
	The winged[10] vengeance overtake such children.	
Cornwall	See 't shalt thou never. Fellows, hold the chair.	
	Upon these eyes of thine I'll set my foot.	
Gloucester	He that will think to live till he be old,	
	Give me some help! – O cruel! O you gods!	75
	Gloucester's eye put out	
Regan	One side will mock another; th' other too.	
Cornwall	If you see vengeance, –	
First Servant	Hold your hand, my lord!	

This refers to bear-baiting, when a bear was tied to a stake and dogs were set on him. Bets were taken on how many 'courses' or sets of dogs it would take to kill the bear. Even in Shakespeare's day, many found this 'sport' disgusting

[7] *Blessed*

[8] *Dreadful*

[9] *Forgiven*

[10] *Swift*

I have served you ever since I was a child;
But better service have I never done you   80
Than now to bid you hold.

Regan   How now, you dog!

First Servant   If you did wear a beard upon your chin,
I'd shake it on this quarrel. What do you mean?

Cornwall   My villain!   85

They draw and fight

First Servant   Nay, then, come on, and take the chance of anger.

Regan   Give me thy sword. A peasant stand up thus?
[Takes a sword, and runs at him behind]

First Servant   O, I am slain! My lord, you have one eye left
To see some mischief on him. O!

Dies

Cornwall   Lest it see more, prevent it. Out, vile jelly!   90
Where is thy lustre now?

Gloucester   All dark and comfortless. Where's my son Edmund?
Edmund, enkindle[11] all the sparks of nature,
To quit this horrid act.

Regan   Out, treacherous villain!   95
Thou call'st on him that hates thee. It was he
That made the overture of thy treasons to us,
Who is too good to pity thee.

Gloucester   O my follies! then Edgar was abus'd.
Kind gods, forgive me that, and prosper him!   100

Regan   Go thrust him out at gates, and let him smell
His way to Dover.

Exit one with Gloucester

How is't, my lord? How look you?

[11] Inflame

Once again, a servant is the one to stand up for what is right, despite servants having very tough lives at the time. Perhaps he is making the point that being aristocratic and wealthy does not make you a good person. This is certainly borne out by history

Gloucester's plea for help to the son who has betrayed him is an example of pathos

Regan's cruelty is shocking – particularly as she is a woman

Cornwall	I have received a hurt: follow me, lady.
	Turn out that eyeless villain; throw this slave 105
	Upon the dunghill. Regan, I bleed apace:
	Untimely comes this hurt: give me your arm.

Exit Cornwall, led by Regan

Second Servant	I'll never care what wickedness I do,
	If this man come to good.
Third Servant	If she live long, 110
	And in the end meet the old course of death,
	Women will all turn monsters.
Second Servant	Let's follow the old earl, and get the Bedlam
	To lead him where he would: his roguish madness
	Allows itself to anything. 115
Third Servant	Go thou: I'll fetch some flax and whites of eggs
	To apply to his bleeding face. Now, Heaven help him!

Exit severally

Despite the horror of this scene, there is hope, because it is Edgar, in disguise, who is chosen to guide Gloucester to Dover

MODERN ENGLISH VERSION

GLOUCESTER'S CASTLE

Enter Cornwall, Regan, Goneril, Edmund, and Servants

Cornwall	Write to Albany straight away and tell him the French army has arrived. Now, where is that traitor Gloucester?

Exit some of the Servants

Regan	Hang him instantly.
Goneril	Pluck out his eyes.
Cornwall	Leave Gloucester to me. You'd better leave, Edmund. You really don't want to see what's going to happen to your father. Keep Goneril company and tell Albany we'll soon be celebrating victory.

Enter Oswald

Where is the King?

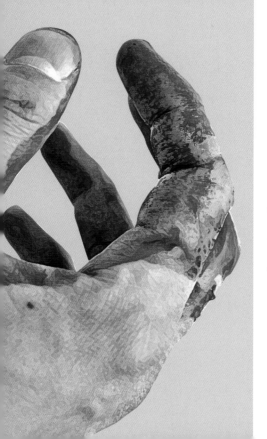

Oswald	He's headed for Dover. Some of his knights are headed that way too, and claim they have more help arriving.
Cornwall	Get horses for your mistress.
Goneril	Goodbye all.
Cornwall	Goodbye, Edmund.
	Exit Goneril, Edmund, and Oswald
	Get Gloucester. Tie him up and drag him here.
	Exit other Servants
	It's a pity we can't kill him, or we'd be in serious trouble. But we can hurt the traitor badly, and there's nothing anyone can do about it.
	Enter Gloucester, brought in by two or three servants
Regan	Ungrateful fox!
Cornwall	Bind his old withered arms good and tight.
Gloucester	What's going on? Don't forget, I am your friend. Please don't hurt me.
Cornwall	Bind him, I said.
	Servants tie him up
Regan	Tighter. Oh, you filthy traitor!
Gloucester	I am not a traitor!
Cornwall	Tie him to this chair, and we'll soon see whether he admits to being a traitor or not.
	Regan pulls his beard
Gloucester	Please don't pull my beard. It's humiliating.
Regan	Such a dignified white beard, and yet you're such a traitor.
Gloucester	Why are you treating me this way? I am your host. This is my home, and to treat me as you would a common criminal is uncalled for!
Cornwall	So, tell us about the letters you have been receiving from France.

Regan   And don't lie about it. We already know the truth.

Cornwall   And who have you been conspiring with? Who else is in on this?

Regan   Where did you send the crazy old king?

Gloucester   I have a letter from someone who is neutral in all this but who just has the king's best interests at heart.

Cornwall   Cunning.

Regan   And a lie.

Cornwall   Where have you sent the king?

Gloucester   To Dover.

Regan   Why Dover?

Cornwall   Answer us, or else … Why Dover?

Gloucester   You may have me trapped, but I will not submit.

Regan   Why Dover?

Gloucester   Because I didn't want you to hurt him. I wouldn't be surprised if you ripped out his eyes or if your sister sank her teeth into his flesh. You sent that poor old man into a storm that would have drowned the sea. An animal shouldn't have been denied shelter during such terrible weather, let alone your vulnerable, generous, royal father!

Cornwall   Hold the chair! I'm going to make him pay for that!
                   [Rips out one eyeball]

Gloucester   Help, someone please help me!

Regan   No point just taking one eye; rip out the other one too! Go on!

First Servant Stop it! I have been your servant since I was a child, and I am telling you not to do this terrible thing. If you listen, it will be the best service I ever gave you!

Regan   How dare you tell us what to do! You're just a servant, a pauper, a nothing!

First Servant I wish you had a beard, and I'd rip it out as you did Gloucester's!

Cornwall   The cheek of you! You'll pay for that.

They draw their swords and fight

Regan Give me that sword. He deserves to die! A servant? Questioning us?

Takes a sword and runs at him from behind

First Servant Oh, she has stabbed me, my lord. You have one eye left, try and protect yourself!

Dies

Cornwall I'd better take it out then. Out it comes, jelly spilling from it! It's useless to you now.

Gloucester Everything has gone black! Edmund! Edmund! Please help me, son!

Regan You idiot, he's gone. He was the one who betrayed you, so why would he help a fool like you? Ha!

Gloucester Edmund betrayed me … what? Oh God, then he must have betrayed his brother too. Forgive me, Edgar, forgive me.

Regan Oh, throw him outside. Let him smell his way to Dover.

Exit a servant with Gloucester

Are you all right, Cornwall?

Cornwall That servant stabbed me. Throw Gloucester out of my sight. Help me to my room, Regan. I think I'm badly hurt.

Exit Cornwall, led by Regan

Second Servant I hope he dies, the bastard.

Third Servant I hope she does too. She doesn't deserve to live to old age after what they've done to Gloucester.

Second Servant Let's follow him and ask that Bedlam beggar to lead him to Dover.

Third Servant Good idea. You go after him. I'll get some bandages and try to patch him up. God help him!

Exit separately

FOCUS ON ACT 3

'Lear feels an affinity with Poor Tom, who has also lost everything. He admires his nakedness, for at least it is honest, and tears off his own clothes in sympathy'

I T IS no accident that Act III is the central act in the play. The first two acts were concerned with setting the scene, establishing characters and allowing events to lead to this calamitous point. A horrific storm rages throughout this act; the rain lashes down and there is flooding as high as the weather vanes. Thunder and lightning complete this apocalyptic scene. It is a measure of Shakespeare's vivid imagery that it is so easy to picture the storm from the Gentleman's description.

This act shows Lear reaching rock bottom. When the trappings of his immense wealth are stripped away from him, he starts to grow and develop as a person. Lear must have led quite a sheltered life. Who tells the king, especially one as capricious as Lear, the truth? Now he is surrounded by the mad and the dispossessed, and it is here we finally start to see signs of the characteristics which make it appropriate to call Lear a tragic hero. He shows compassion for the Fool *(Come on, my boy: how dost, my boy? art cold? / I am cold myself)* and starts to take responsibility for the fact that, as king, he did absolutely nothing for the poor.

Lear feels an affinity with Poor Tom, who has also lost everything. He admires his nakedness, for at least it is honest, and tears off his own clothes in sympathy:

> *Is man no more than this? Consider him well. Thou ow'st the worm no silk, the beast no hide, the sheep no wool, the cat no perfume … Off, off, you lendings! Come, unbutton here.*

This is both an example of imagery and an indication of how we judge by appearances. When Lear gave away his land, he still wanted to keep his title, his knights, his crown – in other words, the trappings of a king. Now Lear realises that clothes do not make the man, and that there are aspects to being king that he has only just begun to understand. As Lear will go on to say in Act IV: *Through*

Lest it see more, prevent it. Out, vile jelly!
Where is thy lustre now?

– CORNWALL (ACT III SCENE VII)

tatter'd clothes, small vices do appear; / Robes and furr'd gowns hide all. Look at how differently Edgar is treated as a gentleman and as a beggar. Even Kent, who has proved to be an exemplary man, shuns Edgar when he is disguised. This theme is possibly even more relevant today when we see so much attention given to superficial things.

The mock court is also held in this act, a pathetic spectacle when Lear asks Poor Tom, the Fool and Kent to judge his daughters. It is a heartbreaking sight to see Lear trying to grapple with his daughters' cruelty, trying to find a reason for their treachery: *Then let them anatomize Regan; see what breeds about her heart. Is there any cause in nature that makes these hard hearts?*

This act also focuses on the sub-plot, notably Edmund's betrayal of his father and his growing involvement with Goneril and Regan. One of the most harrowing scenes in this play is the blinding of Gloucester. Sight is referred to repeatedly, as is blindness. The plucking out of Gloucester's eyes would have been shocking to Shakespeare's audience in an age when, even in battle, there was a strict code of honour, but it is equally shocking to a modern one. Ripping out an old man's eyes is truly horrific. It marks a new level of villainous behaviour and makes us fear for Lear, Cordelia and Gloucester. The fact that it is a servant who tries to save the day by attacking Cornwall shows again that wealth and status don't automatically make you an honourable person. It is a person's actions that count, not his or her words or appearance.

IMPORTANT THEMES IN ACT III

- The theme of learning through suffering is the dominant theme in Act III. The storm is both actual and metaphorical, and Lear suffers physically and emotionally. Facing the truth of what he has done is incredibly difficult but ultimately redemptive. Gloucester also learns through his extreme physical suffering.

- The theme of evil is seen in the appalling actions of Cornwall and Regan, a sad reflection of man's inhumanity to man.

CHARACTER DEVELOPMENT IN ACT III

- Lear is completely lost and vulnerable in this act. This is because he has to reach rock bottom before he can begin to recover his faculties.

- The Fool, who continues to be the uncomfortable voice of truth and reason, abruptly disappears from the play after this act. His dramatic function has been served.

- Gloucester shows integrity and bravery in the face of torture. The audience now sees a principled, loyal man where before they saw a gullible father.

QUESTIONS ON ACT 3

1. **What information do we get from Kent's conversation with the Gentleman?**

2. **How do you picture the weather from the imagery in this act?**

3. **Why does the weather not bother Lear?**

4. **In your opinion, how should an actor play the part of Edgar/Poor Tom? Refer in your answer to costume, props, etc.**

5. **What happens in the mock court?**

6. **Who do you think provides the most comic relief in Act III?**

7. **Do you think Edmund had any idea of how bad his father's punishment would be when he betrayed him?**

8. **How would you stage the blinding scene if you were a director? Give reasons for your answer.**

9. **Pick one scene (which hasn't already been translated) and render it into modern English, i.e. the type of language that you would use yourself.**

10. **Pick ten quotations across a range of characters and themes that you think best sum up Act III. Explain in each case why you have chosen it.**

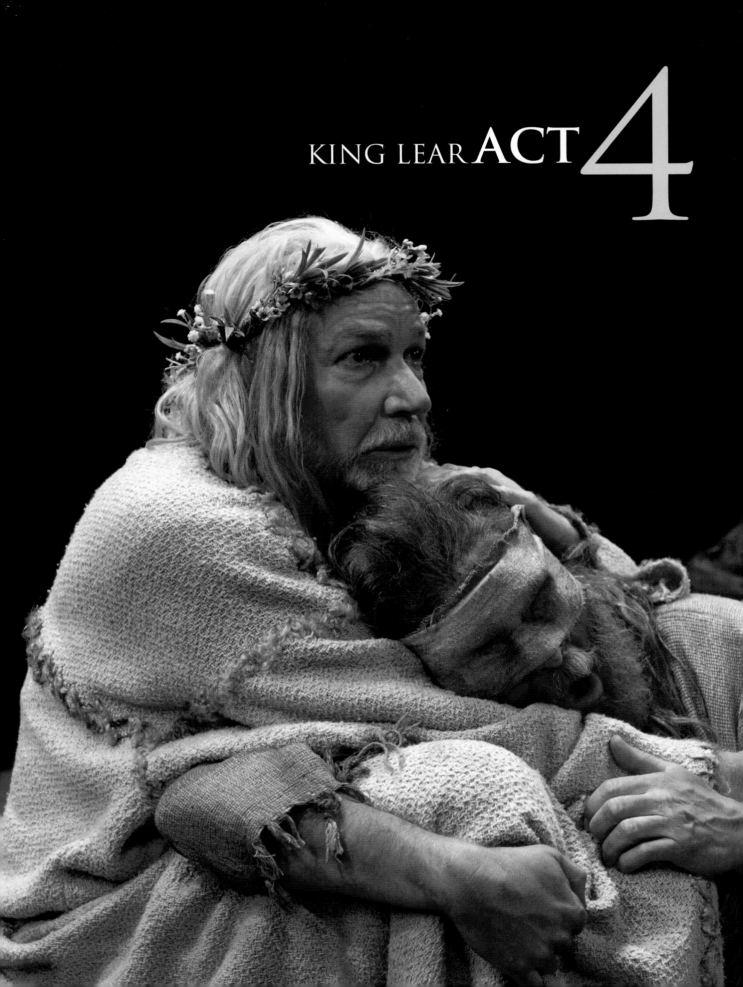

THE HEATH

Enter Edgar

Edgar
Yet better thus, and known to be contemn'd,
Than, still contemn'd and flatter'd, to be worst.
The lowest and most dejected thing of fortune,
Stands still in esperance, lives not in fear.
The lamentable change is from the best;   5
The worst returns to laughter. Welcome, then,
Thou unsubstantial air that I embrace!
The wretch that thou hast blown unto the worst
Owes nothing to thy blasts. But who comes here?

Enter Gloucester, led by an Old Man

My father, poorly led? World, world, O world!   10
But that thy strange mutations make us hate thee,
Life would not yield to age.[1]

Old man
O, my good lord, I have been your tenant, and
your father's tenant, these fourscore years.

Gloucester
Away, get thee away! Good friend, be gone: 15
Thy comforts can do me no good at all;
Thee they may hurt.

Old man
Alack, sir, you cannot see your way.

Gloucester
I have no way, and therefore want no eyes;
I stumbled when I saw. Full oft 'tis seen,   20
Our means secure us, and our mere defects
Prove our commodities. O dear son Edgar,
The food of thy abused father's wrath!
Might I but live to see thee in my touch,
I'd say I had eyes again!   25

Old man
How now! Who's there?

Edgar
[Aside] O gods! Who is't can say 'I am at the worst'?
I am worse than e'er I was.

Old man
'Tis poor mad Tom.

*Edgar must stick to his disguise
in order to keep himself safe*

[1] *We wouldn't grow old if
we could help it*

*Like Lear, Gloucester grows
spiritually through suffering*

'Tis the times' plague, when madmen lead the blind

– *GLOUCESTER*

Edgar	*[Aside]* And worse I may be yet: the worst is not	30
	So long as we can say, 'This is the worst.'[2]	
Old man	Fellow, where goest?	
Gloucester	Is it a beggar-man?	
Old man	Madman and beggar too.	
Gloucester	He has some reason, else he could not beg.	35
	I' th' last night's storm I such a fellow saw;	
	Which made me think a man a worm. My son	
	Came then into my mind; and yet my mind	
	Was then scarce friends with him. I have heard	
	more since.	
	As flies to wanton boys, are we to th' gods.	40
	They kill us for their sport.	
Edgar	*[Aside]* How should this be?	

[2] As long as we can still speak, we haven't hit our lowest point: death

We always know the truth even if we sometimes choose to ignore it

> Bad is the trade that must play fool to sorrow,
> Ang'ring itself and others. – Bless thee, master!

Gloucester   Is that the naked fellow?   45

Old man   Ay, my lord.

Gloucester   Then, prithee, get thee gone. If, for my sake,
Thou wilt o'ertake us hence a mile or twain,
I' th' way toward Dover, do it for ancient love;
And bring some covering for this naked soul,   50
Who I'll entreat to lead me.

Old man   Alack, sir, he is mad.

Gloucester   'Tis the times' plague,[3] when madmen lead the blind.
Do as I bid thee, or rather do thy pleasure;
Above the rest, be gone.   55

[3] *It's a sign of the times*

Old man   I'll bring him the best 'parel[4] that I have,
Come on't what will.

[4] *Clothes (apparel)*

Exit

Gloucester   Sirrah, naked fellow, –

Edgar   Poor Tom's a-cold. *[Aside]* I cannot daub it further.[5]

[5] *He can't pretend any more*

Gloucester   Come hither, fellow.   60

Edgar   *[Aside]* And yet I must. – Bless thy sweet eyes,
they bleed.

Gloucester   Know'st thou the way to Dover?

Edgar   Both stile and gate, horse-way and foot-path. Poor Tom
hath been scar'd out of his good wits. Bless thee, good   65
man's son, from the foul fiend! Five fiends have been
in poor Tom at once; of lust, as Obidicut; Hobbididence,
prince of dumbness; Mahu, of stealing; Modo, of murder;
Flibbertigibbet, of mopping and mowing,[6] who since
possesses chambermaids and waiting-women. So,   70
bless thee, master!

Edgar is talking nonsense to prevent his father discovering his real identity. Shakespeare's audience would have found this entertaining

[6] *Frowning*

[7] *Lecherous*

[8] *Gloucester intends to commit suicide*

Gloucester	Here, take this purse, thou whom the heavens' plagues Have humbled to all strokes. That I am wretched Makes thee the happier; heavens, deal so still! Let the superfluous and lust-dieted[7] man, 75 That slaves your ordinance, that will not see Because he doth not feel, feel your power quickly; So distribution should undo excess, And each man have enough. Dost thou know Dover?
Edgar	Ay, master. 80
Gloucester	There is a cliff, whose high and bending head Looks fearfully in the confined deep: Bring me but to the very brim of it, And I'll repair the misery thou dost bear With something rich about me. From that place 85 I shall no leading need.[8]
Edgar	Give me thy arm; Poor Tom shall lead thee.

Exit

THIS SCENE MARKS the reunion of father and son when Edgar, disguised as Poor Tom, is asked to lead Gloucester to Dover. Like Lear, it is clear that Gloucester has learned much through suffering. He tugs at the heartstrings of the audience both because of his wretched appearance and because of his deep remorse:

I have no way, and therefore want no eyes;
I stumbled when I saw.

Like Lear, Gloucester comments on the unfairness of society and the unequal distribution of wealth. He redresses this by giving Tom some money, and asks to be led towards Dover. Gloucester's literal blindness is a rich metaphor for how we can all be blind, when we choose not to see what we do not want to see.

KEY **POINTS**

- *Edgar and Gloucester are reunited, unbeknownst to Gloucester as Edgar maintains his disguise.*

- *Edgar leads Gloucester to Dover, where the English and French forces will do battle.*

There is a cliff, whose high and bending head Looks fearfully in the confined deep

– *GLOUCESTER*

BEFORE ALBANY'S PALACE

Enter Goneril and Edmund

Goneril Welcome, my lord! I marvel our mild husband
Not met us on the way. –

Enter Oswald

Now, where's your master?

Now we see why there were rumoured tensions between Cornwall and Albany, for, unlike Cornwall, Albany is a good man and is on Lear's side. This is the first sign that Goneril and Regan's plot will not be successful

Oswald Madam, within; but never man so chang'd.
I told him of the army that was landed;   5
He smiled at it. I told him you were coming;
His answer was 'The worse.' Of Gloucester's treachery,
And of the loyal service of his son,
When I inform'd him, then he call'd me sot,
And told me I had turn'd the wrong side out.   10
What most he should dislike seems pleasant to him;
What like, offensive.

[1] He's a coward

Goneril *[To Edmund]* Then shall you go no further.
It is the cowish terror of his spirit,[1]
That dares not undertake; he'll not feel wrongs   15
Which tie him to an answer. Our wishes on the way
May prove effects. Back, Edmund, to my brother;
Hasten his musters[2] and conduct his powers.[3]

[2] Gathering of soldiers [3] Army
[4] Household duties

I must change arms at home, and give the distaff[4]
Into my husband's hands. This trusty servant   20
Shall pass between us. Ere long you are like to hear,
If you dare venture in your own behalf,
A mistress's command. Wear this; spare speech;

[5] A token of affection

[Giving a favour][5]
Decline your head. This kiss, if it durst speak,
Would stretch thy spirits up into the air.   25
Conceive, and fare thee well.

Edmund Yours in the ranks of death.

Goneril My most dear Gloucester!

Exit Edmund

O, the difference of man and man!

	To thee a woman's services are due:	30
	My fool usurps my body.	
Oswald	Madam, here comes my lord.	
	Exit Oswald and enter Albany	
Goneril	I have been worth the whistle.	
Albany	O Goneril!	
	You are not worth the dust which the rude wind	35
	Blows in your face. I fear your disposition:[6]	
	That nature, which contemns its origin,	
	Cannot be border'd certain in itself.	
	She that herself will sliver and disbranch	
	From her material sap, perforce must wither	40
	And come to deadly use.	
Goneril	No more; the text is foolish.	
Albany	Wisdom and goodness to the vile seem vile:	
	Filths savour but themselves. What have you done?	
	Tigers, not daughters, what have you perform'd?	45
	A father, and a gracious aged man,	
	Whose reverence even the head-lugg'd[7] bear would lick,	
	Most barbarous, most degenerate! have you madded.	
	Could my good brother suffer you to do it?	
	A man, a prince, by him so benefited!	50
	If that the heavens do not their visible spirits	
	Send quickly down to tame these vile offences,	
	It will come,	
	Humanity must perforce prey on itself,	
	Like monsters of the deep.	55
Goneril	Milk-liver'd man![8]	
	That bear'st a cheek for blows, a head for wrongs,	
	Who hast not in thy brows an eye discerning	
	Thine honour from thy suffering, that not know'st	
	Fools do those villains pity who are punish'd	60
	Ere they have done their mischief, where's thy drum?	
	France spreads his banners in our noiseless land;	
	With plumed helm thy state begins to threat;	
	Whiles thou, a moral fool, sits still, and criest,	

Goneril defends her overtures to Edmund by saying that Albany does not deserve her

[6] *Character*

Albany echoes Lear's earlier tirade about Goneril not being fit to breed because there is something very wrong with her soul

[7] *Temperamental*

A powerful speech by Albany, which shows that the French have a formidable ally in him

[8] *Coward*

'Alack, why does he so?' 65

Albany
See thyself, devil!
Proper deformity seems not in the fiend
So horrid as in woman.

Goneril
O vain fool!

⁹ *Disguised*

Albany
Thou changed and self-cover'd⁹ thing, for shame, 70
Be-monster not thy feature. Were't my fitness
To let these hands obey my blood,
They are apt enough to dislocate and tear
Thy flesh and bones. Howe'er thou art a fiend,

¹⁰ *Goneril is protected because Albany cannot hit a woman*

A woman's shape doth shield thee.¹⁰ 75

Goneril
Marry, your manhood now –

Enter a Messenger

Albany
What news?

Messenger
O, my good lord, the Duke of Cornwall's dead;
Slain by his servant, going to put out
The other eye of Gloucester. 80

Albany
Gloucester's eye!

¹¹ *Filled*

Messenger
A servant that he bred, thrill'd¹¹ with remorse,
Opposed against the act, bending his sword
To his great master; who, thereat enrag'd,
Flew on him, and amongst them fell'd him dead; 85
But not without that harmful stroke, which since
Hath pluck'd him after.

Albany
This shows you are above,

¹² *Worst*

You justicers, that these our nether¹² crimes
So speedily can venge! But, O poor Gloucester! 90
Lost he his other eye?

Messenger
Both, both, my lord.
This letter, madam, craves a speedy answer;
'Tis from your sister.

Goneril
[Aside] One way I like this well; 95

But being widow, and my Gloucester with her,
May all the building in my fancy pluck
Upon my hateful life.[13] Another way,
The news is not so tart. – I'll read, and answer.

Exit

Albany	Where was his son when they did take his eyes?	100

Messenger   Come with my lady hither.

Albany   He is not here.

Messenger   No, my good lord; I met him back again.

Albany   Knows he the wickedness?

Messenger   Ay, my good lord; 'twas he inform'd against him;   105
And quit the house on purpose, that their punishment
Might have the freer course.

Albany   Gloucester, I live
To thank thee for the love thou show'dst the King,
And to revenge thine eyes. Come hither, friend;   110
Tell me what more thou know'st.

Exit

[13] Regan is now free to marry Edmund, while Goneril cannot marry him as long as Albany lives

EDMUND ESCORTS GONERIL to her castle, where Oswald informs them that Albany is disgusted by the events which took place at Gloucester's home. Goneril and Edmund kiss and she gives him a 'favour', signifying that she is now his. However, Albany's horror at Goneril's behaviour is a sign that her plans may yet be thwarted:

O Goneril! / You are not worth the dust which the rude wind / Blows in your face. Albany's words echo Lear's earlier opinion of Goneril and indicate that the sisters have lost a powerful ally.

A messenger arrives to inform them that Cornwall is dead. Goneril immediately fears for her relationship with Edmund as Regan is now free to marry him.

When Albany hears about Gloucester's blinding he is outraged, and at the close of this scene we can see he is firmly on the side of good. This scene is significant for building up Albany as a heroic character: *Gloucester, I live / To thank thee for the love thou show'dst the King, / And to revenge thine eyes.*

*O Goneril!
You are not worth the dust
which the rude wind
Blows in your face*

– ALBANY

KEY **POINTS**

- *Goneril is in love, or lust, with Edmund.*
- *Albany has realised his wife's duplicity, and it is clear that his loyalties lie with Lear.*

THE FRENCH CAMP NEAR DOVER

Enter Kent and a Gentleman

Kent	Why the King of France is so suddenly gone back, know you the reason?
Gentleman	Something he left imperfect in the state, which since his coming forth is thought of; which imports to the kingdom so much fear and danger that his personal return was most required and necessary.
Kent	Who hath he left behind him General?
Gentleman	The Marshal of France, Monsieur La Far.
Kent	Did your letters pierce the Queen to any demonstration of grief?
Gentleman	Ay, sir; she took them, read them in my presence; And now and then an ample tear trill'd down Her delicate cheek. It seem'd she was a queen Over her passion, who, most rebel-like, Sought to be king o'er her.
Kent	O, then it mov'd her.
Gentleman	Not to a rage: patience and sorrow strove Who should express her goodliest. You have seen Sunshine and rain at once: her smiles and tears Were like a better way; those happy smilets, That play'd on her ripe lip, seem'd not to know What guests were in her eyes; which parted thence, As pearls from diamonds dropp'd. In brief, Sorrow would be a rarity most beloved, If all could so become it.
Kent	Made she no verbal question?
Gentleman	'Faith, once or twice she heaved the name of 'father' Pantingly forth, as if it press'd her heart; Cried 'Sisters! sisters! Shame of ladies! sisters! Kent! father! sisters! What, i' th' storm? i' th' night? Let pity not be believ'd!' There she shook

If France can't personally command the army, the French might not necessarily succeed against the British army

This touching image of Cordelia's gentle nature is in marked contrast with her sisters' horrible personalities

KING LEAR 153

The holy water from her heavenly eyes,
And clamour moisten'd; then away she started
To deal with grief alone.

Kent   It is the stars,   35
The stars above us, govern our conditions;
Else one self mate and mate could not beget
Such different issues. You spoke not with her since?

Gentleman   No.

Kent   Was this before the King return'd?   40

Gentleman   No, since.

Kent   Well, sir, the poor distressed Lear's i' th' town;
Who sometime, in his better tune, remembers
What we are come about, and by no means
Will yield to see his daughter.   45

Gentleman   Why, good sir?

Kent   A sovereign shame so elbows him. His own unkindness,
That stripp'd her from his benediction,¹ turn'd her
To foreign casualties, gave her dear rights
To his dog-hearted daughters, – these things sting   50
His mind so venomously, that burning shame
Detains him from Cordelia.

Gentleman   Alack, poor gentleman!

Kent   Of Albany's and Cornwall's powers you heard not?

Gentleman   'Tis so, they are afoot.   55

Kent   Well, sir, I'll bring you to our master Lear,
And leave you to attend him. Some dear cause
Will in concealment wrap me up a while;
When I am known aright, you shall not grieve
Lending me this acquaintance. I pray you, go   60
Along with me.

Exit

THIS SHORT SCENE takes place in the French camp at Dover. We learn that the King of France himself had to return home, and that Cordelia is at the camp, anxiously awaiting a reunion with her father. Lear, for his part, is too ashamed to meet Cordelia. It is an ominous sign that France will not be there to lead his own troops.

*The stars above us,
govern our conditions;
Else one self mate and
mate could not beget
Such different issues*

– KENT

KEY **POINTS**

- *The King of France has had to return home unexpectedly.*

- *Cordelia wishes to reconcile with her father, but he is so full of shame and remorse that he cannot face her.*

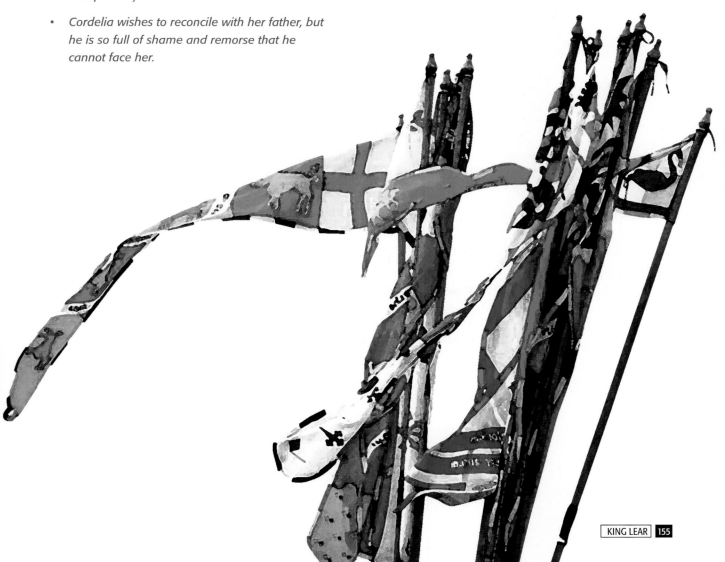

THE FRENCH CAMP NEAR DOVER. A TENT

Enter, with drum and colours, Cordelia, Doctor, and Soldiers

Cordelia	Alack, 'tis he! Why, he was met even now
	As mad as the vex'd sea, singing aloud,
	Crown'd with rank fumiter[1] and furrow-weeds,
	With hardocks, hemlock, nettles, cuckoo-flowers,
	Darnel, and all the idle weeds that grow
	In our sustaining corn. A century send forth;
	Search every acre in the high-grown field,
	And bring him to our eye.

Exit an Officer

What can man's wisdom
In the restoring his bereaved sense?[2]
He that helps him take all my outward worth.

Doctor	There is means, madam.
	Our foster-nurse of nature is repose,
	The which he lacks; that to provoke in him,
	Are many simples operative, whose power
	Will close the eye of anguish.

Cordelia	All blest secrets,
	All you unpublish'd virtues of the earth,
	Spring with my tears! be aidant and remediate
	In the good man's distress! Seek, seek for him;
	Lest his ungovern'd rage dissolve the life
	That wants the means to lead it.

Enter a Messenger

Messenger	News, madam;
	The British powers are marching hitherward.

Cordelia	'Tis known before; our preparation stands
	In expectation of them. O dear father,
	It is thy business that I go about;
	Therefore great France
	My mourning and important tears hath pitied.
	No blown ambition doth our arms incite,
	But love, dear love, and our aged father's right:
	Soon may I hear and see him!

Exit

5

10

15

20

25

30

[1] A herb which was used to treat madness

Lear is wandering the countryside, mad, bedecked with wild flowers, in stark contrast to the rich robes he would have worn as king

[2] Cordelia is asking if it is possible to cure Lear

Cordelia earnestly wishes for her father's return to health

ANOTHER SHORT SCENE, in which Cordelia

describes her father's condition – mad, bedecked with flowers, running through the fields:

> *Alack, 'tis he! Why, he was met even now*
> *As mad as the vex'd sea, singing aloud,*
> *Crown'd with rank fumiter and furrow-weeds,*
> *With hardocks, hemlock, nettles, cuckoo-flowers* …

Cordelia receives news that the British powers are advancing, and she reiterates that she is waging war, not for the sake of it, but to reinstate her father. Her love and concern are clearly evident.

KEY **POINT**

- *Lear is wandering the heath, dressed only with wild flowers, while Cordelia anxiously awaits the reunion with her father.*

Alack, 'tis he! Why, he was met even now
As mad as the vex'd sea, singing aloud

– CORDELIA

GLOUCESTER'S CASTLE

Enter Regan and Oswald

Regan	But are my brother's powers set forth?
Oswald	Ay, madam.
Regan	Himself in person there?
Oswald	Madam, with much ado. Your sister is the better soldier.	5

Regan   Lord Edmund spake not with your lord at home?

Oswald   No, madam.

Regan   What might import my sister's letter to him?

Oswald   I know not, lady.

Regan   Faith, he is posted hence on serious matter.   10
It was great ignorance, Gloucester's eyes being out,
To let him live; where he arrives he moves
All hearts against us. Edmund, I think, is gone,
In pity of his misery, to dispatch[1]
His nighted life; moreover, to descry[2]   15
The strength o' th' enemy.

Oswald   I must needs after him, madam, with my letter.

Regan   Our troops set forth to-morrow; stay with us;
The ways are dangerous.

Oswald   I may not, madam;   20
My lady charg'd my duty in this business.

Regan   Why should she write to Edmund? Might not you
Transport her purposes by word? Belike,
Some things – I know not what: I'll love thee much, –
Let me unseal the letter.   25

Oswald   Madam, I had rather –

[1] *End*

[2] *Spy*

*Regan is just as jealous of
Goneril as Goneril is of her*

Regan	I know your lady does not love her husband;
	I am sure of that, and at her late being here
	She gave strange oeillades³ and most speaking looks
	To noble Edmund. I know you are of her bosom. 30

³ *Loving glances*

| Oswald | I, madam? |

Regan	I speak in understanding; y' are; I know 't.
	Therefore I do advise you, take this note:
	My lord is dead; Edmund and I have talk'd;
	And more convenient is he for my hand 35
	Than for your lady's. You may gather more.
	If you do find him, pray you, give him this;
	And when your mistress hears thus much from you,
	I pray, desire her call her wisdom to her.
	So, fare you well. 40
	If you do chance to hear of that blind traitor,
	Preferment falls on him that cuts him off.⁴

⁴ *Regan will reward whoever kills Gloucester*

| Oswald | Would I could meet him, madam! I should show |
| | What party I do follow. |

| Regan | Fare thee well. 45 |

Exit

OSWALD DELIVERS GONERIL'S letter to Regan, and informs her that the British troops are advancing on the French. Regan really only seems to care about Edmund and the possibility that she might lose him to Goneril. She asks Oswald to deliver Edmund a note from her, casually adding that he should kill Gloucester if he comes across him, as his pathetic state is turning people against her.

KEY **POINTS**

- *The British troops are advancing on Dover.*

- *The love triangle between Goneril, Regan and Edmund is creating tension between the sisters.*

Why should she write to Edmund? Might not you Transport her purposes by word?

– REGAN

FIELDS NEAR DOVER

Enter Gloucester and Edgar dressed like a peasant

Gloucester When shall we come to th' top of that same hill?

Edgar You do climb up it now: look, how we labour.

Gloucester Methinks the ground is even.

Edgar Horrible steep.
Hark, do you hear the sea?   5

Gloucester No, truly.

Edgar Why, then, your other senses grow imperfect
By your eyes' anguish.

Edgar convinces his father that they are climbing a steep cliff by saying that the pain of Gloucester's injury is confusing him

Gloucester So may it be, indeed.
Methinks thy voice is alter'd, and thou speak'st   10
In better phrase and matter than thou didst.

Edgar You're much deceived. In nothing am I changed
But in my garments.

Gloucester Methinks you're better spoken.

Edgar Come on, sir, here's the place; stand still. How fearful   15
And dizzy 'tis, to cast one's eyes so low!
The crows and choughs[1] that wing the midway air
Show scarce so gross as beetles. Half way down
Hangs one that gathers samphire,[2] dreadful trade!
Methinks he seems no bigger than his head.   20
The fishermen, that walk upon the beach,
Appear like mice; and yond tall anchoring bark,[3]
Diminish'd to her cock;[4] her cock, a buoy
Almost too small for sight. The murmuring surge,
That on the unnumb'red[5] idle pebbles chafes,   25
Cannot be heard so high. I'll look no more,
Lest my brain turn, and the deficient sight
Topple down headlong.

Gloucester Set me where you stand.

[1] *Jackdaws*

[2] *A herb*

[3] *Large ship*

[4] *A small rowing boat carried on a large ship*

[5] *Infinite*

Edgar	Give me your hand; you are now within a foot	30
	Of the extreme verge. For all beneath the moon	
	Would I not leap upright.	

Gloucester Let go my hand.
Here, friend, 's another purse; in it a jewel
Well worth a poor man's taking. Fairies and gods   35
Prosper it with thee! Go thou farther off;
Bid me farewell, and let me hear thee going.

Edgar Now fare ye well, good sir.

Gloucester With all my heart.

Edgar explains he is only fooling his father to save him

Edgar Why I do trifle thus with his despair   40
Is done to cure it.

Gloucester *[Kneeling]* O you mighty gods!
This world I do renounce, and in your sights
Shake patiently my great affliction off.

Gloucester is in too much emotional and physical pain to live. His pain is unbearable

If I could bear it longer, and not fall
To quarrel with your great opposeless wills,   45
My snuff and loathed part of nature should
Burn itself out. If Edgar live, O, bless him!
Now, fellow, fare thee well.

He falls forward

Edgar Gone, sir; farewell.
– And yet I know not how conceit may rob   50
The treasury of life, when life itself
Yields to the theft. Had he been where he thought,
By this, had thought been past. Alive or dead? –
Ho, you sir! friend! Hear you, sir! speak! –
Thus might he pass indeed: yet he revives. –   55
What are you, sir?

Gloucester Away, and let me die.

6 Light, cobwebby
7 Thrown headlong

Edgar Hadst thou been aught but gossamer,[6] feathers, air,
So many fathom down precipitating,[7]
Thou'dst shiver'd like an egg: but thou dost breathe;   60
Hast heavy substance; bleed'st not; speak'st; art sound.
Ten masts at each make not the altitude

	Which thou hast perpendicularly fell. Thy life's a miracle. Speak yet again.	
Gloucester	But have I fall'n, or no?	65
Edgar	From the dread summit of this chalky bourn.[8] Look up a-height; the shrill-gorged lark so far Cannot be seen or heard: do but look up.	
Gloucester	Alack, I have no eyes. Is wretchedness depriv'd that benefit, To end itself by death? 'Twas yet some comfort, When misery could beguile[9] the tyrant's rage, And frustrate his proud will.	70
Edgar	Give me your arm: Up: so. How is 't? Feel you your legs? You stand.	75
Gloucester	Too well, too well.	
Edgar	This is above all strangeness. Upon the crown o' the cliff, what thing was that Which parted from you?	
Gloucester	A poor unfortunate beggar.	80
Edgar	As I stood here below, methought his eyes Were two full moons; he had a thousand noses, Horns whelk'd and waved[10] like the enridged[11] sea. It was some fiend; therefore, thou happy father, Think that the clearest gods, who make them honours Of men's impossibilities, have preserv'd thee.	85
Gloucester	I do remember now. Henceforth I'll bear Affliction till it do cry out itself 'Enough, enough,' and die. That thing you speak of, I took it for a man; often 'twould say 'The fiend, the fiend.' He led me to that place.	90
Edgar	Bear free and patient thoughts. But who comes here?	
	Enter Lear, fantastically dressed with wild flowers	
	The safer sense will ne'er accommodate	

Edgar makes out that it is a miracle that Gloucester has survived. He is trying to make his father think he is meant to live. Also, in those days, if you committed suicide you could not be buried in consecrated ground and thus would not go to heaven

[8] From the edge of the white cliffs of Dover

Gloucester ponders whether there is any respite for a man such as he

[9] Thwart

[10] Horny and knobbly   [11] Wavy

Gloucester resolves to endure his life until he dies a natural death

His master thus.

Lear   No, they cannot touch[12] me for coining; I am the   95
King himself.

Edgar   O thou side-piercing sight!

Lear   Nature's above art in that respect. There's your
press-money.[13] That fellow handles his bow like a
crow-keeper;[14] draw me a clothier's yard.[15] Look,   100
look, a mouse! Peace, peace; this piece of toasted
cheese will do 't. There's my gauntlet;[16] I'll prove
it on a giant. Bring up the brown bills.[17] O, well
flown, bird! i' th; clout, i' th' clout: hewgh!
Give the word.[18]   105

Edgar   Sweet marjoram.

Lear   Pass.

Gloucester   I know that voice.

Lear   Ha! Goneril, with a white beard! They flattered
me like a dog; and told me I had white hairs in my   110
beard ere the black ones were there. To say 'ay'
and 'no' to everything that I said! – 'Ay' and 'no'
too was no good divinity. When the rain came to
wet me once, and the wind to make me chatter; when
the thunder would not peace at my bidding; there I   115
found 'em, there I smelt 'em out. Go to, they are
not men o' their words: they told me I was everything;
'tis a lie, I am not ague-proof.[19]

Gloucester   The trick of that voice I do well remember:
Is 't not the King?   120

Lear   Ay, every inch a king:
When I do stare, see how the subject quakes.
I pardon that man's life. What was thy cause?
Adultery?
Thou shalt not die: die for adultery! No: 125
The wren goes to 't, and the small gilded fly
Does lecher[20] in my sight.
Let copulation thrive; for Gloucester's bastard son

---

[12] Punish

[13] Money paid to new army recruits
[14] Someone who shoots crows for a living
[15] A yard-long arrow

[16] Challenge
[17] Foot soldiers

[18] Password

Lear has moved from anger at his daughters' betrayal to an acceptance of his own part in the events that unfolded. He realises he should never have believed them when they told him he was perfect, because no one is perfect. He also acknowledges that he couldn't handle the truth because he was used to being agreed with, whether he was right or wrong

[19] Disease-proof

[20] Copulate

Was kinder to his father than my daughters
Got 'tween the lawful sheets. To 't, luxury, pell-mell!   130
For I lack soldiers. Behold yond simp'ring dame,
Whose face between her forks[21] presageth snow;

[21] Legs

That minces virtue, and does shake the head
To hear of pleasure's name;
The fitchew,[22] nor the soiled horse, goes to 't   135
With a more riotous appetite.

[22] Weasel

Down from the waist they are Centaurs,[23]
Though women all above;

[23] They have the body of a horse

But to the girdle do the gods inherit,
Beneath[24] is all the fiends'; there's hell, there's darkness,   140
there's the sulphurous pit, burning, scalding,

[24] Below the waist

Stench, consumption; fie, fie, fie! pah, pah!
Give me an ounce of civet,[25] good apothecary,

[25] Musk from an animal

To sweeten my imagination:
There's money for thee.   145

Gloucester O, let me kiss that hand!

Lear Let me wipe it first; it smells of mortality.

Gloucester O ruin'd piece of nature! This great world
Shall so wear out to nought. Dost thou know me?

Lear I remember thine eyes well enough. Dost thou squiny   150
at me? No, do thy worst, blind Cupid! I'll not love. Read
thou this challenge; mark but the penning of it.

Gloucester Were all the letters suns, I could not see one.

Edgar I would not take this from report; it is,
And my heart breaks at it.   155

Lear Read.

Gloucester What, with the case of eyes?

Lear O, ho, are you there with me? No eyes in your head, nor
no money in your purse? Your eyes are in a heavy case,
your purse in a light;[26] yet you see how this world goes.   160

[26] He is blind, and poor

Gloucester I see it feelingly.

Lear   What, art mad? A man may see how this world goes
with no eyes. Look with thine ears: see how yond
justice rails upon yond simple thief.[27] Hark, in thine ear:
change places, and, handy-dandy, which is the justice,   165
which is the thief? Thou hast seen a farmer's dog bark
at a beggar?

Gloucester   Ay, sir.

Lear   And the creature run from the cur?
There thou mightst behold the great image of authority: 170
a dog's obeyed in office.
Thou rascal beadle, hold thy bloody hand!
Why dost thou lash that whore? Strip thine own back;
Thou hotly lust'st to use her in that kind
For which thou whipp'st her. The usurer[28] hangs the
cozener.[29]
Through tatter'd clothes small vices do appear;   175
Robes and furr'd gowns hide all. Plate sin with gold,
And the strong lance of justice hurtless breaks;
Arm it in rags, a pigmy's straw does pierce it.
None does offend, none, I say, none; I'll able 'em:
Take that of me, my friend, who have the power   180
To seal the accuser's lips. Get thee glass eyes,
And like a scurvy politician, seem
To see the things thou dost not. Now, now, now, now:
Pull off my boots: harder, harder: so.

Edgar   O, matter and impertinency mix'd!   185
Reason in madness![30]

Lear   If thou wilt weep my fortunes, take my eyes.
I know thee well enough; thy name is Gloucester.
Thou must be patient; we came crying hither.
Thou know'st, the first time that we smell the air,   190
We wawl and cry. I will preach to thee: mark.

Gloucester   Alack, alack the day!

Lear   When we are born, we cry that we are come
To this great stage of fools. – This a good block.
It were a delicate stratagem,[31] to shoe   195
A troop of horse with felt: I'll put 't in proof;
And when I have stol'n upon these sons-in-law,

Then, kill, kill, kill, kill, kill, kill!
Enter a Gentleman, with Attendants

Gentleman   O, here he is: lay hand upon him. Sir,   200
                  Your most dear daughter –

Lear   No rescue? What, a prisoner? I am even
                  The natural fool of fortune. Use me well;
                  You shall have ransom. Let me have surgeons;
                  I am cut to th' brains.   205

Gentleman   You shall have anything.

Lear   No seconds? All myself?
                  Why, this would make a man a man of salt,
                  To use his eyes for garden water-pots,
                  Ay, and laying autumn's dust.   210

Gentleman   Good sir, –

Lear   I will die bravely, like a smug bridegroom. What!
                  I will be jovial. Come, come; I am a king,
                  My masters, know you that.

Gentleman   You are a royal one, and we obey you.   215

Lear   Then there's life in't. Nay, if you get it, you
                  shall get it with running. Sa, sa, sa, sa.

                  Exit running; Attendants follow

Gentleman   A sight most pitiful in the meanest wretch,
                  Past speaking of in a king! Thou hast one daughter,
                  Who redeems Nature from the general curse   220
                  Which twain have brought her to.

Edgar   Hail, gentle sir.

Gentleman   Sir, speed you: what's your will?

Edgar   Do you hear aught, sir, of a battle toward?

Gentleman   Most sure and vulgar: every one hears that,
                  Which can distinguish sound.   225

*This would make a man cry enough
tears to water his garden*

Edgar	But, by your favour, How near's the other army?

The army is expected within an hour. This increases the tension and suspense for the audience

Gentleman	Near and on speedy foot; the main descry Stands on the hourly thought.
Edgar	I thank you, sir: that's all.
Gentleman	Though that the Queen on special cause is here, Her army is mov'd on.
Edgar	I thank you, sir.

Exit Gentleman

Gloucester	You ever-gentle gods, take my breath from me; Let not my worser spirit tempt me again To die before you please!
Edgar	Well pray you, father.
Gloucester	Now, good sir, what are you?

Edgar says that he has suffered himself (remember, he is still in disguise) and that is why he has compassion for Gloucester. This also ties in with one of the themes of King Lear: learning through suffering

Edgar	A most poor man, made tame to fortune's blows; Who, by the art of known and feeling sorrows, Am pregnant to good pity. Give me your hand, I'll lead you to some biding.
Gloucester	Hearty thanks; The bounty and the benison of Heaven To boot, and boot!

Enter Oswald

Oswald is delighted to see Gloucester because he wants to get the reward for killing him

Oswald	A proclaim'd prize! Most happy! That eyeless head of thine was first fram'd flesh To raise my fortunes. Thou old unhappy traitor, Briefly thyself remember; the sword is out That must destroy thee.

[32] *Gloucester obviously doesn't really care if he dies*

Gloucester	Now let thy friendly hand Put strength enough to 't.[32]

Edgar interposes

Line numbers: 230, 235, 240, 245, 250

Oswald	Wherefore, bold peasant,
	Dar'st thou support a publish'd traitor? Hence;
	Lest that the infection of his fortune take	255
	Like hold on thee. Let go his arm.

Edgar   'Chill not let go, zir, without vurther 'casion.[33]

[33] *I won't let him go without a good reason*

Oswald   Let go, slave, or thou diest!

Edgar   Good gentleman, go your gait, and let poor volk
pass. An 'chud ha' bin zwaggered out of my life,   260
'twould not ha' bin zo long as 'tis by a vortnight.
Nay, come not near th' old man; keep out, 'che vor
ye, or Ise try whether your costard or my ballow be
the harder. 'Chill be plain with you.

Edgar, putting on another accent, tells Oswald to get on his way and leave poor folk alone. He says that if big talk could kill him, he would have died years ago, and warns Oswald again to stay away from Gloucester

Oswald   Out, dunghill!   265

Edgar   'Chill pick your teeth, zir: come; no matter vor your foins.[34]

[34] *I'll knock your teeth out, sir. To hell with your sword!*

They fight, and Edgar knocks him down

Oswald   Slave, thou hast slain me. Villain, take my purse.
If ever thou wilt thrive, bury my body;
And give the letters which thou find'st about me
To Edmund Earl of Gloucester; seek him out   270
Upon the British party. O, untimely death!

Now Goneril's treasonous letter proposing the death of Albany has fallen into Edgar's hands. The momentum towards good is gaining pace against the movement of evil

Dies

Edgar   I know thee well: a serviceable villain;
As duteous[35] to the vices of thy mistress
As badness would desire.

[35] *Dutiful*

Gloucester   What, is he dead?   275

Edgar   Sit you down, father; rest you.
Let's see these pockets; the letters that he speaks of
May be my friends. He's dead; I am only sorry
He had no other death's-man.[36] Let us see.
Leave, gentle wax; and, manners, blame us not.   280
To know our enemies' minds, we'd rip their hearts;
     Their papers, is more lawful. [Reads]
     'Let our reciprocal vows be remembered. You have

[36] *Edgar is only sorry he had to be the one to kill Oswald*

Goneril's letter is as blatant as Edgar would have hoped. She is telling Edmund to take advantage of the confusion of battle to kill Albany. This is treason, which is punishable by death

37 Unlimited

*many opportunities to cut him off; if your will
want not, time and place will be fruitfully offered.* 285
*There is nothing done, if he return the conqueror;
then am I the prisoner, and his bed my goal; from
the loathed warmth whereof deliver me, and supply
the place for your labour.*
Your – wife, so I would say – Affectionate servant, 290
Goneril.
O undistinguish'd³⁷ space of woman's will!
A plot upon her virtuous husband's life;
And the exchange my brother! Here, in the sands,

38 Edgar will bury Oswald in the sand

Thee I'll rake up,³⁸ the post unsanctified 295
Of murderous lechers: and in the mature time
With this ungracious paper strike the sight
Of the death-practis'd Duke. For him 'tis well
That of thy death and business I can tell.

Edgar is going to wait for the right time to show Albany the letter

Gloucester   The King is mad: how stiff is my vile sense, 300
That I stand up, and have ingenious feeling
Of my huge sorrows! Better I were distract:
So should my thoughts be sever'd from my griefs,
And woes by wrong imaginations lose
The knowledge of themselves. 305

Gloucester wishes for the oblivion of insanity so that he does not have to think about his mistakes and what he has suffered

Edgar   Give me your hand:

Drum afar off

Far off, methinks, I hear the beaten drum:
Come, father, I'll bestow you with a friend.

Exit

EDGAR SAVES HIS father from suicide by tricking him into thinking he has jumped off a cliff. Gloucester then resolves to bear what he must from now on.

Lear and Gloucester meet in this scene. The meeting between the vulnerable old men is heartbreaking. They have been emotionally and physically battered by events. Gloucester's eye sockets are no doubt bleeding, and Lear is pathetically bedecked with flowers. One is blind, the other is mad. Their hearts have been broken and, in every sense of the word, they are lost. And yet, in their vulnerability, both show the great men that they really are, deep inside. We see Lear's radical sympathy for the poor and the dispossessed, and Gloucester's awareness of how he stumbled when he saw. It is one of the most affecting key moments of the play, not least because of the touching fact that Gloucester is still utterly loyal to Lear.

KEY **POINTS**

- Edgar rescues his father from suicide in an altruistic gesture of love, and also kills Oswald to protect him.

- Lear and Gloucester, two vulnerable old men with a long history, meet in a pathetic and poignant scene.

- Edgar has Goneril's treasonous letter in his possession. This marks a reversal of fortune for the two evil sisters.

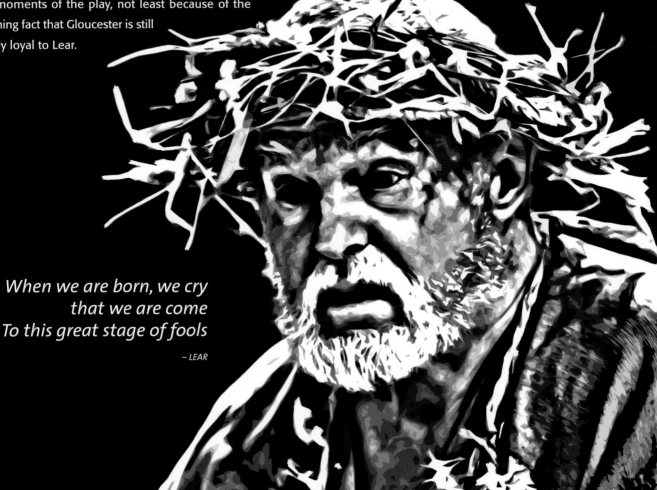

When we are born, we cry
that we are come
To this great stage of fools

– LEAR

A TENT IN THE FRENCH CAMP. LEAR ON A BED ASLEEP,
Soft music playing; Gentleman, and others attending

Enter Cordelia, Kent, and Doctor

Cordelia	O thou good Kent, how shall I live and work,
	To match thy goodness? My life will be too short,
	And every measure fail me.

Kent	To be acknowledg'd, madam, is o'erpaid.[1]	
	All my reports go with the modest truth;	5
	Nor more nor clipp'd, but so.	

[1] Cordelia's kind words are payment enough for Kent

Cordelia	Be better suited:
	These weeds are memories of those worser hours.
	I prithee, put them off.

Kent	Pardon me, dear madam;	10
	Yet to be known shortens my made intent.	
	My boon[2] I make it, that you know me not	
	Till time and I think meet.	

[2] Advantage

Cordelia	Then be't so, my good lord. *[To the Doctor]* How does
	the King?

Doctor	Madam, sleeps still.	15

Cordelia	O you kind gods,
	Cure this great breach in his abused nature!
	Th' untun'd and jarring senses, O, wind up
	Of this child-changed[3] father!

[3] Lear is like a child in his madness

Doctor	So please your Majesty	20
	That we may wake the King? He hath slept long.	

Cordelia	Be govern'd by your knowledge, and proceed
	I' th' sway of your own will. Is he array'd?[4]

[4] Dressed appropriately

Gentleman	Ay, madam; in the heaviness of his sleep	
	We put fresh garments on him.	25

Doctor	Be by, good madam, when we do awake him;
	I doubt not of his temperance.[5]

[5] The doctor doesn't know how Lear will be when he wakes

Cordelia	Very well.

Doctor	Please you, draw near. – Louder the music there!	
Cordelia	O my dear father! Restoration hang	30
	Thy medicine on my lips; and let this kiss	
	Repair those violent harms that my two sisters	
	Have in thy reverence made!	

Cordelia hopes that when Lear wakes his sanity will be restored

Kent	Kind and dear princess!	
Cordelia	Had you not been their father, these white flakes[6]	35
	Had challenged pity of them. Was this a face	
	To be oppos'd against the warring winds?	
	To stand against the deep dread-bolted thunder?	
	In the most terrible and nimble stroke	
	Of quick, cross lightning? to watch – poor perdu! –	40
	With this thin helm?[7] Mine enemy's dog,	
	Though he had bit me, should have stood that night	
	Against my fire; and wast thou fain, poor father,	
	To hovel[8] thee with swine, and rogues forlorn,[9]	
	In short and musty straw? Alack, alack!	45
	'Tis wonder that thy life and wits at once	
	Had not concluded all. He wakes; speak to him.	

[6] Grey hair

[7] Thin, balding hair

[8] House   [9] The Fool and Poor Tom

Doctor	Madam, do you; 'tis fittest.	
Cordelia	How does my royal lord? How fares your Majesty?	
Lear	You do me wrong to take me out o' th grave:	50
	Thou art a soul in bliss;[10] but I am bound	
	Upon a wheel of fire,[11] that mine own tears	
	Do scald like molten lead.	

[10] An angel in heaven
[11] He is in hell

Cordelia	Sir, do you know me?	
Lear	You are a spirit, I know: when did you die?	55
Cordelia	Still, still, far wide!	
Doctor	He's scarce awake; let him alone a while.	
Lear	Where have I been? Where am I? Fair daylight?	
	I am mightily abused. I should e'en die with pity,	
	To see another thus. I know not what to say.	60
	I will not swear these are my hands. Let's see;	
	I feel this pin prick. Would I were assured	

Of my condition!

[12] Blessing

Cordelia   O, look upon me, sir,
And hold your hands in benediction[12] o'er me: 65
No, sir, you must not kneel.

*Lear's return to sanity is
realistically gradual. It is
almost too much for him to
accept that he has a second
chance with Cordelia*

Lear   Pray, do not mock me:
I am a very foolish fond old man,
Fourscore and upward, not an hour more nor less.
And, to deal plainly,   70
I fear I am not in my perfect mind.
Methinks I should know you, and know this man;
Yet I am doubtful; for I am mainly ignorant
What place this is; and all the skill I have
Remembers not these garments; nor I know not   75
Where I did lodge last night. Do not laugh at me;
For, as I am a man, I think this lady
To be my child Cordelia.

Cordelia   And so I am, I am.

Lear   Be your tears wet? Yes, 'faith. I pray, weep not.   80
If you have poison for me, I will drink it.
I know you do not love me; for your sisters
Have, as I do remember, done me wrong:
You have some cause, they have not.

Cordelia   No cause, no cause.   85

Lear   Am I in France?

Kent   In your own kingdom, sir.

Lear   Do not abuse me.

Doctor   Be comforted, good madam; the great rage,
You see, is kill'd in him: and yet it is danger   90
To make him even o'er the time he has lost.[13]
Desire him to go in; trouble him no more
Till further settling.

[13] The doctor warns that Lear is still fragile

Cordelia   Will't please your Highness walk?

*There is a stark contrast
between Lear's humility here
and his earlier arrogance*

Lear   You must bear with me: 95
Pray you now, forget and forgive; I am old and foolish.

Exit all but Kent and Gentleman

Gentleman   Holds it true, sir, that the Duke of Cornwall was so slain?

Kent   Most certain, sir.

Gentleman   Who is conductor of his people?

Kent   As 'tis said, the bastard son of Gloucester.

Gentleman   They say Edgar, his banished son, is with the Earl of   100
Kent in Germany.

Kent   Report is changeable. 'Tis time to look about; the
powers of the kingdom approach apace.[14]   [14] *Quickly*

Gentleman   The arbitrement[15] is like to be bloody. Fare you well, sir.   [15] *Fight*

Exit

Kent   My point[16] and period will be throughly wrought,   105   [16] *Aim*
Or well or ill, as this day's battle's fought.

Exit

MODERN ENGLISH VERSION

A TENT IN THE FRENCH CAMP. LEAR ON A BED ASLEEP,
Soft music playing; Gentleman, and others attending

Enter Cordelia, Kent, and Doctor

Cordelia   Oh Kent, how can I repay you for everything you have done?
My lifetime is too short for all I owe you.

Kent   The thanks you have given me is more than enough. I don't
need anything more.

Cordelia   Those rags and weeds my father is wearing belong in the bin.
I'll ask the servants to put clean clothes on him.

Kent   I don't want to reveal my identity just yet. Will you keep my
secret?

Cordelia   Of course. *[To the Doctor]* How is the king?

Doctor   Madam, he is still asleep.

Cordelia   Oh God, please help him to make a full recovery.

Doctor   I think we should wake him up. He has slept for an awfully long time.

Cordelia   Well, you're the expert. Wake him up if you think it is the right thing to do.

Gentleman   We put fresh clothes on him while he slept – he didn't even stir.

Doctor   Stay close, I don't know how we'll find him when we do wake him.

Cordelia   Very well. Oh father, let my kisses repair the harm that my sisters did to you.

Kent   Kind and dear princess!

Cordelia   Even if he wasn't their father, how could they have put such a frail old man out in the storm? The thunder, the lightning … how could they do it? I would have given my enemy's dog a place by the fire during that terrible storm, even if he had bitten me. Yet they cast our old father out. It's amazing he didn't lose his life along with his mind. Oh, he's waking up!

Doctor   Speak to him. You're the person he needs to see.

Cordelia   Hi Dad, it's me, are you all right?

Lear   You're wrong to take me out of the grave. You belong in heaven, but I belong in hell for the mistakes I have made.

Cordelia   Do you know me?

Lear   I know you're a ghost. When did you die?

Cordelia   He's still very confused.

Doctor   He's still half asleep. Just give him a few minutes.

Lear   Where am I? What has happened? Am I dead or alive?

Cordelia   Hold your hands in blessing over me, Dad … no … don't kneel at my feet!

Lear	Please don't make fun of me. I'm over eighty years old. But I can't remember where I slept last night, or where I got these new clothes. I feel like I recognise you, and this man. In fact, I think you are my child Cordelia.
Cordelia	And so I am, I am.
Lear	Are you crying? Please don't cry. If you have poison for me, I'll drink it. You have good reason to hate me, but your sisters don't.
Cordelia	No reason, I don't hate you. I love you.
Lear	Am I in France?
Kent	In your own kingdom, sir.
Lear	Do not lie to me.
Doctor	Don't ask him too many questions; he's not able for it.
Cordelia	Can you walk a little?
Lear	Just be patient and forgive me. I am old and foolish.
	Exit all but Kent and Gentleman
Gentleman	Is it true that the Duke of Cornwall was killed?
Kent	Yes, it's true all right.
Gentleman	Who's in charge, so?
Kent	Rumour has it that Gloucester's bastard son is in charge.
Gentleman	They say Edgar, his banished son, is with the Earl of Kent in Germany.
Kent	Don't believe everything you hear. The powers of England and of France will soon meet.
Gentleman	The fight is likely to be bloody.
	Exit
Kent	Everything depends on how this battle is fought – who wins and, of course, who loses.
	Exit

FOCUS ON ACT 4

'Cordelia's concern and love for her father is remarkable. She is visibly moved when she hears Lear has lost his mind and is wandering the heath, dressed only in wild flowers'

WHILE ACT III might be said to focus on psychological and physical suffering, Act IV is full of action and crucial events. It could also be described as one of reunion, even if some of the reunions occur in secret.

The act begins with a soliloquy by Edgar, who is, ironically, comforting himself that things cannot get any worse. He then sees his blinded father, and one can only imagine Edgar's horror when he sees the horrible punishment inflicted upon a weak old man: ***Bless thy sweet eyes, they bleed.***

Father and son are reunited, but Edgar maintains his disguise. Gloucester seems quite philosophical about his injury ***(I have no way, and therefore want no eyes; / I stumbled when I saw)***, but we soon see that this is because he has resolved to end his life. It is also clear that Gloucester, like Lear, is realising how blind he was emotionally, even before he was blinded physically.

Edgar is asked to lead Gloucester to Dover, and naturally he agrees. It is obvious how thoughtful Gloucester is, requesting that clothing be procured for Poor Tom: ***And bring some covering for this naked soul, / Who I'll entreat to lead me.*** He also showed this generosity of spirit in bringing Lear to shelter and communicating with Cordelia, despite the consequences. Since the only mistake Gloucester made in the play was to believe one son over the other, his crime is a lesser one than Lear's own.

Gloucester, like Lear, comments on the unfairness of their society, where just a few hold all the wealth and the many go without: ***So distribution should undo excess, / And each man have enough.*** Perhaps it is Shakespeare himself who wanted to highlight the fundamental unfairness of society, as he was a man who believed in

Give me your hand; you are now within a foot
Of the extreme verge. For all beneath the moon
Would I not leap upright

– EDGAR (ACT IV SCENE VI)

honour and justice. Certainly, in Shakespeare's day, the distribution of wealth was extremely uneven. The royals, aristocrats and merchants had an obscene amount of wealth, but most people had very little or none.

In the second scene of this act, there is a marked change in Albany after he learns of Gloucester's punishment. We see the growing relationship between Goneril and Edmund (*Yours in the ranks of death*) and the declining one between Goneril and Albany:

I fear your disposition:

That nature, which contemns its origin,

Cannot be border'd certain in itself.

She that herself will sliver and disbranch

From her material sap, perforce must wither

And come to deadly use.

What is really concerning Goneril in this scene, however, is not her husband's disgust at her behaviour, but her fear that her widowed sister might marry Edmund now she is free to do so: *being widow, and my Gloucester with her, / May all the building in my fancy pluck / Upon my hateful life.*

Regan is just as determined as Goneril not to let her sister have Edmund: *My lord is dead; Edmund and I have talk'd; / And more convenient is he for my hand / Than for your lady's.* Regan's casual cruelty is shocking. Shakespeare's audience would have been particularly shocked by cruelty in a woman, but would a modern audience also tend to think it is mostly men who commit violent acts? Regardless, Regan's instructions to kill Gloucester are horribly callous: *It was great ignorance, Gloucester's eyes being out, / To let him live …*

There is also great pathos in the scene where Edgar supposedly leads the suicidal Gloucester to the edge of the cliff. The still-disguised Edgar confuses his father and makes him think he is walking up a steep incline:

Methinks the ground is even. Edgar goes to great lengths to convince Gloucester, and his description of the view 'below' is filled with excellent imagery: *The fishermen, that walk upon the beach, / Appear like mice.* When Gloucester jumps – blessing his son Edgar, in another example of dramatic irony – and survives, he assumes that it is a sign that he must suffer until his life ends naturally. In Shakespeare's day, there was much unfortunate superstition around suicide. Someone who committed suicide could not be buried in consecrated ground and so could not go to heaven. By his rather elaborate strategy, Edgar is ensuring his father will get to heaven. He adopts yet another persona at the 'bottom' of the cliff to further convince Gloucester he has fallen from a great height. But, however convoluted this scene is, it is ultimately effective, and Gloucester resolves: *Henceforth I'll bear / Affliction till it do cry out itself / 'Enough, enough,' and die.* The significance of the importance of

> *O, look upon me, sir,*
> *And hold your hands in*
> *benediction o'er me*
>
> *– CORDELIA (ACT IV SCENE VII)*

the afterlife to Shakespeare's audience cannot be underestimated. In those days, life was very hard. Most people were very poor, and mortality rates were high. People preferred to believe that they would find happiness in the afterlife, and they wanted to get there without a prolonged spell in purgatory.

Lear and Gloucester meet each other at this crucial point, with Lear dressed in wild flowers and at the height of his madness. It is a pathetic sight, the two old, fragile men, one literally blinded, the other who had chosen

blindness. But just as Gloucester acknowledged his metaphorical blindness about his sons, we can see that a great deal of self-knowledge is now apparent in Lear:

> *Ha! Goneril, with a white beard! They flattered*
> *me like a dog; and told me I had white hairs in my*
> *beard ere the black ones were there. To say 'ay'*
> *and 'no' to every thing that I said! – 'Ay' and 'no'*
> *too was no good divinity ... they told me I was*
> *everything; 'tis a lie, I am not ague-proof.*

He realises that the central problem of the love test was that he should never have believed it when Goneril and Regan told him he was perfect, because no one is perfect. This is a massive development in Lear's character.

Ironically, he is at his most admirable when he acknowledges how imperfect he is, how human.

Oswald chances upon Gloucester and Edgar, and before he can kill Gloucester, Edgar kills him. Unfortunately for Goneril, Edgar is now in possession of her treasonous letter, and this will be the means by which she is destroyed. This helps build suspense for Act V. It also increases the sense that good is ultimately about to triumph over evil.

Finally, we come to the long-awaited reunion between Cordelia and Lear. This is the most important moment in the act. It is interesting that Cordelia, whom we have not seen since Act I, and the Fool are never on stage at the same time. It is sometimes claimed that the same actor would always have played both parts in Shakespeare's day and, as this play is full of disguise, perhaps Cordelia and the Fool are in fact one and the same. It's more probable, however, that the dramatic function of both characters is the same, and so there is no need for the Fool when Cordelia returns. Both characters are honest, uncomfortably so at times, and both characters speak the truth, no matter what the cost to themselves.

Cordelia's concern and love for her father is remarkable. She is visibly moved when she hears Lear has lost his mind and is wandering the heath, dressed only in wild flowers:

> *O dear father,*
>
> *It is thy business that I go about* …
>
> *No blown ambition doth our arms incite* …

While Lear sleeps, Cordelia has him dressed in appropriate garments. This is another example of how clothing imagery is used throughout the play to symbolise the relationship between appearance and reality. Far from having any residual anger at her father, Cordelia demonstrates what filial love actually is: it is unconditional. Lear does not have to ask for her forgiveness because, as far as she is concerned, there is nothing to forgive. He is ashamed and so contrite he volunteers to drink poison to show how sorry he is, a far cry from the last time he spoke to his daughter during the love test:

> *If you have poison for me, I will drink it.*
>
> *I know you do not love me; for your sisters*
>
> *Have, as I do remember, done me wrong:*
>
> *You have some cause, they have not.*

The whole point of the play has been to show that, when it comes to love, actions speak louder than words. A real 'love test' involves showing the people you love, by your everyday actions, how much you love them. Words, despite this play being a work created with words, aren't always enough. But it is still heartening to hear Lear's heartfelt plea, perhaps as much to the audience as to Cordelia: *Pray you now, forget and forgive; I am old and foolish.*

IMPORTANT THEMES IN ACT IV

- The theme of learning through suffering is seen in the transformed characters of Lear and Gloucester. This is a key source of the optimism in the play, for none of the suffering has been in vain.

- The theme of reconciliation is seen vividly in the reunion between Cordelia and Lear.

CHARACTER DEVELOPMENT IN ACT IV

- Lear's journey to self-knowledge is complete. His humility towards Cordelia proves how his suffering has broken him, and while he is now more fragile, his vulnerability allows him to genuinely feel.

- Gloucester's horrific blinding allows him to reconnect with his other senses. Now he is not blinded by appearances, he truly sees for the first time.

- Edgar shows admirable loyalty to his father, which runs in parallel with Cordelia's loyalty towards Lear.

- Goneril and Regan are utterly without any redeeming characteristics.

QUESTIONS ON ACT 4

1. Were you surprised that Edgar did not reveal himself to his father in Scene I?

2. What is the significance of Edgar preventing his father from committing suicide?

3. Write a diary entry for Albany in which he expresses his changed feelings for Goneril.

4. Imagine you are a French soldier at Dover. Write a description of what you see.

5. Who kills Oswald and why?

6. How does Cordelia react to news of her father's madness?

7. What is the dramatic purpose of the meeting between Lear and Cordelia?

8. Did you find the reunion between Cordelia and Lear touching? Give reasons for your answer.

9. Describe how you would stage one scene from Act IV, if you were directing a new version of King Lear.

10. Pick ten quotations across a range of characters and themes that you think best sum up Act IV. Explain in each case why you have chosen it.

THE BRITISH CAMP, NEAR DOVER

Enter, with drum and colours, Edmund, Regan,
Gentlemen, and Soldiers

Edmund	Know of the Duke if his last purpose[1] hold,		[1] *Decision*
	Or whether since he is advis'd by aught		
	To change the course. He's full of alteration[2]		[2] *According to Edmund, Albany keeps changing his mind*
	And self-reproving; bring his constant pleasure.		
	[To a Gentleman, who goes out]		

| Regan | Our sister's man is certainly miscarried.[3] | 5 | [3] *Regan realises that something has happened to Oswald* |

| Edmund | 'Tis to be doubted,[4] madam. | | [4] *There is no doubt about it* |

Regan	Now, sweet lord,		
	You know the goodness I intend upon you.		
	Tell me – but truly – but then speak the truth,		
	Do you not love my sister?		

| Edmund | In honour'd love.[5] | 10 | [5] *Platonically* |

| Regan | But have you never found my brother's way | | ***Regan is asking Edmund if he has slept with Goneril*** |
| | To the forfended[6] place? | | [6] *Forbidden* |

| Edmund | That thought abuses you.[7] | | [7] *How dare you think that!* |

| Regan | I am doubtful[8] that you have been conjunct[9] | | [8] *Worried* [9] *Close* |
| | And bosom'd with her,[10] as far as we call hers. | 15 | [10] *In her confidence* |

| Edmund | No, by mine honour, madam. | | |

| Regan | I never shall endure her. Dear my lord, | | |
| | Be not familiar with her. | | |

| Edmund | Fear me not: | | |
| | She and the Duke her husband! | 20 | |

Enter, with drum and colours, Albany, Goneril
and Soldiers

| Goneril | *[Aside]* I had rather lose the battle than that sister | | [11] *Goneril would rather lose the war than have Regan come between her and Edmund* |
| | Should loosen him and me.[11] | | |

Albany	Our very loving sister, well be-met.

Albany
Our very loving sister, well be-met.
Sir, this I hear; the King is come to his daughter,
With others whom the rigour[12] of our state   25
Forc'd to cry out. Where I could not be honest,
I never yet was valiant.[13] For this business,
It toucheth us, as France invades our land,
Not bolds the King, with others, whom, I fear,
Most just and heavy causes make oppose.   30

Edmund
Sir, you speak nobly.

Regan
Why is this reason'd?

Goneril
Combine together 'gainst the enemy;
For these domestic and particular broils[14]
Are not the question here.   35

Albany
Let's then determine
With the ancient of war[15] on our proceedings.[16]

Edmund
I shall attend you presently at your tent.

Regan
Sister, you'll go with us?

Goneril
No.   40

Regan
'Tis most convenient; pray you, go with us.

Goneril
[Aside] O, ho, I know the riddle. – I will go.

As they are going out, enter Edgar disguised

Edgar
If e'er your grace had speech with man so poor,
Hear me one word.

Albany
I'll overtake[17] you. – Speak.   45

Exit all but Albany and Edgar

Edgar
Before you fight the battle, ope this letter.
If you have victory, let the trumpet sound
For him that brought it. Wretched though I seem,
I can produce a champion that will prove
What is avouched[18] there. If you miscarry,   50

Side notes:

Some of the invaders are not attacking England for Lear but because they have other grievances. Therefore, Albany may support Lear, but he will still have to defeat the French in battle

[12] Harshness
[13] Brave
[14] They'll have to forget about their domestic squabbles for the moment
[15] Senior, in command [16] Strategy

Tensions are clearly growing between Goneril and Regan

[17] Catch up with
[18] Claimed

Your business of the world hath so an end,
And machination ceases. Fortune love you!

Albany   Stay till I have read the letter.

Edgar   I was forbid it.
When time shall serve, let but the herald cry,   55
And I'll appear again.

Albany   Why, fare thee well; I will o'erlook thy paper.[19]

*Exit Edgar and re-enter Edmund without seeing
one another*

Edmund   The enemy's in view; draw up your powers.
Here is the guess of their true strength and forces
By diligent discovery; but your haste   60
Is now urg'd on you.

Albany   We will greet the time.[20]

Exit

Edmund   To both these sisters have I sworn my love;
Each jealous of the other, as the stung
Are of the adder. Which of them shall I take?   65
Both? one? or neither? Neither can be enjoy'd,
If both remain alive. To take the widow
Exasperates, makes mad her sister Goneril;
And hardly shall I carry out my side,
Her husband being alive. Now then we'll use   70
His countenance for the battle; which being done,
Let her who would be rid of him devise
His speedy taking off. As for the mercy
Which he intends to Lear and to Cordelia,
The battle done, and they within our power,   75
Shall never see his pardon; for my state
Stands on me to defend, not to debate.

Exit

[19] Read the letter

Edmund has intelligence on the enemy's movements. This shows how clever he is, and what a good man he could have been if he hadn't been so focused on revenge

[20] Be ready in time

This is the most important of all Edmund's speeches. It is a soliloquy, so it can be trusted. He is not lying or trying to manipulate. He doesn't have any genuine feelings for either sister. They are simply a means to an end. Callously, he decides to kill Lear and Cordelia, because they stand in the way of Edmund himself being king

THIS SCENE IS one of the most dramatic of the play. Goneril and Regan are growing increasingly hostile to each other because of their mutual love for Edmund. The tension increases when Edgar appears in disguise to present Albany with the treasonous letter. Edmund is smug in his new-found position. His place in both the sisters' affections means he could soon have a huge kingdom of his own. Not bad for a man who, just days previously, stood to inherit nothing at all from his father's estate. But pride comes before a fall, and Edmund is unaware that he is about to lose all he has gained and more.

KEY **POINTS**

- *Goneril and Regan are turning on each other.*

- *Edgar gives Goneril's treasonous letter to Albany.*

*Before you fight the battle, ope this letter.
If you have victory, let the trumpet sound
For him that brought it*

– EDMUND

A FIELD BETWEEN THE TWO CAMPS

Alarum within. Enter, with drum and colours, Lear, Cordelia, and Soldiers, over the stage; and exit

Edgar Here, father,[1] take the shadow of this tree
For your good host; pray that the right may thrive.
If ever I return to you again,
I'll bring you comfort.

Gloucester Grace go with you, sir!   5

Exit Edgar
Alarum and retreat within. Re-enter Edgar

Edgar Away, old man; give me thy hand; away!
King Lear hath lost, he and his daughter ta'en:
Give me thy hand; come on.

Gloucester No farther, sir; a man may rot even here.

Edgar What, in ill thoughts again? Men must endure   10
Their going hence, even as their coming hither;[2]
Ripeness is all. Come on.

Gloucester And that's true too.

Exit

[1] A term of respect. Edgar still hasn't revealed his true identity to Gloucester

[2] You can't choose your time of death any more than you can choose your time of birth

THIS BRIEF SCENE serves two purposes. It is the last time Gloucester will be on stage; we will learn of his fate through flashbacks. The other purpose of the scene is to inform us, via Edgar, that the French have lost the battle and Lear and Cordelia have been taken prisoner.

Just as the audience is, perhaps, relaxing in anticipation of a happy ending, this scene throws everything into turmoil once more.

KEY **POINT**

- *King Lear and Cordelia have been taken prisoner, which renews tension and intrigue at this crucial part of the play.*

King Lear hath lost, he and his daughter ta'en

— *EDGAR*

THE BRITISH CAMP NEAR DOVER

*Enter, in conquest, with drum and colours, Edmund, Lear
and Cordelia, prisoners; Captain, Soldiers, etc*

Edmund   Some officers take them away. Good guard,
Until their greater pleasures first be known
That are to censure[1] them.

Cordelia   We are not the first
Who, with best meaning, have incurr'd the worst.   5
For thee, oppressed king, am I cast down;
Myself could else out-frown false Fortune's frown.
Shall we not see these daughters and these sisters?

Lear   No, no, no, no! Come, let's away to prison:
We two alone will sing like birds i' th' cage.   10
When thou dost ask me blessing, I'll kneel down,
And ask of thee forgiveness. So we'll live,
And pray, and sing, and tell old tales, and laugh
At gilded butterflies, and hear poor rogues
Talk of court news; and we'll talk with them too,   15
Who loses and who wins; who's in, who's out;
And take upon's the mystery of things,
As if we were God's spies: and we'll wear out,
In a wall'd prison, packs and sects[2] of great ones,
That ebb and flow by th' moon.[3]   20

Edmund   Take them away.

Lear   Upon such sacrifices, my Cordelia,
The gods themselves throw incense.[4] Have I caught thee?
He that parts us shall bring a brand from heaven,
And fire us hence like foxes. Wipe thine eyes;   25
The good-years shall devour them, flesh and fell,
Ere they shall make us weep. We'll see 'em starve first.
Come.

Exit Lear and Cordelia, guarded

Edmund   Come hither, captain; hark.
Take thou this note; *[Giving a paper]*   30
Go follow them to prison:
One step I have advanc'd thee; if thou dost

---

[1] Judge

Cordelia wisely acknowledges that they are not the first good people to have suffered badly

Even the prospect of prison cannot dampen Lear's enthusiasm at being reunited with Cordelia. As long as they are together, he can bear anything. Lear has finally realised what is truly important

[2] Groups

[3] That come and go according to who or what is in fashion

[4] A sweet-smelling spice, often used in celebratory or religious ceremonies

As this instructs thee, thou dost make thy way

To noble fortunes:[5] know thou this, that men

Are as the time is; to be tender-minded   35

Does not become a sword. Thy great employment

Will not bear question; either say thou'lt do 't,

Or thrive by other means.

Captain   I'll do 't, my lord.

Edmund   About it; and write happy when thou hast done.   40

Mark, I say, instantly; and carry it so

As I have set it down.

Captain   I cannot draw a cart, nor eat dried oats;

If it be man's work, I'll do 't.[6]

Exit

Flourish. Enter Albany, Goneril, Regan, another

Captain, and Soldiers

Albany   Sir, you have shown to-day your valiant strain,[7]   45

And fortune led you well. You have the captives

That were the opposites of this day's strife;

We do require them of you, so to use them

As we shall find their merits and our safety

May equally determine.   50

Edmund   Sir, I thought it fit

To send the old and miserable King

To some retention and appointed guard;

Whose age has charms in it, whose title more,

To pluck the common bosom on his side,   55

And turn our impress'd lances in our eyes

Which do command them. With him I sent the Queen,

My reason all the same; and they are ready

To-morrow, or at further space, t' appear

Where you shall hold your session. At this time   60

We sweat and bleed: the friend hath lost his friend;

And the best quarrels, in the heat, are curs'd

By those that feel their sharpness:

The question of Cordelia and her father

Requires a fitter place.   65

Albany   Sir, by your patience,

---

[5] *He will be financially rewarded*

Edmund goes so far as to ensure that the Captain is capable of murder. But, yet again, he does not get his own hands dirty

[6] *Jobs are hard to come by – the Captain attempts to justify this murder*

[7] *Bravery*

Edmund explains he sent Lear to prison for his own safety, and also because the soldiers might give him their loyalty instead. He suggests Albany can meet with Lear and Cordelia the next day or the day after that. Edmund is trying to buy time to ensure Lear and Cordelia are killed. Once again, he proves himself a convincing liar

	I hold you but a subject of this war, Not as a brother.	
Regan	That's as we list to grace him.[8] Methinks our pleasure might have been demanded, Ere you had spoke so far. He led our powers; Bore the commission of my place and person; The which immediacy may well stand up, And call itself your brother.	70
Goneril	Not so hot: In his own grace he doth exalt himself, More than in your addition.[9]	75
Regan	In my rights, By me invested, he compeers the best.	
Goneril	That were the most, if he should husband you.	
Regan	Jesters do oft prove prophets.[10]	80
Goneril	Holla, holla! That eye that told you so look'd but a-squint.	
Regan	Lady, I am not well; else I should answer From a full-flowing stomach. General, Take thou my soldiers, prisoners, patrimony; Dispose of them, of me; the walls are thine. Witness the world, that I create thee here My lord and master.	85
Goneril	Mean you to enjoy him?	
Albany	The let-alone lies not in your good will.	90
Edmund	Nor in thine, lord.	
Albany	Half-blooded fellow, yes.	
Regan	[To Edmund] Let the drum strike, and prove my title thine.	
Albany	Stay yet; hear reason. Edmund, I arrest thee On capital treason; and, in thine attaint, This gilded serpent [Pointing to Goneril]	95

Side notes:

[8] *That's for us to decide*

Regan claims that Edmund is effectively her husband and therefore Albany's brother

[9] *Edmund is enough in his own right. He doesn't need Regan*

[10] *'Many a true word is spoken in jest'*

Regan is feeling sick, which arouses the suspicions of the audience. She says she wants to give everything she has to Edmund

ACT 5 SCENE III

Albany plays his trump card: the treasonous letter and his knowledge of the love triangle between Goneril, Edmund and Regan

	For your claim, fair sister,	
	I bar it in the interest of my wife:	
	'Tis she is sub-contracted to this lord,	
	And I, her husband, contradict your bans.	
	If you will marry, make your loves to me,	100

11 Spoken for

My lady is bespoke.[11]

Goneril An interlude!

Albany Thou art arm'd, Gloucester: let the trumpet sound.
If none appear to prove upon thy head

12 Wicked

Thy heinous,[12] manifest, and many treasons, 105

13 Promise

There is my pledge;[13] *[Throwing down a glove]*
I'll prove it on thy heart,
Ere I taste bread, thou art in nothing less

14 Albany is determined to prove Edmund's guilt

Than I have here proclaim'd thee.[14]

Regan Sick, O, sick! 110

Goneril *[Aside]* If not, I'll ne'er trust medicine.

Edmund stoutly defends his name, even though he knows the accusations are true. It is as though he now believes his own lies

Edmund There's my exchange: *[Throwing down a glove]*
What in the world he is
That names me traitor, villain-like he lies.
Call by thy trumpet; – he that dares approach, 115
On him, on you, who not? I will maintain
My truth and honour firmly.

Albany A herald, ho!

Edmund A herald, ho, a herald!

Edmund is on his own. Albany drafted the soldiers, and he has also discharged them

Albany Trust to thy single virtue; for thy soldiers, 120
All levied in my name, have in my name
Took their discharge.

Regan My sickness grows upon me.

Albany She is not well; convey her to my tent.

Exit Regan, led

Come hither, herald, *[Enter a Herald]* 125
Let the trumpet sound – And read out this.

Not so hot:
In his own grace he doth exalt himself,
More than in your addition

— GONERIL

Captain	Sound, trumpet!

A trumpet sounds

Herald	*[Reads]* 'If any man of quality or degree within the lists of the army will maintain upon Edmund, supposed Earl of Gloucester, that he is a manifold traitor,[15] let him appear by the third sound of the trumpet. He is bold in his defence.'

130

[15] *A traitor in many different ways*

Edmund	Sound! *[First trumpet]*
Herald	Again! *[Second trumpet]*

Herald	Again! *[Third trumpet]*	135
	Trumpet answers within	
	Enter Edgar at the third sound, armed, with a	
	trumpet before him	
Albany	Ask him his purposes, why he appears	
	Upon this call o' th' trumpet.	
Herald	What are you?	
	Your name, your quality?[16] And why you answer	
	This present summons?	140
Edgar	Know, my name is lost;	
	By treason's tooth bare-gnawn and canker-bit,[17]	
	Yet am I noble as the adversary	
	I come to cope.	
Albany	Which is that adversary?	145
Edgar	What's he that speaks for Edmund Earl of Gloucester?	
Edmund	Himself: what say'st thou to him?	
Edgar	Draw thy sword.	
	That, if my speech offend a noble heart,	
	Thy arm may do thee justice; here is mine.	150
	Behold, it is the privilege of mine honours,	
	My oath, and my profession. I protest,	
	Maugre[18] thy strength, youth, place, and eminence,	
	Despite thy victor sword and fire-new[19] fortune,	
	Thy valour[20] and thy heart, thou art a traitor;	155
	False to thy gods, thy brother, and thy father;	
	Conspirant[21] 'gainst this high-illustrious prince;[22]	
	And, from the extremest upward of thy head	
	To the descent and dust below thy foot,[23]	
	A most toad-spotted traitor. Say thou 'No,'	160
	This sword, this arm, and my best spirits, are bent	
	To prove upon thy heart, whereto I speak,	
	Thou liest.	
Edmund	In wisdom I should ask thy name;	
	But, since thy outside looks so fair and warlike,	165
	And that thy tongue some say of breeding breathes,	
	What safe and nicely I might well delay	

Side notes:
[16] Rank
[17] Eaten away
[18] Despite
[19] Brand new
[20] Bravery
[21] Conspirer [22] Albany
[23] From head to toe

By rule of knighthood, I disdain and spurn.
Back do I toss these treasons to thy head;
With the hell-hated lie o'erwhelm thy heart;   170
Which, for they yet glance by and scarcely bruise,
This sword of mine shall give them instant way,
Where they shall rest for ever. Trumpets, speak!

Alarums. They fight. Edmund falls

Albany   Save him, save him!

Goneril   This is mere practice,[24] Gloucester: 175
By th' law of arms thou wast not bound to answer
An unknown opposite. Thou art not vanquish'd,[25]
But cozen'd[26] and beguil'd.[27]

Albany   Shut your mouth, dame,
Or with this paper shall I stop it. Hold, sir, –   180
Thou worse than any name, read thine own evil.
No tearing, lady; I perceive you know it.

Gives the letter to Edmund

Goneril   Say, if I do, the laws are mine, not thine:
Who can arraign[28] me for't?

Albany   Most monstrous! oh! –   185
Know'st thou this paper?

Goneril   Ask me not what I know.

Exit

Albany   Go after her; she's desperate; govern her.[29]

Edmund   What you have charged me with, that have I done;
And more, much more; the time will bring it out.   190
'Tis past, and so am I. But what art thou
That hast this fortune on me? If thou'rt noble,
I do forgive thee.

Edgar   Let's exchange charity.
I am no less in blood than thou art, Edmund;   195
If more, the more thou hast wrong'd me.

Edmund doesn't have to fight an unnamed opponent but, curiously, he decides to. He claims it is because he can tell Edgar is of noble rank, but it is more likely that he is confident he will win

[24] *A trick*

[25] *Beaten*

[26] *Tricked* [27] *Fooled, deceived*

[28] *Punish*

[29] *Albany predicts Goneril is about to do something dreadful*

There is a dramatic change in Edmund's character in the moments before his death. In Shakespeare's day, it was thought that a person's true character was seen at the end of their life. Also, to avoid hell, it was vital to confess and ask forgiveness

My name is Edgar, and thy father's son.

The gods are just, and of our pleasant vices,

Make instruments to plague us:

The dark and vicious place where thee he got   200

Cost him his eyes.[30]

[30] Edgar quite rightly lays the blame for Gloucester's blinding upon Edmund

Edmund   Thou'st spoken right, 'tis true.

The wheel is come full circle: I am here.

Edmund has ended up back where he started. The moral is a common one in Shakespearean tragedies: crime never pays

Albany   Methought thy very gait did prophesy

A royal nobleness. I must embrace thee: 205

Let sorrow split my heart, if ever I

Did hate thee or thy father!

Edgar   Worthy prince, I know't.

Albany   Where have you hid yourself?

How have you known the miseries of your father?   210

Edgar   By nursing them, my lord. List a brief tale;

And when 'tis told, O, that my heart would burst!

The bloody proclamation to escape,

That follow'd me so near,[31] – O, our lives' sweetness!

That we the pain of death would hourly die   215

Rather than die at once! – taught me to shift

Into a madman's rags; t' assume a semblance[32]

That very dogs disdain'd; and in this habit

Met I my father with his bleeding rings,[33]

Their precious stones[34] new lost; became his guide,   220

Led him, begg'd for him, sav'd him from despair;

Never, – O fault! – reveal'd myself unto him,

Until some half-hour past, when I was arm'd.

Not sure, though hoping, of this good success,

I ask'd his blessing, and from first to last   225

Told him my pilgrimage; but his flaw'd heart,

Alack, too weak the conflict to support!

'Twixt two extremes of passion, joy and grief,

Burst smilingly.

[31] The order of death that was put upon Edgar

[32] An appearance

[33] His bloody eye sockets
[34] Eyeballs – what could be more precious?

When Edgar revealed all to Gloucester, it was too much for the old man to take. He died full of joy at his reunion with his son, but tempered with sadness at Edmund's treachery and Edgar's ordeals

Edmund   This speech of yours hath moved me,   230

And shall perchance do good. But speak you on;

You look as you had something more to say.

Edmund is clearly rethinking his decision to have Lear and Cordelia killed but does not immediately act. This increases suspense for the audience

Albany   If there be more, more woeful, hold it in;

Draw thy sword.
That, if my speech offend a noble heart,
Thy arm may do thee justice; here is mine

– EDGAR

	For I am almost ready to dissolve,[35]	[35] *Albany is close to tears*
	Hearing of this. 235	
Edgar	This would have seem'd a period	
	To such as love not sorrow; but another,	
	To amplify too much, would make much more,	
	And top extremity.[36]	[36] *There are even sadder stories than Gloucester's*
	Whilst I was big in clamour came there in a man, 240	
	Who, having seen me in my worst estate,	
	Shunn'd my abhorr'd society; but then, finding	
	Who 'twas that so endured, with his strong arms	
	He fastened on my neck, and bellow'd out	

	As he'd burst heaven; threw him on my father;	245
	Told the most piteous tale of Lear and him	
	That ever ear receiv'd; which in recounting	
	His grief grew puissant, and the strings of life	
	Began to crack. Twice then the trumpets sounded,	
	And there I left him tranc'd.	250
Albany	But who was this?	
Edgar	Kent, sir, the banish'd Kent; who in disguise	
	Follow'd his enemy king, and did him service	
	Improper for a slave.	

Enter a Gentleman, with a bloody knife

Gentleman	Help, help, O, help!	255
Edgar	What kind of help?	
Albany	Speak, man.	
Edgar	What means that bloody knife?	
Gentleman	'Tis hot, it smokes;	
	It came even from the heart of – O, she's dead!	260
Albany	Who dead? Speak, man.	

Gentleman	Your lady, sir, your lady: and her sister	
	By her is poisoned; she hath confess'd it.	
Edmund	I was contracted to them both: all three	
	Now marry in an instant.[37]	265
Edgar	Here comes Kent.	
Albany	Produce their bodies, be they alive or dead:	
	This judgement of the heavens, that makes us tremble,	
	Touches us not with pity.[38]	

Exit Gentleman
Enter Kent

	– O, is this he?	270

	The time will not allow the compliment	
	Which very manners urges.	
Kent	I am come	
	To bid my king and master aye good night:	
	Is he not here?	275
Albany	Great thing of us forgot!	
	Speak, Edmund, where's the King? and where's	
	Cordelia?	
	See'st thou this object, Kent?	

The bodies of Goneril and Regan are brought in

Kent	Alack, why thus?	
Edmund	Yet Edmund was beloved!	280
	The one the other poison'd for my sake,	
	And after slew herself.	
Albany	Even so. Cover their faces.	
Edmund	I pant for life. Some good I mean to do,	
	Despite of mine own nature. Quickly send,	285
	Be brief in it, to the castle; for my writ[39]	
	Is on the life of Lear and on Cordelia.	
	Nay, send in time.	
Albany	Run, run, O, run!	
Edgar	To who, my lord? Who hath the office? Send	290
	Thy token of reprieve.	
Edmund	Well thought on: take my sword,	
	Give it the captain.	
Albany	Haste thee, for thy life.	

Exit Edgar

Edmund	He hath commission from thy wife and me	295
	To hang Cordelia in the prison, and	
	To lay the blame upon her own despair,	
	That she fordid[40] herself.	

Kent wants to say goodbye to Lear before he dies

Edmund's vulnerable side reveals itself in the moments before his death. He is glad of having been loved, showing that this is probably all he wanted all along

These lines are crucial as they redeem Edmund to some degree, at least

[39] Death sentence

[40] Killed herself

	Albany	The gods defend her! Bear him hence a while.	

Edmund is borne off
Re-enter Lear, with Cordelia dead in his arms;
Edgar, Captain, and others following

Lear's grief is almost too much for an audience to bear

Lear　Howl, howl, howl, howl! O, you are men of stones!　300
Had I your tongues and eyes, I'd use them so
That heaven's vault should crack. She's gone for ever!
I know when one is dead, and when one lives;
She's dead as earth. Lend me a looking-glass;
If that her breath will mist or stain the stone,　305
Why, then she lives.

Kent　Is this the promised end?

Edgar　Or image of that horror?

Albany　Fall, and cease!

Lear is unable to fully comprehend that Cordelia is dead

Lear　This feather stirs; she lives! If it be so,　310
It is a chance which does redeem all sorrows
That ever I have felt.

Kent　[*Kneeling*] O my good master!

Lear　Prithee, away.

Edgar　'Tis noble Kent, your friend.　315

Lear　A plague upon you, murderers, traitors all!
I might have saved her; now she's gone for ever!
Cordelia, Cordelia! stay a little. Ha!
What is't thou say'st? Her voice was ever soft,
Gentle, and low; an excellent thing in woman.　320

The old king managed to kill Cordelia's murderer

I kill'd the slave that was a-hanging thee.

Captain　'Tis true, my lords, he did.

41 Sword

Lear　Did I not, fellow?
I have seen the day, with my good biting falchion[41]
I would have made them skip. I am old now,　325

42 Suffering has weakened him

And these same crosses spoil me.[42] Who are you?
Mine eyes are not o' th' best. I'll tell you straight.

Kent	If Fortune brag of two she loved and hated, One of them we behold.	
Lear	This is a dull sight. Are you not Kent?	330
Kent	The same, Your servant Kent. Where is your servant Caius?	
Lear	He's a good fellow, I can tell you that; He'll strike, and quickly too. He's dead and rotten.	
Kent	No, my good lord; I am the very man, –	335
Lear	I'll see that straight.	
Kent	– That, from your first of difference and decay, Have follow'd your sad steps –	
Lear	You are welcome hither.	
Kent	Nor no man else: all's cheerless, dark, and deadly. Your eldest daughters have fordone themselves, And desperately are dead.	340
Lear	Ay, so I think.	
Albany	He knows not what he says; and vain it is That we present us to him.	345
Edgar	Very bootless.[43]	

Enter a Captain

Captain	Edmund is dead, my lord.	
Albany	That's but a trifle here. – You lords and noble friends, know our intent. What comfort to this great decay may come Shall be appli'd. For us, we will resign, During the life of this old majesty, To him our absolute power; *[To Edgar and Kent]* you, to your rights: With boot, and such addition as your honours Have more than merited. All friends shall taste	350 355

In his lifetime, Lear experienced the most extreme highs and lows possible

Tragically, Kent tries to reveal himself to Lear, but Lear is too far gone to understand

[43] *Pointless*

Albany intends handing over power to Lear for however long he lives

The wages of their virtue, and all foes
The cup of their deservings.[44] O, see, see!

Lear And my poor fool[45] is hang'd! No, no, no life!
Why should a dog, a horse, a rat, have life,
And thou no breath at all? Thou'lt come no more,   360
Never, never, never, never, never!
Pray you, undo this button. Thank you, sir.
Do you see this? Look on her, look, her lips,
Look there, look there!

Dies

Edgar He faints! My lord, my lord!   365

Kent Break, heart; I prithee, break!

Edgar Look up, my lord.

Kent Vex not his ghost; O, let him pass! He hates him much
That would upon the rack of this tough world
Stretch him out longer.   370

Edgar He is gone, indeed.

Kent The wonder is, he hath endur'd so long;
He but usurp'd his life.[46]

Albany Bear them from hence. Our present business
Is general woe. *[To Kent and Edgar]*   375
Friends of my soul, you twain
Rule in this realm, and the gor'd state sustain.

Kent I have a journey, sir, shortly to go.
My master calls me; I must not say no.

Albany The weight of this sad time we must obey;   380
Speak what we feel, not what we ought to say.
The oldest hath borne most; we that are young
Shall never see so much, nor live so long.

Exit, with a dead march

THE BRITISH CAMP NEAR DOVER

Enter, in conquest, with drum and colours, Edmund, Lear and Cordelia, prisoners; Captain, Soldiers, etc.

Edmund   Take them away until the princesses judge them and decide their fate.

Cordelia   We're not the first good people to have something bad happen to them. I can deal with this unfair world, but it's you I feel sorry for, Dad. Will we see your daughters, my sisters, do you think?

Lear   No, who cares about them? They can imprison our bodies but not our souls. We'll sing like birds in a cage, and I'll tell you again and again how sorry I am. And we'll chat and laugh about fake people who pretend to be what they are not, and we'll join in the prison gossip and laugh at the silliness of it all.

Edmund   Take them away.

Lear   Don't cry, Cordelia. It will all be OK.

Exit Lear and Cordelia, guarded

Edmund   Here, Captain, take this. *[Giving him a paper]* Follow them to prison and do as I have instructed you. I'll reward you well for carrying out my wishes. But first I want to make sure, are you up to the job?

Captain   Yes, that kind of work doesn't bother me.

Edmund   Do exactly as I have told you and let me know the minute it's done.

Captain   I'm not an animal, but if it's something a man can do, then I'll do it.

Exit
Flourish. Enter Albany, Goneril, Regan, another Captain, and Soldiers

Albany   You have been brave today, Edmund, I have to admit. Where are Lear and Cordelia?

Edmund   I thought it was best to imprison them. Lear is dangerous, because many people are still loyal to him, and the same goes for Cordelia. We can decide in a day or two. Now is not the time.

Albany	Edmund, I've admitted you were brave, but you are not my equal. It is not your decision.
Regan	Well, actually, I've given him my powers, so he is your equal.
Goneril	Take it easy; he doesn't need you! His bravery speaks for itself.
Regan	Well, I've given him all the powers my husband had.
Goneril	Oh, sounds like you want him to be your next husband. What a joke!
Regan	The truest things are often said in jest.
Goneril	Yeah, right, in your dreams.
Regan	You're lucky I'm not feeling well or else … Edmund, I want to give you everything. My land, my wealth, my title, me …
Goneril	You want to be with him? I don't think so.
Albany	It's none of your business!
Edmund	Or yours!
Albany	You bastard, how dare you!
Regan	*[To Edmund]* Let the drum strike, to show I mean what I say.
Albany	Sorry to ruin your plans, Edmund, but I am arresting you for treason, and I'm also arresting that snake over there. *[Pointing to Goneril]* As for you, Goneril, did you not realise that my own wife was planning to kill me and marry Edmund? So it seems he is already spoken for!
Goneril	Oh, shut up!
Albany	Let the trumpet sound. Let's see who comes to fight Edmund. If no one comes, I'll fight him myself. *[Throwing down a glove]* I'll prove what a traitor and a creep you are.
Regan	I feel like I'm going to vomit. Oh God, I feel like I'm dying …
Goneril	*[Aside]* So the poison worked.
Edmund	I can't believe anyone would call me a traitor! I am a hero, an honourable man. I'll fight anyone who says otherwise. *[Throwing down a glove]*

Albany	You'll be fighting your own battles. I've discharged all your soldiers.
Regan	I'm really dying. I mean it.
Albany	She looks awful. Take her to my tent.
Herald	[Reads] If there is anyone who agrees that Edmund is a traitor, let them show themselves before the third trumpet.
	First trumpet
	Second trumpet
	Third trumpet
	Trumpet answers within
	Enter Edgar, at the third sound, armed, with a trumpet before him
Albany	Ask who he is and why he wishes to fight Edmund.
Herald	What are you? Your name? Your rank? Why do you wish to fight?
Edgar	My name has been stolen from me, but I am Edmund's equal. I can assure you of that.
Albany	Who is that adversary?
Edgar	Will you fight me? You can see that I am an honourable man. Look at my sword. It is a symbol of my honour, my rank, and my status. Despite your courage, your recent victory and your good fortune, I declare that you're a traitor. You've betrayed your gods, your brother and your father. If you have any guts, any integrity, you'll meet my challenge.
Edmund	I don't have to fight you when you haven't even revealed your name, and yet there is something about you that tells me you are a gentleman. I'll prove my innocence and I'll prove I'm the better man.
	The two men, almost identical in size and stature, fight in an impressive display of swordsmanship. It is as close a contest as you can get. But then Edmund falls
Albany	Save him! Save him!
Goneril	You idiot, Edmund, you didn't have to fight an unnamed

attacker, so why the hell did you do it? What will I do if anything happens to you?

Albany   Shut your mouth, Goneril, or I'll shut it with this letter – the letter you wrote, which proves you are guilty of treason too!

Gives the letter to Edmund

Goneril   Whatever. I own this country, and so I own the law. I can do whatever I want, and there is nothing you can do about it.

Albany   You are unbelieveable! Heartless witch.

Exit

Albany   Someone go after her; she's dangerous.

Edmund   I'm too tired to fight any more. I know I'm dying, and everything you accused me of is true, so I deserve it.
If you are a good man, I forgive you.

Edgar   Then I forgive you, too, Edmund *[removes helmet]*. I am a good man. I'm your brother, Edmund. I didn't deserve what you did to me. I always loved you as much as any brother could.

Edmund   I'm sorry, brother. Everything has come full circle now, but thank you for forgiving me.

Albany   Edgar! I thought it was you. Please forgive me for ever believing ill of you.

Edgar   That's all right, I certainly don't blame you.

Albany   How did you avoid being captured? Survive being apart from your poor father?

Edgar   I survived by disguising myself as a madman, Poor Tom, and I wasn't apart from my father for long. I found him, wandering blindly, his eyes having been plucked out and his eye sockets streaming blood. He did not know me, but I stayed with him and protected him. I never left his side. And when I saw that he was dying, I told him who I was. He died happy, knowing I had never betrayed him.

Edmund   I feel so guilty, and I want to redeem myself by telling you something. But finish what you were saying first.

Albany   Please don't tell me anything else that is so tragic. I am almost in tears hearing of you and your father's reunion.

Edgar   I met another man, in a terrible state, who told me the tragic tale of Lear. His heart was broken, not because he had endured so much, but for Lear.

Albany   But who was this?

Edgar   Kent, the man Lear banished. He came back in disguise and did not leave Lear's side. What Lear endured, he endured. I don't think he has long to live. He's a broken man.

Enter a Gentleman, with a bloody knife

Gentleman   Help!

Edgar   What's happened?

Albany   For God's sake, tell us what's going on.

Edgar   Why are you holding that bloody knife?

Gentleman   I took it from her chest! She killed herself!

Albany   Who killed herself?

Gentleman   Your wife, sir. She poisoned her sister and then killed herself! What an awful mess.

Edmund   I was engaged to marry both, now we're all dead.

Edgar   Here comes Kent.

Kent   I came to say goodbye to the king, my master. Where is he?

Albany   Oh God, we almost forgot the king!

Edmund   At least someone loved me. Goneril poisoned Regan to be with me. It's a comfort in a way. But I'm finding it hard to breathe, and I want to do something good before I die. I ordered the deaths of Lear and Cordelia. For God's sake, get to the prison quick and rescind my order.

Albany   Run, Edgar, quickly. Stop it from happening!

Exit Edgar

Edmund   Your wife and I told the Captain to hang Cordelia, to make it look like she had taken her own life. I feel so awful. What a terrible person I have been. Please forgive me.

Albany   Take him to a tent. Let him die in peace.

Edmund is carried off
Re-enter Lear, with Cordelia dead in his arms; Edgar, Captain, and others following

Lear   No! No! My daughter is dead! Only a man of stone could stop tears pouring down his face on witnessing the loss of such an angel. She is dead, I can't bear it. I cannot bear it. Or maybe she's alive – get me a mirror, let's see if she is still breathing … Or a feather, I have a feather … I think it moves slightly when I put it close to her face. Maybe she is alive? Please God, let her be alive!

Kent   [Kneeling] O my good master!

Lear   Please, leave me alone. I need to be alone.

Edgar   But it is Kent, your true friend.

Lear   What an awful world we live in. How could something like this happen to my beautiful daughter? I only just got her back. The only comfort is that I killed her hangman with my bare hands.

Captain   It's true, my lords, he did.

Lear   I did, didn't I? Even though I'm old and not as strong as I was, I did kill him. But I feel so tired now. Where am I again? Who are you, sir?

Kent   If ever there was a man who experienced the best life has to offer, but also the worst, it is you.

Lear   Are you my old friend Kent?

Kent   I am, and where is Caius?

Lear   I don't know, but I can tell you he's a good friend. He looked after me and protected me. But I think he must be dead now.

Kent   No, I'm Caius, I'm …

Lear   What? I don't understand.

Kent   I've been with you all this time.

Lear   You are welcome.

Kent   Goneril and Regan are dead. They can't hurt you any more.

Lear   Ay, so I think.

Albany   He's confused and in total shock. I don't think he can take anything in, the poor man.

Captain   Edmund is dead, my lord.

Albany   I don't really care. This is a tragic day all around, and Edmund's death pales into insignificance compared to the death of Cordelia. I'm going to restore Lear as king immediately and restore both of you to your rightful place, along with extra rewards for your loyalty.

Lear   My poor fool is hanged. Why should a horse have life but not her? Or any creature? Why should anyone have life when the best person in the world is dead? *[Dies]*

Edgar   He has fainted. I think he is dying.

Kent   At least he is not suffering any more. The world has tortured his poor mind and body enough.

Edgar   He's gone.

Kent   It's amazing he survived this long. It shows what a strong man he was. What a hero.

Albany   My friends, you both can rule alongside me now.

Kent   Thank you, sir, but I'm going to go with my master. I've never left his side, and I'm not going to do so even in death.

Albany   It will take us a long time to get over this. We need to say how we feel, and not what we think we ought to say. We need to be honest. Please God, those of us who are young will never live to see such tragedy and treachery in our country again.

         Exit, with a dead march

FOCUS ON ACT 5

'The final scene is as atmospheric, tense, poignant and tragic as it could possibly be'

THE FINAL act of this play is catastrophic, as befits a classic tragedy. In the eighteenth and nineteenth centuries, the events of this act were often changed to avoid upsetting the audience too much. Cordelia, for example, was often allowed to live. However, the version in this text is the one favoured today.

The act begins by showing the tensions between Goneril *(I had rather lose the battle than that sister / Should loosen him and me)* and Regan *(But have you never found my brother's way / To the forfended place?)*. Throughout the play, the audience is appalled by how evil both sisters are and how richly they deserve to be punished. It is a stroke of brilliance that Shakespeare has them destroy one another – and all for a man who is really not all that bothered about them:

> *To both these sisters have I sworn my love;*
> *Each jealous of the other, as the stung*
> *Are of the adder. Which of them shall I take?*
> *Both? one? or neither? Neither can be enjoy'd,*
> *If both remain alive* …

Albany becomes a very stong character during this act, making it clear that he is only fighting France because he has a duty to protect his country. He does not wish harm to either Lear or Cordelia.

Edgar aids Albany by giving him Goneril's treasonous letter to Edmund (the letter that suggests Edmund kill Albany and marry her). This increases the suspense greatly, and makes Edmund's speech rich in dramatic irony. He is like the proverbial cat who got the cream. The audience, however, knows he is about to fall off his pedestal.

We see Gloucester for the last time in Scene II, and it is perhaps surprising that Edgar has not yet revealed his true identity. This scene's dramatic function is mainly to

*She's gone for ever!
I know when one is dead,
and when one lives;
She's dead as earth*

– LEAR (ACT V SCENE III)

tell us that the French army has been defeated, and the audience is well aware of the possible implications of this. Note how skilfully Shakespeare balances the action. He gives us hope, and then he takes it away, and then he gives it back again. He is masterful at maintaining suspense right up until the end of the play.

The final scene is as atmospheric, tense, poignant and tragic as it could possibly be. Shakespeare felt that the first scene and the final scene were the most important ones. The first scene engages the audience and, especially in his day, keeps them interested enough not to leave the theatre and demand their money back. But the final scene is the one that the audience will remember. It is the one that they will discuss most, and, crucially, it is the one that will tend to dictate their overall impression of the play. This was particularly important for Shakespeare and his troupe of actors. They wanted the audience members to recommend the play so that more people would come and see it. It was their livelihood, after all.

Edmund appears to have it all as the play draws towards its tragic conclusion. He has managed to keep his hands relatively clean until this point in the play. Yes, he betrayed his father, but he was not actually there when Gloucester was tortured. So the audience can still choose to believe that he would have stopped the blinding had he been present. But now he orders the deaths of Lear and Cordelia. The last thing he wants is either of them regaining power. All he needs to do is marry Goneril or Regan, and he will be king. Edmund is not about to lose this opportunity, yet once again he gets someone else to do his dirty work, bribing a captain to carry out the murders:

> *Come hither, captain; hark …*
> *go follow them to prison:*
> *One step I have advanc'd thee; if thou dost*

> *As this instructs thee, thou dost make thy way*
> *To noble fortunes*

The entire country is Edmund's for the taking, it seems, were it not for the letter, which Albany has now read. This, understandably, has completely destroyed his view (already diminished in Act IV) of both Goneril and Edmund. Albany shapes up to be a powerful adversary: *I hold you but a subject of this war, / Not as a brother.*

Goneril and Regan engage in an unseemly tug of war over Edmund. Shakespeare's audience would have been shocked by this:

Regan   **In my rights,**
              By me invested, he compeers the best.

Goneril **That were the most, if he should husband you.**

Regan   **Jesters do oft prove prophets.**

Goneril **Holla, holla!**
              That eye that told you so look'd but a-squint.

Regan   **Lady, I am not well; else I should answer**
              From a full-flowing stomach. General,
              Take thou my soldiers, prisoners, patrimony;
              Dispose of them, of me; the walls are thine:
              Witness the world, that I create thee here
              My lord and master.

Goneril **Mean you to enjoy him?**

Edgar arrives, in disguise, and challenges Edmund to a duel. Edmund does not have to answer the challenge from someone who does not disclose their name, and yet he does:

In wisdom I should ask thy name;
But, since thy outside looks so fair and warlike,
And that thy tongue some say of breeding breathes,
What safe and nicely I might well delay
By rule of knighthood, I disdain and spurn.

Perhaps this is because he cannot resist a challenge and is confident he will win. Or he may feel he has no choice. It might even be an innate recognition of his own brother, a subconscious need to right the wrongs that he has done.

The sword fight also serves an important dramatic function as a visual spectacle. The audience would have been enthralled by such a scene. Most modern films have fight scenes, too, even if they are totally gratuitous, so clearly people haven't changed that much in what they like to see acted out. It is Edgar, the elder and 'legitimate' brother (in the sense that he did not betray Edmund as Edmund did him), who is victorious. This is an example of poetic justice, but it is also crucial to the plot.

Goneril has already shown herself capable of poisoning her own sister. She is seen to be capable of more when Albany reveals his possession of the letter proving treason:

Shut your mouth, dame,
Or with this paper shall I stop it. Hold, sir, –
Thou worse than any name, read thine own evil.
No tearing, lady; I perceive you know it…

She takes matters into her own hands and kills herself, just as Regan dies of the poison. Suddenly, all Lear's comments about the pair being like serpents, snakes, vultures, kites, etc. seem all the more insightful.

However, in Shakespeare's day, a person's true character was thought to be most evident in the moments before death. Edmund shows that he is, perhaps, a good person after all when his brother fatally wounds him:

What you have charged me with, that have I done;
And more, much more; the time will bring it out:
'Tis past, and so am I. But what art thou
That hast this fortune on me? If thou'rt noble,
I do forgive thee.

Forgiving Edgar is important, because otherwise Edmund's death would prevent Edgar from getting to heaven. It is also noble of Edmund – or maybe he is just trying to save himself from hell!

Edgar finally reveals himself, to the shock of the other characters, and eloquently explains how he continued to look after his father in disguise. He also recalls how Gloucester died, and it is hard not to be as moved as Albany and Edmund clearly are:

Never, – O fault! – reveal'd myself unto him,
Until some half-hour past, when I was arm'd.
Not sure, though hoping, of this good success,
I ask'd his blessing, and from first to last
Told him my pilgrimage: but his flaw'd heart,
Alack, too weak the conflict to support!
'Twixt two extremes of passion, joy and grief,
Burst smilingly.

Edgar also describes meeting Kent, who, like Lear, has suffered so much. News arrives of Goneril's suicide and Regan's death, but is greeted with indifference. Edmund talks about the wheel coming full circle, and we see how true this is when he has a complete change of heart regarding Lear and Cordelia:

I pant for life. Some good I mean to do,
Despite of mine own nature. Quickly send,
Be brief in it, to the castle; for my writ
Is on the life of Lear and on Cordelia.
Nay, send in time.

Edmund is saying that, because of his nature, it is difficult for him to do the right thing, but he tries to overcome this, which is admirable.

In any case it is too late, and we are greeted with the heartwrenching sight of the old king carrying Cordelia's corpse in his arms. His anguish and pain are difficult to witness:

> *Howl, howl, howl, howl! O, you are men of stones!*
> *Had I your tongues and eyes, I'd use them so*
> *That heaven's vault should crack. She's gone for ever!*
> *I know when one is dead, and when one lives;*
> *She's dead as earth. Lend me a looking-glass;*
> *If that her breath will mist or stain the stone,*
> *Why, then she lives.*

This is an incredibly poignant scene, as Lear desperately looks for some signs of life in his beloved daughter. Kent tries to reveal his true identity to console Lear, but Lear is past understanding. Yet the old man still managed to kill his daughter's murderer, and this hints at the great soldier he must once have been:

> *I kill'd the slave that was a-hanging thee …*
> *I have seen the day, with my good biting falchion*
> *I would have made them skip. I am old now,*
> *And these same crosses spoil me. Who are you?*
> *Mine eyes are not o' the best. I'll tell you straight.*

Convincing himself that Cordelia is still breathing, Lear himself dies, worn out by the physical and emotional suffering he has undergone in the course of the play. His death is all the more profound because of the person he had proved himself to be in the latter part of the play. He dies a great man, a great king, having learned who he really was, and what love really is, through his suffering. Some critics think this is too tragic, but the real tragedy would have been if Lear had died an unrealised, egotistical and self-centred man, as he would have without the experience he endured.

It is also comforting to know that Kent will still be at

This sword, this arm, and my best spirits, are bent
To prove upon thy heart, whereto I speak,
Thou liest

– EDGAR (ACT V SCENE III)

Lear's side, even in death: *I have a journey, sir, shortly to go; / My master calls me, I must not say no.*

The play concludes with just Albany and Edgar left alive. Edgar is to be ruler alongside Albany, and Albany stresses the importance of saying what one really feels, not what you think you should say, which is, of course, just what Cordelia did. Her death, therefore, has not been in vain. She reminds us of the importance of being true.

IMPORTANT THEMES IN ACT V

- The theme of Forgiveness is seen when Edgar and Edmund forgive each other.

- The theme of Redemption is seen in the character of Edmund, and also in Edgar's description of his reunion with Gloucester.

- The theme of Justice is seen in the way Goneril and Regan destroy one another; in how Edgar survives, while Edmund dies; and in how Albany inherits the throne.

- The theme of Love is seen most notably in the relationship between Cordelia and Lear. Cordelia's unconditional love for her father is inspirational, and Lear's candid expression of his love for her shows how

much he has developed as a person, as a father, and as a character. We also see love between Gloucester and Edgar, and in Kent's loyalty to Lear.

CHARACTER DEVELOPMENT IN ACT V

- Goneril and Regan prove themselves to be even more evil than we could possibly have imagined.

- Lear becomes a great man, one who truly knows himself and the value of love.

- Gloucester dies of sorrow and joy; sorrow at his gullibility and Edmund's betrayal, but joy at Edgar's unconditional love.

- Edmund displays both his worst characteristics (greed, opportunism, disloyalty) and his best (the ability to forgive, remorse) in this act.

- Kent continues to be as selfless and steadfast as ever, but, tragically, never gets the recognition from Lear that he so craves.

- By his rejection of Goneril and his attempts to save Lear and Cordelia, Albany develops into a heroic figure in this act. He is also willing to share power with Edgar and Kent.

QUESTIONS ON ACT 5

1. **Which sister do you think Edmund prefers? Give reasons for your answer.**

2. **Why do you think Edmund agrees to fight an unnamed challenger?**

3. **Why does Edmund order the deaths of Lear and Cordelia?**

4. **Taking all the evidence into account, which sister, Goneril or Regan, is the more evil, in your view?**

5. **If Goneril left a suicide note, what do you think it might have said?**

6. **Is Edmund gracious in defeat, in your opinion?**

7. **Write the dialogue that might have occurred between Edgar and Gloucester, before the latter's death.**

8. **Is Cordelia's death going too far, even in a tragedy?**

9. **Write a diary entry for Albany, on the evening of the day Lear and Cordelia died.**

10. **Pick ten quotations, across a range of characters and themes, which you think best sum up Act V. Explain in each case why you have chosen it.**

KING LEAR

KEY WORDS TO DESCRIBE HIM

egotistical
arrogant
narcissistic
impetuous
rash
reckless
incensed
wrathful
anguished
humiliated
livid
volatile
remorseful
chastened
humble
kind
tolerant
self-aware

*THERE IS A SAMPLE ESSAY ON THE
CHARACTER OF LEAR ON PAGE 263*

L EAR IS a typical tragic hero. Despite possessing a *hamartia* or fatal flaw (arrogance, rashness, vanity), he earns our earnest goodwill because of, and not despite, his human frailty.

Remember that the intention of a tragedy is to bring about a catharsis in the audience; that is to say, a purging of negative emotions. It was believed that the act of crying caused the expulsion of pain from the body, and so, theoretically, after seeing a tragedy like *King Lear* you should feel a lot happier. Lear is the main character and thus the main figure on whom the tragic events will centre.

At the beginning of the play, Lear is impetuous, egotistical, hasty, volatile and exercises poor judgement. But when Lear's domestic circumstances change from being the king of a huge kingdom to the unwanted aged father of two devious daughters whose care he had relied upon, Lear himself starts to change.

In poverty, Lear starts to share and to demonstrate compassion and a capacity for self-analysis. Instead of a royal retinue, he is surrounded by the poor and the dispossessed: Poor Tom, the Fool and Caius. Yet he appreciates their loyalty and acknowledges the truth of the Fool's many comments about his mistakes.

In madness, Lear discovers the truth about his own flawed character. It is ironic that he shows his most attractive traits when he has lost his reason and stops putting on an act.

When Lear's intellect fails, he begins to engage with

*When thou dost ask me blessing,
I'll kneel down,
And ask of thee forgiveness*

– LEAR (ACT V SCENE III)

his senses. This primal simplicity serves him much better than his previously complex 'kingly' approach.

Lear learns self-awareness and humility, and discovers the rawness and vulnerability of newly awakened emotions when he reunites with Cordelia, realises his great love for her, and then loses her to death.

Lear dies having learned the inestimable value of Cordelia's love. Just as he offers his unconditional love, he loses her. His own subsequent death is, at least, that of a fully realised man, a true tragic hero, who has discovered that you cannot quantify love.

GONERIL & REGAN

KEY WORDS TO DESCRIBE THEM

selfish
evil
scheming
mercenary
malevolent
greedy
manipulative
deceitful
treacherous
corrupt
immoral
unscrupulous

GONERIL AND Regan present similar characteristics to the audience. They do what they must to get their inheritance, and then they really just want to get rid of their father. Their motivation is primarily greed. Later, of course, they are both motivated by their love of, or more probably lust for, Edmund. Goneril and Regan are on a path to self-destruction because they care about nobody but themselves. Like all the worst characters, their partnership in time turns to hatred and jealousy of one another.

Goneril is generally considered the worse of the two sisters. But how do you quantify evil? Yes, it is Goneril who poisons Regan, but isn't that just a case of her getting there first? Unlike Regan, Goneril is married to a good man, Albany. Surely the fact that Albany chose to marry Goneril shows that there was once some good in her?

It is Goneril who sets the events of the play in motion with her treatment of Lear, but Regan quickly proves herself Goneril's match in evil doings. Also, *King Lear* has the stereotypical scenario of the youngest sister being the best, so by extension it is probably typical that we would regard Goneril, being the eldest, as the worst.

Should we take Goneril's suicide as redeeming her in any way? Certainly the case could be made that her

Combine together 'gainst the enemy;
For these domestic and particular broils
Are not the question here

– GONERIL (ACT V SCENE I)

guilt at causing her own sister's death leads to her suicide. However, it would be more consistent with the character she has exhibited throughout the play to say that Goneril realises that her plans had ended with Albany's discovery of her letter to Edmund. The punishment for adultery in those days was death, and the treason she was also guilty of due to her treatment of her father meant that Goneril's death was a certainty anyway. She merely took Albany's power to punish her into her own hands.

As for Regan, at first she seems to be in Goneril's shadow, obeying her sister without question. She has the advantage of having a husband who is just as greedy and cruel as she is. Cornwall is also too caught up in his own

sense of self-importance to have any conception of the attraction she is harbouring for Edmund.

Regan's blinding of Gloucester proves her to be Goneril's match for cruelty. She shows little concern when her husband is slain by Gloucester's servant; indeed, her first thought seems to be that now the way is clear for her and Edmund to marry.

Both Goneril and Regan die terrible deaths, and far from being accomplices, each turns out to be the other's greatest enemy. There is very little humanity to be found in their characters. They are portrayed as melodramatically heinous, and their role is to show how low human beings can sink when they are in thrall to greed, jealousy and a complete disregard for the binding ties of family.

CORDELIA

candid
honest
exemplary
noble
faithful

authentic
true
forthright
angelic
forgiving
merciful
moral
magnanimous

CORDELIA IS not intended to be a woman realistically portrayed. She is an exemplary character who embodies perfection. Her role is that of a whiter-than-white persona, against which all the other characters appear as various shades of black and grey. Just as her sisters represent absolute evil, Cordelia represents absolute good.

Cordelia's reluctance to voice her love for her father seems curiously at odds with the character who declares her love so profusely at the end of the play. Many critics wonder at this verbosity in one who could not heave her heart into her mouth. But what Cordelia objected to was the test of her love, and Lear's intention to make performing seals of his daughters before he gave them what would eventually be their due anyway. She would not play that game, and suffered the consequences of her integrity: first banishment, then military defeat, and finally death.

Cordelia is the truly hopeful part about the play *King Lear*. Her unconditional love is a lesson both to the characters and to us, the audience.

*I love your Majesty
According to my bond;
nor more nor less*

– CORDELIA (ACT I SCENE I)

GLOUCESTER

KEY WORDS TO DESCRIBE HIM

credulous
naive
vain
gullible
weak
exploitable
remorseful
brave
enlightened
loyal
redeemed
noble

GLOUCESTER'S CHARACTER is closely allied to Lear's. He is not a bad man, and his embarrassment about his illegitimate son should be seen as a quality of restraint rather than an immoral one. Many a titled man of this time, and throughout the centuries, in fact, would have had quite a number of illegitimate children. Most of the English kings are thought to have had hundreds of illegitimate children all told. This presented a practical difficulty because of the notion of 'blue blood', i.e. noble blood. Illegitimate children, though normally shunned in society, were given a measure of social acceptance if their fathers were of a high social rank. Gloucester seems fond of his illegitimate son and tells us that ***there was good sport at his making***!

Gloucester is extremely gullible, and deeply insecure to believe that his eldest son, Edgar, would plot against him. Yet it might also be said that he is manipulated by Edmund easily simply because he loves him. He is an innocent man who believes evidence that is put before him. As an honest person, he does not always see deceit in others.

Gloucester is also an honourable man, utterly loyal to Lear. An earl, he fulfills his duty to the king with admirable bravery, risking his life when he intervenes to prevent Goneril, Regan and Cornwall's ill-treatment of Lear. His horrific punishment makes him the literal embodiment of Lear; both are blind, one physically, the other mentally.

O my follies! then Edgar was abus'd.
Kind gods, forgive me that, and prosper him!

– GLOUCESTER (ACT III SCENE VII)

Gloucester's torture was devised by Shakespeare to provide a gory spectacle for his audience. They would have been appalled at the scene, but also entertained, as we are when we watch a horror film. His blinding is also significant because it mirrors his earlier emotional blindness. Gloucester is a far wiser man after he loses his sight. It takes blindness for him to see clearly.

Gloucester wishes to die when his sight is taken, not out of weakness but out of utter devastation. He is fooled once again by one of his sons, when Edgar leads him to jump off a log rather than a cliff. Gloucester's belief in his amazing survival is rather far-fetched, but this is an instance where you must suspend your disbelief; that is, just ignore the practical discrepancies and enjoy the scene. After all, we do this with television all the

time. The point Shakespeare makes over and over in this play is that we believe what we want to believe, and on that account Gloucester probably does want to be saved.

We never get to see Gloucester and Edgar's reunion on stage, but Edgar relates it through flashback:

I ask'd his blessing, and from first to last
Told him my pilgrimage: but his flaw'd heart,
Alack, too weak the conflict to support!
'Twixt two extremes of passion, joy and grief,
Burst smilingly.

Gloucester always wore his heart on his sleeve, and his death is entirely believable. Edgar's poignant words move Edmund so much that he tries to save Lear's and Cordelia's lives. This shows that both sons loved their father, and this adds to the pathos of Gloucester's death.

EDGAR

KEY WORDS TO DESCRIBE HIM

clever

resourceful

trusting

dignified

heroic

loyal

principled

noble

virtuous

moral

dutiful

honest

brave

humble

E DGAR AS a character starts off rather sketchily but develops through the play into a believable, well-rounded individual. Edgar is a well-brought-up nobleman's son. He is very like his father, innocent and trusting, but his journey teaches him to be tougher and more discriminating.

Edgar believes in his father's wrath all to easily. But he also believes in his brother, despite Edmund's bitterness towards him. Edgar's only 'crime' against his brother is to be older by a year and to have been born within marriage.

Edgar flees from his father's supposed anger, in an act of self-preservation that shows his inner strength, but he does not go far. Just as he shares Gloucester's innocence and lack of guile, so too does he share his loyalty. He does not leave his father, no matter what. Like Cordelia, he displays unconditional love for his parent.

Edgar disguises himself as a beggar called Poor Tom, or Tom o' Bedlam, meaning from Bedlam, the infamous lunatic asylum. His filthy appearance and pretence of madness allow him to remain undiscovered, as he becomes a kind of guardian angel, first to Lear and then to his father. His choice of disguise shows real intelligence, for he is, essentially, hiding in plain sight. Poor Tom is a very realistic depiction, and his character is also a vehicle for social criticism. How terrible that a beggar's disguise should mean that a person becomes virtually invisible in society.

The gods are just, and of our pleasant vices,
Make instruments to plague us

– EDGAR (ACT V SCENE III)

Edgar shows loyalty, determination, and even a touch of ruthlessness in his killing of Oswald, and in his tense duel with his brother, Edmund. Edgar is more real than his counterpart in the main plot, Cordelia, because he gets his hands dirty. He deals with Edmund decisively, and yet has the capacity to forgive him all that he has done.

Edgar is *Lear*'s one true success story. At the end of the play, he has survived all its evil scheming. His reinstatement as an earl demonstrates renewed faith in the aristocracy, and shows that good will ultimately triumph over evil.

EDMUND

KEY WORDS TO DESCRIBE HIM

cunning
shrewd
duplicitous
manipulative
ruthless
pitiless
wily
opportunistic
devious
deceitful
sly
unscrupulous
cold-hearted
redeemed

THERE IS A SAMPLE ESSAY ON THE
CHARACTER OF EDMUND ON PAGE 260

E DMUND BETRAYS his father and is ultimately responsible for his death. He tries to disinherit his brother, and turns father and son against one another in order to do so. He turns two sisters into mortal enemies, and he orders the deaths of Lear and Cordelia. Yet he is also one of the most charismatic characters in the play and never truly makes the audience despise him, even though he certainly does enough to deserve our contempt.

There are certain mitigating factors that prevent a blanket condemnation of Edmund's actions. First, there are the circumstances of his birth, for which he is blameless but yet has suffered the consequences. He has been hidden from society thus far and will be sent away again. Edmund is bitter as a result, and to a certain extent that bitterness is understandable. He resents his brother, and this is understandable too.

Second, Edmund views his manipulation of those around him as a game. He is like a child in a sweet shop. He is taking all he can get, not because he needs it, or even necessarily wants it, but because he can. His enthusiasm for the game and his glee when he wins are infectious.

Third, Edmund is the cause of Goneril and Regan's downfall, and though he did not orchestrate the events leading to their deaths, he uses them as they used their father. He does not treat either of them with respect, but did they deserve to be treated in any way other than

To both these sisters have I sworn my love;
Each jealous of the other, as the stung
Are of the adder

– EDMUND (ACT V SCENE I)

how they themselves have treated their families and their husbands?

Fourth, Edmund does repent as he is dying. He treats death with the casual nature he treats life. He does not really seem to mind that he is dying, but he does want to make some sort of amends before he dies. He warns Edgar and Albany about the two deaths he has ordered, and though the warning comes too late for Cordelia, it redeems Edmund's character somewhat.

Edmund succeeds as a character because he is an enigma. We never quite understand him, but there is enough good in him to warrant a closer look. He is realistic – neither wholly bad nor wholly good. Above all, he is a fallible human being and perhaps the most interesting character in *King Lear*. He has the most soliloquies in the play, because he is in league with no one but himself. Edmund's duplicity makes him intriguing, and he is the catalyst for many plot developments.

ALBANY

principled

dignified

firm

decisive

authoritative

magnanimous

noble

commanding

confident

honourable

calm

trustworthy

sensible

strong

A S ALBANY is married to Goneril, at the end of the play it is he who will accede to the throne. Shakespeare had the ending of the play clearly in sight in the delineation of his character, and this accounts for many of the inconsistencies of his role in the play.

Remember that this play is about the British monarchy and was acted out before a British public. The public enjoyed plays about the monarchy as that was the closest most of them would ever get to royalty (and also, of course, because royalty, being larger than life, were allowed to have larger-than-life characters).

However, that posed a practical problem for Shakespeare, because he needed to leave one upstanding member of the monarchy alive, or there would have been an outcry on the part of the audience. Yet because of the intimate nature of the action in *King Lear,* and with the whole point of the play being to depict family set against family, who in the end was to be left standing? One of the husbands of the three daughters was the obvious choice, but how to keep them from sullying themselves while being married to a bad character?

Shakespeare's answer was to have Albany disappear at times of crisis and reappear to voice his disapproval at what has transpired in his absence. It is not entirely successful. Albany seems blind for much of the play, and so his role in the latter half – of a brave hero – is a

The weight of this sad time we must obey; Speak what we feel, not what we ought to say

little hard to swallow.

Albany seems merely disgusted by Goneril's association with Edmund, not angry or jealous. Yet he is the character who remains to fly the banner of righteousness, so to speak, and his steady air of calm as the devastating repercussions of *King Lear* come to light does make it seem as though he will indeed make a fine king. His assurances to Edgar and Kent that they may rule with him shows a magnanimous character also, which bodes well for the future.

KENT

KEY WORDS TO DESCRIBE HIM

noble
steadfast
honest
admirable
resourceful
principled
loyal
devoted
brave
dependable
dutiful
honourable
valiant
trustworthy

KENT IS a relatively minor character in the play, but his role is still important. Kent is Lear's loyal servant. He epitomises the perfect servant, loyal to the death. He is brave enough to assert himself to Lear for Cordelia's sake, and receives a harsh punishment for his troubles.

Undeterred, Kent disguises himself as Caius and immediately returns to Lear's service. He stays with him through his madness and unsheltered nights. He is also an enjoyable character, particularly when it comes to his skirmishes with the slimy Oswald. Kent's dramatic function is often underestimated, but he adds a lot to this play.

When Lear dies, Kent's heart breaks. Kent announces his intention of following his master into death, despite Albany's offer of a share in the kingdom. It is tragic that Lear is too far gone to realise what Kent is trying to tell him at the end of the play, but at least Cordelia, Edgar and Albany tell Kent how much his loyal service meant.

Kent's main purpose in the play, however, is to show how a mere servant knows his duty so that, in contrast with him, Goneril and Regan seem all the more dastardly.

See better, Lear; and let me still remain
The true blank of thine eye

— KENT (ACT I SCENE I)

THE FOOL

KEY WORDS TO DESCRIBE HIM

witty

honest

droll

funny

entertaining

wise

shrewd

truthful

comical

blunt

outspoken

pithy

astute

clever

THERE IS A SAMPLE ESSAY ON THE
ROLE OF THE FOOL ON PAGE 252

IN ROYAL courts there was a very specific code of conduct. You had to behave in a certain way, dress in a certain way, talk in a certain way. Far from power and status equalling freedom, the higher up in society you stood, the more rigorously were you governed by a code of conduct. In this context, a king was the least free of all citizens.

Who was free, then? It was the 'freaks' and fools who assembled in court for the entertainment of the nobility. Children born with a deformity were often sold to the castle, where their malformed bodies provided amusement for the higher classes. They often had dwarves, conjoined twins and anyone who was in any way different wandering around the castle. It was considered a mark of status to have as many of these 'fools' as possible.

For that reason, the Fool in *Lear* is a person on the very periphery of 'civilised' society. It is from this unique vantage point that he can see the evils of the world from which he is excluded. The Fool does not need to behave in a certain way: he can say exactly what he likes, and so he is the only character in the play who can see the wood for the trees, so to speak. It was the special privilege of the court jester to tell the truth, and he could do so without fear of reprisal.

Lear is genuinely fond of the Fool, despite the Fool's constant reminders of how Lear has brought this terrible situation upon himself. The Fool has nothing to lose and,

If thou wert my fool, nuncle,
I'd have thee beaten
for being old before thy time

– THE FOOL (ACT I SCENE IV)

paradoxically, is in fact the wisest person in the play. All the great truths are spoken by the Fool, often in a humorous way, which serves to lighten the tone of this often sombre drama. Lear probably has just one soliloquy because the Fool assumes the role of voicing his interior thoughts.

The theatrical role of the Fool is to provide a visual spectacle. He would have been dressed in a traditional fool's costume, and he would have danced and pranced on the stage. He also provided a link between the audience and the action of the play: because he tends to voice what we ourselves are thinking, the importance of his role in the play should not be dismissed.

The Fool does not remain until the end of the play, but disappears quite abruptly in Act III. His last line in the play is: ***And I'll go to bed at noon***. By this the Fool means that he will die early, worn out by what he has learned of man's inhumanity to man. He leaves us with a very different Lear, one who, due in no small way to the Fool's contribution, is steadily on the path to redemption.

IMPORTANT
THEMES
IN KING LEAR

LOVE AND HATE

Love and hate are very important themes in *King Lear*, as they are in life in general. The love of Cordelia, Kent, Albany and Gloucester for Lear, the love of France for Cordelia, and the love of Edgar for Gloucester means that the play contains optimism as well as pessimism, hope as well as despair. Unconditional love provides a balance for unfathomable hatred.

FILIAL INGRATITUDE

Goneril, Regan and Edmund do not know how to be grateful for what they have. They take what they can, and rather than thanking anybody, they try to grab more. Their ingratitude is a motivating force in the play. It is particularly disgusting because the natural order is for children to love and protect their aged parents. It is unnatural for them to treat them badly.

GOOD AND EVIL

Good and evil are set in opposition constantly throughout *King Lear:* that is the whole premise of the play. As Cordelia herself says, good does not always win the day. The avenging French army is defeated by the British; Cordelia and Lear die. But so too do Goneril, Regan, Edmund, Cornwall and Oswald. Not one evil person is left standing, and so good does eventually win, by a very narrow margin.

BLINDNESS

The theme of blindness recurs throughout the play. References to blindness are made even before Gloucester's blinding. Lear's self-blindness is the crux of his dilemma, and Gloucester's literal blinding serves to emphasise this *hamartia* in Lear and make it all the sadder.

THE VALUE OF SUFFERING / THE MEANING OF LIFE

When critics say that *King Lear* is an overwhelmingly pessimistic play, they are missing a crucial theme of the tragedy. The Lear who dies in the final scene of the play is very different from the vain, pompous Lear proposing the love test in Act I, Scene I. His suffering has value, because it makes him a better man, worthy of the title of tragic hero. This also applies to Gloucester, Edgar and Kent.

Even Edmund changes dramatically in a very short space of time as he is suffering the final throes of death. The shallowness of the characters in the play shows the truth of Socrates' aphorism that 'the unexamined life is not worth living'. Even though some characters die immediately after learning the value of suffering, they die enlightened as to the meaning of life, something everyone searches for at some point.

JUSTICE AND REDEMPTION

The theme of justice is also intrinsic to *King Lear*. The quality of justice is often represented in our courts by a statue of a woman holding a scales. She is blindfolded to show that, ideally at least, justice should be blind. In practice, this means that a poor man is entitled to the same justice as a rich man, and a beggar, in the eyes of the law, is equal to a king.

Lear only discovers what justice really means when he stops being appalled at the injustices in his own life and becomes accountable for the injustice he sees around him. Poetic justice in a work of literature means that vice is punished and virtue rewarded. Shakespeare has the dramatic licence to make the 'bad guys' of *King Lear* pay heavily for their crimes. To his credit, he does not use this licence as much as he could. As a result, while the search for justice motivates much of the action in *King Lear,* when it comes it is not melodramatic but realistic. Goneril and Regan receive their just desserts at each other's hands, while Edgar punishes the brother who betrayed him.

Justice also means redemption, and the opportunity for an individual to effect justice by redeeming him or herself. The redemption in *King Lear* shows that no matter how lost you become, like Edmund you can still make amends, and like Lear you can become a different and better person.

INTER-FAMILY RELATIONSHIPS

The relationship between Lear and his daughters and Gloucester and his sons is another major theme of the play. Lear and Gloucester are both old men and need the kindness of their children at this point in their lives. The family is the smallest unit of society, and Shakespeare underlines its importance. When a family goes badly wrong, as Lear's family and Gloucester's family do, there are repercussions for society at large. That is why when you hear of a murder on the news and are then told that a family member committed it, you tend to be far more shocked than if you heard a perfect stranger had done it. Family members are meant to love, protect and nurture one another, not betray and hurt one another. *King Lear* explores the breakdown of family relationships and how this can impact on the state itself.

MAIN
IMAGERY
IN KING LEAR

The imagery in *King Lear* can be divided into several distinct categories: blindness, clothing, animals, disease/ suffering and storm imagery. Each of these types of imagery serves a distinct purpose. Also, remember that this is a drama, so when discussing imagery, also discuss what you have seen on stage or film, particularly the images that have stuck in your mind. It could be the Fool cavorting about the stage or Kent's ignominious position in the stocks.

ANIMAL IMAGERY

Fifty-seven different types of animals are mentioned in *King Lear.* Normally, people are compared to animals in order to highlight a particular characteristic. Goneril and Regan are often compared to birds of prey (vultures, kites, etc.) for example, because they too prey on the weak. Lear is a ***pelican*** because it was thought then that pelicans fed their young on their own blood. So that makes Goneril and Regan ***blood-suckers***! Bears, dogs, serpents, wolves, tigers and cuckoos are all mentioned too. A cuckoo is a simple image, but the fact that it bites the head of the sparrow that has fed it shows vividly how children can turn against their parents. The different breeds of dogs are also a way of characterising different types of people.

BLINDNESS / SIGHT

Throughout the play, there are numerous references to seeing and not seeing. Kent is the **true blank** of Lear's eye, and Goneril refers to sight as the most precious sense we possess. The blinding of Gloucester and the description of his **bleeding rings** is incredibly powerful. The imagery here is also thematic, a constant reminder of how we can choose, even subconsciously, what we see and acknowledge, and what we don't.

SUFFERING / DISEASE

In Shakespeare's day, beds were full of bedbugs, heads were full of lice, and many people suffered from boils, carbuncles, and more. They were not sterile times, so these images were very immediate to the audience. Disease imagery can also be used to show how we can be biologically connected to people, in a bad way. For example, Lear says to Regan: *thou art a boil, / A plague-sore, an embossed carbuncle, / In my corrupted blood.* Suffering images include the blind Gloucester stumbling towards Dover, and the tragic sight of Lear cradling the dead Cordelia in his arms.

Detested kite! thou liest

– LEAR (ACT I SCENE IV)

STORM IMAGERY

In a theatre with limited props and little or no special effects, Shakespeare summons up a ferocious storm using only words. It is a measure of his talent as a writer that this imagery is so effective:

Blow, winds, and crack your cheeks! rage! blow!
You cataracts and hurricanoes, spout
Till you have drench'd our steeples, drown'd
the cocks!
You sulph'rous and thought-executing fires,
Vaunt-couriers to oak-cleaving thunderbolts,
Singe my white head!

MAIN PLOT &
SUB-PLOT
IN KING LEAR

The role of the sub-plot in the play is to make the events of the main plot all the more dramatic, to exaggerate them, if you will. Many of the abstract elements of the main plot are mirrored in a tangible way in the sub-plot, for example the literal blindness of Gloucester as opposed to the emotional blindness of Lear.

LEAR AND GLOUCESTER

- Lear and Gloucester are similar in many ways. They are old friends and share many of the same characteristics. Lear is rash, impetuous and, as Regan so shrewdly says: ***hath ever but slenderly known himself.***

- Gloucester, too, is quick to assume the worst and acts impulsively. Later on, when he is literally blinded and is wandering on the heath, he is the physical manifestation of Lear's emotional and mental blindness.

- However, Gloucester was presented with a more compelling case for the rejection of his child than Lear. Since Gloucester truly believes that Edgar was plotting against him, his only real crime is believing one son over another. In many ways it could almost be seen as a good quality in Gloucester that he does not automatically assume Edmund is less trustworthy than Edgar just because he is illegitimate.

- Just as Gloucester's social ranking is a watered-down version of Lear's, so too is he a less dramatic and more well-rounded character. He does not reach the lows that Lear experiences, but neither does he reach the heights of Lear's eventual self-knowledge.

GONERIL, REGAN AND EDMUND

- In many ways Goneril and Regan are interchangeable. There is no fundamental difference in their characters other than the fact that Goneril seems the more assertive of the two. Though it is Goneril who kills Regan, it could easily have been the other way around. Goneril and Regan are paralleled by Edmund. They are all malicious, scheming and greedy.

- The main difference is that Edmund is actually illegitimate and, because of the prejudice against him, has some motive for his actions. Goneril and Regan are legitimate but do not act like proper daughters, so in a sense they too are illegitimate.

- Edmund is an anti-hero, but he does redeem himself at the end of the play by showing genuine remorse for his actions. Goneril and Regan never show remorse or any kind of human feeling. They are rather two-dimensional, like caricatures of evil rather than realistic portrayals. Edmund is a realistically portrayed character and in the end invites our sympathy.

CORDELIA AND EDGAR

- Cordelia and Edgar are the truly good characters in the play, but as with the relationships between the other characters in the main plot and sub-plot, Cordelia and Edgar are not completely equal.

- Both Cordelia and Edgar are wronged by their fathers. However, Cordelia is banished by Lear as a direct result of the love test. There is nothing she can do to avoid her punishment, and she is blameless in the affair. Edgar is wronged by Gloucester in light of the latter's readiness to believe one brother over another. But Edgar himself is taken in by Edmund, so he is as guilty as Gloucester of being easy to deceive. He runs scared at the news of the rumour that his father is angry with him, and this shows bad judgement on his part.

- Cordelia and Edgar are both unfortunate in their siblings. Edgar, however, kills Edmund. While no one could say that Edmund did not deserve to be punished, there are other ways to punish someone, and so Edgar does have blood on his hands while Cordelia never does. Both Edgar and Cordelia are good characters, the best in the play, but Cordelia is an exemplary picture of perfection, like an angel or a saint. Edgar is more realistically portrayed, just as Edmund and Gloucester are.

HOW TO WRITE ESSAYS ON KING LEAR

In the Leaving Certificate exam, you will always have a choice of two essays on *King Lear*. The essay is worth 60 marks, which is 15 per cent of your total mark for English.

Your essay should consist of: an introduction (which repeats the wording of the question); a minimum of six paragraphs (although you can write more) which deal with one point or one topic each; and a conclusion (which refers back to the question and ties up any loose ends).

Throughout your essay, you must *answer the question*. Stick rigidly to what is asked. Do not waffle or go off the point. Remember, you only get marks for relevant points. You must also quote as much as possible, and you can also refer to the text. Two quotations per paragraph would be ideal, but it is quality, not quantity, that counts. When choosing quotations to memorise, pick ones that are versatile and can be used in lots of different essays. For example, when Gloucester says, ***I stumbled when I saw***. You could use this quotation for a question on Gloucester, or the sub-plot, or imagery, or blindness (including Lear's).

For any Shakespearean text, there are four possible styles of question:

1. On a theme (sample essay, page 266)
2. On a character (sample essays, page 260 and 263)
3. On imagery or style or a specific scene (sample (essay, page 254)
4. An opinion question; for example, 'Is *King Lear* still relevant to a modern audience?' (sample essay, page 257)

The character who comes up in a question on his own most often is Lear himself, but you could be asked questions on any of the main characters, or perhaps a group of characters, such as the three characters in the sub-plot. Sometimes there will be a question on the Fool.

Any of the main themes can come up. A stylistic question on imagery seems quite difficult, but the main thing is to know relevant quotations.

When answering a question on *King Lear:*

- Always write about the play chronologically – go from the very first scene onwards.

- Start by underlining the important words in the question; make sure you know exactly what the examiner is looking for. Keep repeating the wording of the question to demonstrate clear focus.

- Don't summarise the play. The examiner will assume you have a thorough knowledge of it and is looking for your ability to *analyse,* not summarise.

- If the question takes the form of a statement with which you are asked to agree or disagree, as a general rule it is better to agree. Of course there are exceptions, but mostly it is easier to argue for the statement rather than against it.

- Shape the question to your individual needs. Make it work for you. For example, if you're asked about imagery, you can also use what you know on the theme of blindness. Or if you're asked what makes the play enjoyable, and you know Edmund's character well, you could write a paragraph or two on how you enjoyed Shakespeare's characterisation, particularly the character of Edmund.

- Plan your answer carefully. A plan should consist of approximately six to ten points which you can develop throughout the essay. This will ensure that you:

  1. Do not run out of ideas after a page or two.
  2. Do not become irrelevant.
  3. Do not spend too much time exploring just one or two issues, or spend time on just one character.
  4. Do not run out of time.
  5. Do not forget any quotations that pop into your mind – you can simply jot them on your plan, and slip them in where appropriate.

When you are preparing for your Leaving Certificate, have pen and paper in hand and plan, plan, plan! Whether it is a bubble plan, a spider plan or bullet points, once you get used to planning, it is easy to do well in this question.

Finally:

- Use personal opinion. 'I' is the most important word in any Leaving Certificate English essay.

- Refer to a performance (either a play or a film) you have seen. Remember, this is a drama.

- Refer to the original audience for whom, let's not forget, Shakespeare intended this play.

- Remember the marking scheme.

SAMPLE PLANS ON KING LEAR

Below are examples of some of the most common questions on *King Lear* and advice on how to tackle the essay titles. Before you start any essay, however, forget about having the text open in front of you as you write. Learn off your quotations, read through your notes, then shut your books and do the question in 50 to 60 minutes. This may sound tough, but you must recreate exam conditions as closely as possible in order to get the best possible mark.

SAMPLE PLAN 1

'Shakespeare's depiction of evil in the play **King Lear** *is far more interesting than his depiction of goodness.'*
Discuss this statement, supporting your answer by quotation from or reference to the play.

What the question is simply asking is: are the evil characters more interesting than the good characters? You can either agree or disagree; both options are equally valid.

Sample introduction: The introduction will be more or less repeating the wording of the question. So a good example would be the following:
I disagree with the statement that Shakespeare's depiction of evil in the play *King Lear* is far more interesting than his depiction of goodness. Most of the 'evil' characters, with the exception of Edmund, seem shallow and stereotypically evil, particularly in contrast with more substantial and three-dimensional good characters such as Cordelia.

Discuss the evil characters for the first 4 paragraphs.

Paragraph 1: Discuss how Goneril and Regan's characters are fascinating on a sensationalist level. They are the equivalent of the kind of characters we might read about in the tabloids or see on a tacky chat show today. But ultimately they lack Cordelia's substance and depth.

Paragraphs 2 and 3: Discuss Edmund's charisma: he appeals to the audience despite his evil qualities; he appeals to us because of the good aspects of his character, not the evil ones.

Paragraph 4: Cornwall is the typical villainous sidekick – his blinding of Gloucester is appalling, although it does make the play interesting. No one cares when he dies, though, because he is like a caricature of evil.

Discuss the good characters for the next 3 paragraphs.

Paragraph 5: Cordelia is indeed an exemplary character, but she stands up to her sisters and fights a war for her father – nothing boring about that. Also, if she is in fact the Fool in disguise, she becomes very interesting indeed.

Paragraph 6: Edgar allows himself to be manipulated by Edmund, but that is only because he alone does not hold Edmund's illegitimacy against him and he trusts him. Edgar may lack the magnetism of his brother, but his various disguises are ingenious, and he speaks some of the most powerful words in the entire play.

Paragraph 7: Albany may start off as an uninteresting character, but he quickly grows into a heroic character who consistently does the right thing, no matter what the personal cost.

Sample conclusion: In conclusion, as I have demonstrated through my essay, I think it is fundamentally erroneous to say that the evil characters intrigue us and engage us more than the good characters. I found many of the evil characters such as Goneril and Regan mere caricatures, while the good characters such as Lear and Cordelia were fascinating, memorable and very real. Edmund may seem to be the exception to this rule, but as I discussed in my essay, it is the good elements of Edmund's character which make him interesting, and not the bad. Had Edmund died without remorse, he would have been just as forgettable as the other villains. Therefore, it is true to say that the good characters in *King Lear* are the most remarkable.

SAMPLE PLAN 2

'The play King Lear *offers us one central experience – pessimism.'*
Discuss this statement, supporting your answer with reference to *King Lear*.

Paragraph 1: Disagree. Yes, there are many pessimistic elements – greed, treachery, disloyalty, filial ingratitude – and the play can be bleak, gloomy and challenging. Give examples.

Paragraph 2: However, there is always optimism to be observed, due to the inspirational characters of Cordelia, Kent and the Fool, not to mention the loyalty of Gloucester, Edgar, Kent and many servants.

Paragraph 3: Many key scenes are quite dark, yet Shakespeare is always careful to balance them out. For example, the love test's cruelty is balanced by France's true love and Kent's loyalty, or the servants' loyalty when Gloucester is blinded, etc.

Paragraph 4: The storm scenes are considered bleak, but we also see Lear's growing compassion, and he learns through suffering, which is hardly depressing.

Paragraph 5: Edgar's devoted service to his father, Cordelia's unconditional forgiveness, Edmund's 'deathbed' confession are all hopeful.

Paragraph 6: There are many pessimistic elements, and the ending is (as it must be according to the rules of tragedy) catastrophic. But pessimism is only one experience this complex play offers. That is why *King Lear* is rightly judged the pinnacle of Shakespeare's career.

SAMPLE PLAN 3

'The play King Lear offers us characters who represent the very worst and the very best in human nature.'

Paragraph 1: Agree. Goneril, Regan, Cornwall and Oswald represent the very worst human characteristics possible: greed, avarice, selfishness, cruelty, treachery, evil.

Paragraph 2: Some scenes are utterly shocking in showing how low a human being can sink: the blinding of Gloucester, the poisoning of Regan by her own sister, the love triangle.

Paragraph 3: Lear himself is capable of terrible behaviour (disowning Cordelia and banishing Kent) but he goes on to behave in a very admirable way. This is also true of Gloucester, even if to a lesser extent.

Paragraph 4: Edmund seems to represent the very worst in human nature, but this is mostly due to his resentment at his upbringing and future prospects. So, sometimes human nature appears irredeemable, but this is not always the case.

Paragraph 5: Cordelia, the Fool, Edgar, Kent and Albany display love, loyalty, integrity, kindness and selflessness.

Paragraph 6: Ultimately, we see that good human characteristics are constructive, while bad ones are destructive. This is the moral of the play.

SAMPLE PLAN 4

'The redemptive power of love is a major theme in King Lear.'

Sample introduction: I agree that a central theme in Shakespeare's compelling play *King Lear* is the redemptive power of love. Although this play is often bleak and gloomy, and many characters behave appallingly, beneath this there is always a current of love, reassuring us that, ultimately, good will prevail.

Certain extraordinary characters are responsible for this: Cordelia, Kent, Edgar and, later, Gloucester and Lear. The hatred in the play serves to contrast and heighten the power of love to redeem, to make whole again.

Paragraph 1: Even with the fake love expressed during the love test, we see real love in the characters of Cordelia, and also France, who is willing to marry without a dowry, practically unheard of at that time.

Paragraph 2: Kent's love for Lear is inspirational and unconditional.

Paragraph 3: Edgar's love for Gloucester doesn't go away when his father betrays him.

Paragraph 4: Gloucester's love for Lear and, later, his love for Edgar.

Paragraph 5: The Fool stays with Lear through everything, and Lear loves him, despite his painfully true words.

Paragraph 6: Lear's love for Cordelia, in contrast with the pain Goneril and Regan cause him.

SAMPLE PLAN 5

'The sub-plot in King Lear *is essential to the play's success.'*

Paragraph 1: The sub-plot didn't appear in original versions of *King Lear*. Shakespeare added it himself, and it's so effective, it is hard to imagine the play without it.

Paragraph 2: The theme of parents and children is very similar, yet different enough to be interesting. Gloucester is gullible, whereas Lear is egotistical. Contrast the love test with the forged letter.

Paragraph 3: Cordelia and Edgar are very similar in their display of unconditional love and loyalty, although Cordelia is like a saint and Edgar is more real. Also, Poor Tom adds a lot to the play as a visual spectacle, comic relief and pathos. Explore the link, if only thematic, between Cordelia and the Fool.

Paragraph 4: We get to know Edgar better than Cordelia, plus he is not perfect. Cordelia and Edgar show how the characters in the main plot tend to be more extreme and melodramatic.

Paragraph 5: However, Edmund is far more interesting than Goneril and Regan. He is charismatic and compelling. They are too evil for the audience to be emotionally involved with, but the addition of Edmund, and the love triangle, adds much interest to the play.

Paragraph 6: The love triangle adds the extra ingredient of sex and brings about the downfall of Goneril and Regan.

Paragraph 7: The meeting of Gloucester and Lear in Act IV is very poignant.

Paragraph 8: The resolution of the sub-plot is crucial to the drama of the final scene of the play.

SAMPLE PLAN 6

'The theme of blindness is explored in great detail throughout Shakespeare's tragedy King Lear.'

Sample introduction: I agree that the theme of blindness is a central one in Shakespeare's play *King Lear*. Sight and blindness, both literal and metaphorical, are contrasted throughout the play. 'Seeing is believing' is shown to be an untrustworthy method of ascertaining the truth, as appearances can often be deceptive. Lear and Gloucester are the two main characters through which this theme is expressed, and their acknowledgment of their past blindness leads to their redemption.

Paragraph 1: From Act I, Scene I, eyesight is mentioned; 'dearer than eyesight …' This establishes sight/blindness as a recurring theme.

Paragraph 2: Lear says 'Out of my sight …' to Cordelia and Kent, while Kent implores Lear to 'See better, Lear …' Clearly showing Lear seeing what he wants to see, and not what is really there.

Paragraph 3: Likewise, in the sub-plot, Gloucester sees a (forged) letter and makes assumptions about a son who has never before given him reason to doubt him.

Paragraph 4: Gloucester's blinding is horrific, not only for Shakespeare's audience (who were, in some ways, less innocent than we are, as they saw hangings and beheadings on a regular basis) but for any audience. 'Out, vile jelly!' is absolutely gruesome. But

Gloucester goes on to say: 'I stumbled when I saw …'

Paragraph 5: When Lear and Gloucester meet, sight is mentioned once again as Lear remembers Gloucester's eyes.

Paragraph 6: Lear's last words to Cordelia are 'wipe thine eyes …' Some of his final words in the play are: 'Mine eyes are not o' th' best / I'll tell you straight …' This is his acknowledgment of his own human frailty.

SAMPLE PLAN 7

'Scenes of great suffering and of great tenderness help to make King Lear *a very memorable play.'*
Discuss this statement, supporting your answer with reference to the play *King Lear*.

Agree with this statement, and point out that many scenes combine both elements of 'suffering' and 'tenderness' to great effect.

Paragraph 1: In Act I, Scene I, the love test causes two characters in particular, Cordelia and Kent, to suffer. They are badly hurt by Lear.

Paragraph 2: Lear's rejection by both Goneril and Regan is heartbreaking to witness.

Paragraph 3: The storm scenes of Act III combine both suffering and tenderness. Lear is suffering and incredibly vulnerable, but he cares for the Fool and Poor Tom, and they for him.

Paragraph 4: The utterly horrific blinding of Gloucester is the ultimate scene of suffering. Gloucester's loyalty to Lear, however, is deeply touching, as is the servant's loyalty when he slays Cornwall. The disguised Edgar's devoted loyalty to his blinded father is another example of tenderness.

Paragraph 5: Cordelia and Lear's reunion is one of the most touching scenes in the play. Lear's humility and love is in marked contrast to his casual dismissal of his daughter in Act I.

Paragraph 6: The final scene of the play is full of both elements. It contains the greatest suffering in the play when Lear carries the dead Cordelia in his arms.

SAMPLE
ESSAYS
ON KING LEAR

SAMPLE ESSAY 1

The Role of the Fool in King Lear

I found the character of the Fool in *King Lear* fascinating. Through my study of this challenging play, I discovered that members of the royal family had to behave in a way that befitted their very strict royal etiquette, as well as having numerous advisors dictating their every word and movement. In this context, a king was often the least free of all citizens and it was the 'freaks' and fools who assembled in court for the entertainment of the nobility who were the only ones with the freedom to speak the truth. I thought at first that we have no modern equivalent, but I think comedians in today's society often perform a similar role. By holding human beings up to ridicule, by forcing us to laugh at our own failings, they help us acknowledge our human frailty.

A fool was dressed in a jester's costume and was often a scapegoat, a target of abuse. But the fool also had an advantage in that he was a person on the very periphery of 'civilised' society, and it is from this unique vantage point that he could see all the evils of the world he was excluded from taking part in. Lear's Fool does not need to act in a certain way; he can say exactly what he likes, and so he is the only character in the play who can see the wood for the trees, so to speak. It was the special privilege of the court jester to tell the truth, and he could do so without fear of reprisal. The Fool doesn't even have a name, yet he is one of the most important characters in the play.

Lear is genuinely fond of the Fool, despite the Fool's constant reminders of how Lear has brought this terrible situation upon himself: 'Fathers that wear rags

/ Do make their children blind; / But fathers that bear bags / Shall see their children kind.' Because he has nothing to lose, the Fool is paradoxically the wisest person in the play. All the great truths are spoken by the Fool, often in a humorous way which serves to lighten the tone of this often sombre drama. 'Thou hadst little wit in thy bald crown, when thou gav'st thy golden one away.' The reason why Lear has just one soliloquy is probably because the Fool assumes the role of voicing his interior monologue. I think this is the most important aspect of the Fool's dramatic function, the insight he shines on Lear's true self. 'I did her wrong.'

I also noticed that the Fool and Cordelia are never on stage together at the same time. He appears for the first time only after Cordelia has left for France. Then he disappears quite abruptly in Act III, just before Cordelia's reappearance in Act IV. His last line in the play is: 'And I'll go to bed at noon.' By going to bed early, maybe the Fool means he will die early, worn out by what he has learned of man's inhumanity to man. Yet I thought it an interesting coincidence that he conveniently dies just before Cordelia returns. After all, the play is full of characters in disguise, Kent as Caius and Edgar as Poor Tom, for example. I found out that the same actor would play both parts in Shakespeare's day.

Even if it is going too far to believe that Cordelia and the Fool are one and the same, I think that the Fool certainly represents Cordelia thematically. For Cordelia's blunt yet admirable honesty ('I cannot heave / My heart into my mouth: I love your Majesty / According to my bond ...') is markedly similar to the Fool's brutal words to the dispossessed Lear: 'I am a Fool, thou art nothing.' Both characters are catalysts for

Lear to learn who he really is, and what is true and what is false. Both have a selfless integrity and are Christ-like figures in a way, because they do the right thing no matter what the cost to themselves. I think the original Christian audience would really have enjoyed this religious aspect, but I did too. We always need heroes, and I found both these honourable characters heroic. And, when Cordelia dies, Lear cradles her body and says 'My poor fool.' Perhaps these are just the confused words of a devastated old man, but I think they are significant.

Another reason why I found the Fool so entertaining was the amount of imagery his character is responsible for generating. I also liked how accessible this imagery is. I'm sure Shakespeare's original audience may not have seen tigers, vultures, pelicans and all the other animals that are referred to throughout the play, but they certainly would have found the Fool's comparisons accessible: 'The hedge-sparrow fed the cuckoo so long / That it had it head bit off by it young.' The theatrical role of the Fool is to provide a visual spectacle. He would have been dressed in a traditional fool's costume, and he would have danced and pranced upon the stage. This was an added dimension to the Fool's role that is not always seen in modern performances.

The Fool, and Poor Tom, are also responsible for redeeming Lear in the eyes of the audience. Lear is quite a repellent character at the start of the play. I found his treatment of his daughter Cordelia disgusting. 'Come not between the dragon and his wrath.' But his concern for the Fool's welfare is very touching. When they are out in the storm, he is more concerned about the Fool's welfare than his own: 'how dost, my boy? art cold? / I am cold myself.' He leaves us as a very different Lear, who, due in no small way to the Fool's contribution, is steadily on the path to redemption.

In conclusion, as I have demonstrated throughout my essay, the Fool is undoubtedly a crucial character in *King Lear.* I found myself nodding in agreement at his pithy comments and laughing at his droll asides. His connection with Cordelia was really intriguing too, and these two characters are definitely my favourites. The Fool also provides a link between the audience and the action of the play because he tends to voice what we ourselves are thinking. I think this is essential in a play of *King Lear*'s complexity. My favourite quotation from the Fool is 'Who thou / clovest thy crown i' th' middle, and gavest away / both parts, thou borest thine ass on thy back o'er / the dirt …' because it is funny and true in equal measure, and shows what an important dramatic function the Fool serves in the play.

SAMPLE ESSAY 2

Imagery and Symbolism in King Lear

When Shakespeare wrote *King Lear,* he was aware of the limitations of theatre at that time. The stage he used most often was that of the Globe Theatre. A simple rectangular stage projected into a semicircular theatre. Covered balconies sheltered the richer members of the audience, but most people could only afford to stand in the pit around the stage, for which they paid the princely sum of one penny. There were very few props and no 'special effects'. Total reliance was placed upon the acting, and even more on the script. So Shakespeare came up with a way to overcome this; he wrote plays full of rich and evocative imagery, so the audience could simply imagine what he could not physically show them.

King Lear is a deeply psychological play, so it does not really require the type of imagery many other plays would. Instead, Shakespeare used imagery for characterisation and for emphasis. There are several distinct types of imagery in the play: animal imagery, clothing imagery, storm imagery, as well as images of blindness, torture and suffering. In such a stark, stripped-back play, the importance of this imagery cannot be overstated, and in this essay I will demonstrate this.

The first type of imagery I will discuss, animal imagery, is arguably the most powerful. This is always used in derogatory terms. For example, when Goneril first confronts Lear (for the 'bad' behaviour of his knights when he has gone to live with her after the love test), he berates her and calls her a 'detested kite' and says that Regan would show her nails to her 'wolvish visage'. When Lear speaks to Regan about Goneril's attitude, he describes it in terms of animal behaviour: 'O Regan, she hath tied / Sharp-toothed unkindness, like a vulture, here.'

Albany also speaks of the two sisters in comparison to animals; he calls them, 'Tigers, not daughters', and names Goneril a 'gilded serpent'. All of these images – tigers, vultures, kites and pelicans – are of animals who eat other animals, satisfying their hunger at the expense of others. The audience would never have seen some of these creatures, but they would have had a clear mental image of them from the vivid descriptions in fairy tales and other stories. Other creatures such as cuckoos would have been familiar to all. The Fool calls Goneril and Regan cuckoos: 'the hedge-sparrow fed the cuckoo so long / That it had it head bit off by it young.' This animal imagery is very effective in articulating the sadistic sisters' personalities. It is also powerfully suggestive. 'Vulture', for example, has connotations of a scary-looking bird hovering in wait around vulnerable prey, the perfect description of Goneril's and Regan's treatment of their father.

This comparison of Goneril and Regan to animals is similar to Edmund's affiliation with animal nature, and these three characters embody Albany's sentiment that 'Humanity must perforce prey on itself, / Like monsters of the deep.' Animal appetite is the downfall of both Regan and Goneril, just like Edmund, who decides that since he is considered to be outside nature because he is illegitimate, he will act just as his nature dictates. Both women lust after Edmund and, as he notes, 'To both these sisters have I sworn my love; / Each jealous of the other, as the stung / Are of the adder.' This suspicion leads to their deaths, as Goneril poisons Regan and kills herself with a knife. Two poisonous snakes destroy one another. In a society so obsessed with correct etiquette, humans behaving like animals was a scary concept. I find this ironic, as few animals would behave as badly as Goneril, Regan and Edmund!

A recurring symbol is that of sight or vision, a simple but effective idea since sight is precious to us all and a sense few sighted people could imagine living without. Although Lear can physically see, he is blind in that he lacks insight, understanding and direction. Goneril declares that Lear is 'dearer than eye-sight' to her (though she is the one who later suggests putting Gloucester's eyes out for his 'treachery'). Regan goes further, proclaiming, 'I profess / Myself an enemy to all other joys, / Which the most precious square of sense possesses'; presumably the most precious sense is that of sight. Crossed by Kent, Lear cries in his wrath, 'Out of my sight!', only to be reproved with Kent's 'See better, Lear; and let me still remain / The true blank of thine eye.' So obviously Kent's role in the court has been to see what Lear cannot. Lear has been blinded by his luxurious, decadent lifestyle, surrounded by yes-men. With no insight, Lear only sees what is on the surface and cannot look beyond the words.

The storm imagery in the play is raw and brutal. Here, imagery is vital. How to convey lashing rain and rumbling thunder in the most simple of theatres?

'Blow, winds, and crack your cheeks! rage! blow!
You cataracts and hurricanoes, spout
Till you have drench'd our steeples, drown'd
the cocks!
You sulph'rous and thought-executing fires,
Vaunt-couriers to oak-cleaving thunderbolts,

Singe my white head!'

Lear's railing at the tempest powerfully conveys the full horror of this terrible storm. I could picture sheets of rain bucketing down until even the weather vanes were flooded over, and thunderbolts shattering oak trees apart, while forked lightning illuminated this Armageddon-like scene in a nightmarish way. I'm sure Shakespeare's original audience, much more used to braving the elements than we are, found this imagery even more affecting.

The blinding of Gloucester is full of distressing imagery, such as 'Out, vile jelly!' Yet the destruction of Gloucester's eyes leads to greater insight on his part ('I stumbled when I saw'), and his literal blindness forms a powerful parallel with Lear's spiritual blindness. The stumbling, blinded old man is no different from the mad Lear. Ironically, Gloucester seems to almost ask for his horrific punishment when he says: 'Because I would not see thy cruel nails / Pluck out his poor old eyes; nor thy fierce sister / In his anointed flesh stick boarish fangs.' This is yet another example of superb, disturbing imagery.

There are many references to clothing and nakedness throughout *King Lear*. The importance of clothing in defining one's status seems to have fascinated Shakespeare, as there is also a proliferation of clothing imagery in *Macbeth* and *Hamlet*. In Shakespeare's day, clothing was expensive and hard to acquire, but not only could the poor not afford the clothing of the wealthy, they were not allowed to wear it. The really poor, such as Poor Tom, could not afford clothes at all. Their nakedness makes them vulnerable in every sense, whereas the luxurious robes of the wealthy cover a multitude of sins. Cordelia's exit speech in the first scene reveals some similar

thoughts: 'Time shall unfold what plighted cunning hides: / Who cover faults, at last shame them derides.' 'Plighted' means 'pleated', which makes one think of clothing. It appears as if she is saying much the same thing that Lear says in Act IV, Scene VI: those who hide their evil with their clothing (Goneril and Regan) are in the end exposed and shamed. 'Through tatter'd clothes small vices do appear; / Robes and furr'd gowns hide all.' In wearing tattered clothes one's wickedness easily shows through, but when one is splendidly dressed, their inner rottenness is hidden. Lear ends this speech with 'Pull off my boots: harder, harder: so' as he tears off his clothes, as if ridding himself of the lies and falsity that went with them. I think this might also have been Shakespeare's way of commenting on appearances not necessarily chiming with reality. One can dress like a king, or a queen, but does that make you a good person?

When Lear enters in Act IV, Scene VI, the stage direction reads 'fantastically dressed with wild flowers'. His lack of clothing symbolises his madness, but also his spiritual awakening. He is being honest at last. When he returns from madness in Act IV, Scene VII, the Gentleman says, 'in the heaviness of his sleep / We put fresh garments on him'. Since clothes represent one's identity, it appears as if being reclothed symbolises a new identity. When King Lear is stripped down to his bare essentials, he realises who he is. At the end of the play, he is still referring to clothing: 'Pray you, undo this button', as if he is suffocating in his clothes. This imagery is undoubtedly effective, and universal, as we all wear clothes, and many of us wear disguises.

Also notable in the play is that it is somewhat ironic that the character who is least blinded and has the most insight is the Fool. He has more wisdom than others in the play realise. He is blunt, honest and always says things the way he sees them. He might actually be considered the voice of sanity in Lear's crazy life. He is also the source of some of the most vivid imagery in the play. For example: 'Thou hadst little wit in thy bald crown, / when thou gav'st thy golden one away' and 'The hedge-sparrow fed the cuckoo so long, / That it had it head bit off by it young.'

In conclusion, as I have demonstrated throughout my essay, *King Lear* is a play full of amazing imagery, which is absolutely essential to its dramatic impact. The version of the play I watched was the 1978 BBC version, and it used very basic scenery and props. Yet, even to me, a modern viewer, used to seeing amazing special effects on TV, I felt that Shakespeare's words were sufficient backdrop to the tragedy. The imagery serves so many purposes: background, characterisation, themes. Shakespeare's words help us to conjure up our own pictures and ideas. This makes the play an interactive experience, something the original audience in their penny standing room would really have appreciated, for they lived in a world without the visual media we are saturated in today.

SAMPLE ESSAY 3

The Appeal of King Lear, *for a 21st Century Audience*

There are many reasons why *King Lear* is appealing for a 21st century audience. Although it was written over 400 years ago, *King Lear* is, quite simply, a great story, and great stories never date. The play is full of intrigue, suspense and drama. It has universal themes such as love, hate, betrayal and loyalty, not to mention murder and sex. I think *King Lear* has all the ingredients we find in successful dramas today, dramas such as *Skins* which have dramatic scenes and sub-plots, just like *King Lear*. *King Lear* has amazing scenes which may shock, provoke or even inspire us, fantastic scenes such as the love test and Gloucester's gory blinding. These scenes are so gripping they fascinate and appeal to us. I think, though, that it is the characters that are most important in determining the success of a film or a TV programme or a play. *Friends* wouldn't have been a success if it hadn't had exactly the right blend of characters. Similarly, in *King Lear* we have Lear, an astounding dramatic invention, but I personally found Edmund enigmatic and engaging, and I really loved the Fool too.

The whole premise of *King Lear* centres on an absurd love test, which Lear stages to find out which of his daughters loves him best. Lear clearly believes that words speak louder than actions, and the rest of the play is devoted to showing him the folly of this: 'Which of you shall we say doth love us most? / That we our largest bounty may extend / Where nature doth with merit challenge?' The love test is what catches our attention immediately, and it accounts for much of *King Lear's* continued appeal. In Shakespeare's day, the first few minutes of a play were crucial. A dissatisfied audience could still get their money back at this point. But, for a modern audience, there are other reasons for this scene's appeal. Not only is it interesting from a historical perspective, but it also really shows how the other half lives. It actually reminded me of *My Super Sweet Sixteen,* a television programme where spoiled brats briefly pretend to love their doting parents in order to get the party/car/money they desire. Shakespeare is also showing how wealth can corrupt, and how some people will, literally, do anything for money. The Christian ethos seen in Cordelia's integrity is diametrically opposed to her sisters' greed, and I think this is just as attractive to us as it was to Shakespeare's original audience: 'my love's / More ponderous than my tongue.' Now we have less money, a lot of people are finding that the most important things in life, like family and love, are free, and they always were.

The themes in *King Lear* are still relevant, and this is also appealing. In my opinion, no themes are more relevant than the theme of learning through suffering and the theme of love. In a way, the Leaving Cert can be compared to *King Lear.* Studying for hours upon end is definitely a form of torture, but throughout this, or any ordeal, is the hope that it will all be worth it, and that is what gets us through. Many characters in the play learn how to be better people because of what they go through. Gloucester sees how blind he was to the truth: 'I stumbled when I saw'. Lear recognises how misled he was because of his ego: ' 'tis a lie, I am not ague-proof.' Even Edmund sees the error of his ways when he is fatally slain: 'The wheel is come full circle: I am here.' Not only is this theme of suffering universal, it is also philosophical, and ultimately inspirational.

Life throws challenges at us all, but Shakespeare seems to be saying that our greatest challenge is in becoming the best version of ourselves that we can possibly be. I really like this idea, and it's certainly something I want to achieve in my life. Hopefully, I won't wait until I'm in my eighties, as Lear does!

There is no more relevant theme in *King Lear,* or in life itself, than love. Love is what motivates us in everything we do. Love really does make the world go around. In *King Lear,* we see the power of love to redeem in the unconditional love of Edgar and Cordelia for their fathers. We use the phrase 'unconditional love' a lot, but then we do impose conditions on it. I think I only really understand the concept of unconditional love through studying this play. Shakespeare shows that if you love someone, you can't let them push you away, and also you don't stop loving them. He also shows that love will ultimately win out in the end. Edgar adopts a complicated disguise to stay close to his father, and it is often thought that the Fool may actually be Cordelia in disguise. I like how Shakespeare is saying that love is its own reward, and in our cynical time, I think that's why we find this theme in particular so appealing.

Lear is the central character, and we witness his journey to redemption in almost painful detail throughout the play. We see him live through the physical and emotional pain of the central theme of learning through suffering. Initially, I hated Lear. I found him obnoxious and petulant in the first scene. Just one example of this is: 'Come not between the dragon and his wrath.' However, Shakespeare then shows how adversity can break us, but, if we are determined enough, it can also make us. Lear does not change abruptly, as many characters in modern films unrealistically do. Lear's learning is so gradual, it is utterly, painfully believable:

'You think I'll weep

No, I'll not weep:

I have full cause of weeping; but this heart

Shall break into a hundred thousand flaws,

Or ere I'll weep. O Fool, I shall go mad!'

It is as if we are on this journey with Lear, and we witness how much he has learned when we see his humility when he is reconciled with Cordelia: 'Pray you now, forget and forgive; I am old and foolish.' I think we can all identify with Lear to an extent. He may be flawed, but aren't we all? The original audience would not have found his death depressing, for they knew he would be rewarded in heaven. But I didn't find it depressing either, because he had lived a complete and real life by the close of the play.

Edmund is the anti-hero of this play. In many ways, he steals the show (like Sue Sylvester in *Glee*), not just because of his Machiavellian strategies and his opportunism, but because he is so realistic. For a start, Edmund's anger is initially justified. Unlike Goneril and Regan, he has valid reasons for his resentment of his family: 'Why bastard? Wherefore base? / When my dimensions are as well compact, / My mind as generous, and my shape as true, / As honest madam's issue?' And we see that Gloucester can actually change the inheritance laws if he chooses to: 'Loyal and natural boy, I'll work the means / To make thee capable.' It is, however, Edmund's involvement in the love triangle that really grabs the audience's attention. His casual disdain for both Goneril and Regan shouldn't really be appealing, but it is. I think Edmund definitely accounts for a lot of the continuing appeal of *King Lear*. He is a loose cannon. We never know what he

is going to get up to next, and he is also charismatic and charming – a truly great and enthralling villain.

When I saw *King Lear* being performed, I saw the full potential of the Fool. I had always loved him, especially the way he had dared to say what no one else would: 'I am a Fool, thou art nothing.' And it was also intriguing how Lear would hear the truth from him, but not from anyone else. However, when we saw the *King Lear Review*, the actor who played the Fool played a miniature guitar and sang, while dancing and prancing all over the stage. I saw then how the Fool is intended as a visual spectacle. His humour also balances out the tragedy, and he is very much like comedians I love, such as Des Bishop, who are hilarious because they dare to say what no one else would. The Fool had the entire audience in stitches when he said things such as:

'He that has a house to put's head in has a good head-piece.

The cod-piece that will house

Before the head has any,

The head and he shall louse;

So beggars marry many.'

And I think, because he is unique, he is definitely a huge part of the play's continuing appeal. He certainly made us laugh.

There are so many contrasting scenes in *King Lear* that it is no wonder we still enjoy the play today. There are scenes of incredible suffering juxtaposed with scenes of deep tenderness. It is impossible to get bored because of Shakespeare's careful balance of suspense and tension.

A scene which I found horrific, but utterly absorbing, was Act III, Scene VII, the blinding of Gloucester. Considering the type of horror films most teenagers have seen today, I didn't think there would be anything in *King Lear* to shock me in this way, but I stand corrected. When we saw *King Lear* performed, you could have heard a pin drop during this scene. The original audience, though used to violence, would have nonetheless found the plucking out of Gloucester's eyes shocking: 'Out, vile jelly!' They may have seen people hanged, flogged and beheaded, but blinding was a taboo that few would have broken.

In conclusion, as I have demonstrated throughout my essay, it is small wonder that we continue to enjoy *King Lear*. There are so many reasons for its continued appeal, time constraints mean that I have only been able to mention those reasons which were most significant to me. The more I study *King Lear*, the more I realise how brilliant Shakespeare's characterisation is, how fantastically he balances the action, and how relevant the themes and issues still are today.

SAMPLE ESSAY 4 (CHARACTER OF EDMUND)

'Edmund's insensitivity to others is evident from the fact that he treats men and women merely as obstacles or aids to his ambition.'
Discuss this statement with quotation from or reference to *King Lear*

In Shakespeare's gripping psychological drama *King Lear*, I find one character particularly interesting. Despite his insensitivity to others, Edmund fascinates me, especially in the way he treats all those around him as either obstacles or aids to his ambition. The obstacles must be got rid of by whatever means possible. The aids are used and abused until they have served their purpose. Although I would never want to be like Edmund, his amoral outlook is intriguing. To view Edmund's actions is to catch a rare glimpse of a person who will do anything to succeed.

The first obstacle to Edmund's advancement is Edgar, his brother. Edgar is a double threat: he is older and he is legitimate. Thus, it is Edgar who will succeed his father as Earl of Gloucester and inherit everything. In Act I, Scene II, we see Edmund gleefully hatch a plan to get rid of this obstacle. Edmund has decided that since he is 'illegal' and not recognised in law, he should not hold himself to upholding any law. So he forges a letter in Edgar's handwriting, in which Edgar is apparently plotting against their father. Gloucester is easily persuaded that his eldest son has simply turned on him (not surprising given Lear's daughters' behaviour), and Edgar just as easily accepts the need to flee. Edmund may view his brother as a mere obstacle, but Edgar loves his brother and does not see him as being any lesser because of his illegitimacy.

Edmund does not see this loyalty, just his good fortune in having 'a credulous father! and a brother noble … My practices ride easy.'

Gloucester is also a threat to Edmund's ambition, and it has to be said that as soon as Edmund turns the gullible Gloucester against Edgar, Gloucester rapidly changes his stance on the question of Edmund inheriting: 'Loyal and natural boy, I'll work the means / To make thee capable.' So Gloucester can change the laws if he so wishes, but obviously, until now, he didn't wish to do so. I admit to feeling some sympathy for Edmund at this point. Indeed, the way he has been hidden away from society because of a 'crime' he had nothing to do with means the audience tends to give Edmund much leeway, even when he no longer deserves it. Also, everything that follows from Edmund's original treachery is probably not planned – opportunities or aids come his way after this point, and he simply takes advantage: 'Briefness and fortune, work!'

Goneril, Regan and Cornwall prove to be vital in advancing Edmund's cause. Ironically, he first comes to their attention because of how he 'stood up' to his 'traitorous' brother. Cornwall compliments his loyalty: 'I hear that you have shown your father / A child-like office.' No less ironically, Edmund answers, ''Twas my duty, sir.' Cornwall and Regan are impressed with Edmund, although it is baffling that they admire him for his filial loyalty, when they have shown none to Lear. Edmund knows that, with the fertile ground of their admiration, he can make great rewards grow for himself. The 'seed' he uses is the letter about the French invasion, about which Gloucester had foolishly confided in him. Edmund not only betrays his father, he manages to look good while doing so. 'How

malicious is my fortune, that I must repent to be just!' Ever the great opportunist, Edmund's huge ambition cannot be checked because of his indifference, his total insensitivity towards others. People are merely pawns to him. Cornwall promises to reward him for snitching on his father: 'I will lay trust upon thee; and thou shalt find a dearer father in my love.'

Although ambition is not, in my opinion, a bad thing, it was certainly considered to be so in Shakespeare's day. Macbeth proves this. However, ambition is usually controlled by conscience, but Edmund's conscience doesn't really trouble him until the very end of the play. We see this in the love triangle between Goneril, Regan and Edmund. His charisma and good looks have provided him with yet more momentum, and he uses this opportunity with the same lack of ethics with which he betrayed Gloucester. Indeed, he delights in his duplicity, like a child in a sweet shop. When Regan asks if he has slept with Goneril ('have you never found my brother's way / To the forfended place?'), Edmund feigns indignation: 'That thought abuses you.' A natural politician, he reminded me of someone like Bill Clinton, who didn't just deny, but made everyone feel bad for asking the question. Edmund revels in his power: 'To both these sisters have I sworn my love; / Each jealous of the other, as the stung / Are of the adder. Which of them shall I take? / Both? one? or neither?' Edmund has no affection whatsoever for either sister. Yet, because the two duped women in question are the repulsive Goneril and Regan, I didn't feel any sympathy for them, and hence no real anger towards Edmund. In fact, Edmund being the weapon with which they destroy one another probably elevates him in my regard. He used and abused them, and they used and abused their father. There's a certain poetic justice in it.

Edmund's opportunistic crimes are one thing: how he treats those he perceives as obstacles is quite another. We witnessed his diabolical treatment of two innocents, Edgar and Gloucester, earlier in the play. Now he turns his attention to Lear and Cordelia. Newly reunited, Lear and Cordelia present Edmund with a real threat to his ambition. Edmund will defend his position by whatever means, fair or foul. Again, we witness his complete insensitivity to those around him, even an old man who has suffered so terribly already and a young girl who has never been less than exemplary in her behaviour. In many ways, Edmund personifies selfishness by his shocking decision at the end of Act V, Scene I:

> 'As for the mercy
> Which he intends to Lear and to Cordelia,
> The battle done, and they within our power,
> Shall never see his pardon; for my state
> Stands on me to defend, not to debate.'

Personally speaking, this was the point at which I began to see Edmund as actually capable of evil, rather than a flawed opportunist. I felt quite protective of both Lear and Cordelia after their poignant reconciliation, and I felt angry at Edmund's casual disregard for their lives.

The final scene of *King Lear* is full of tension, suspense and drama. Ultimately, everything is resolved, including Edmund's treachery being discovered because of Goneril's letter. Goneril poisons her own widowed sister to stop her marrying Edmund, and then kills herself. All these events have Edmund as the common denominator. However, in his duel with Edgar we discover more about Edmund than in the rest of the play put together. Fatally wounded, he admits his guilt almost with pride: 'What you have charged me with, that I have done; / And more, much more.' Yet his earlier insensitivity also starts to give way. He forgives Edgar for fatally stabbing him, and says that Edgar's story of reunion with his father has touched him: 'This speech of yours hath moved me.' With nothing left to lose, Edmund's character becomes almost unrecognisable. Shakespeare's audience believed that your true character was revealed in the moments before your death, so Edmund's remorse significantly redeems him.

Yet Edmund's real crime (ordering the officer to kill Lear and Cordelia and to make their deaths look like suicide) is being carried out at the very time he is urging Edgar to 'speak on'. Surely he realises that time is of the essence? But then we see his surprising response to the news of Goneril's and Regan's deaths: 'Yet Edmund was beloved! / The one the other poison'd for my sake, / and after slew herself.' It seems that Edmund really just wanted to be loved and accepted, and this was what lay behind his actions. His last words partly redeem him, when he tells the others what has been planned for Lear and Cordelia: 'I pant for life. Some good I mean to do, / Despite of mine own nature. Quickly send, / Be brief in it, to the castle; for my writ / Is on the life of Lear and on Cordelia.' This quotation is often used as proof of Edmund's redemption, but I think it is really too little, too late. I think that Edmund is a consummate actor and that this half-hearted apology is simply a way for him to go out with greater drama. And if I did feel any sympathy, the heart-wrenching sight of the frail old king clutching the corpse of the angelic Cordelia definitely extinguished it!

In conclusion, as I have demonstrated throughout

my essay, it is abundantly clear that Edmund's insensitivity to others is very evident from how he treats men (Edgar, Gloucester, Lear) and women (Goneril, Regan, Cordelia) merely as obstacles or aids to his ambitions. While I agree that Edmund is a compelling character who performs important dramatic functions in the play (the sub-plot, the love triangle), ultimately he is responsible for heinous crimes, such as the blinding of his father and the murder of Cordelia, that make it impossible to like him. However, Edmund is the puppet master who really does dominate this play. He is a highly entertaining character, despite his moral ambiguity, and this play would be far less successful without him.

SAMPLE ESSAY 5 (CHARACTER OF LEAR)

'... a man more sinn'd against than sinning ...'
Do you agree with Lear's own self-description? Discuss with quotation from or reference to the play.

I agree wholeheartedly with the statement that King Lear is indeed 'a man more sinn'd against than sinning'. Initially, I was shocked at the character of Lear. The egotistical love test, his appalling treatment of Cordelia and Kent, and his petulance throughout Act I, Scene I all combined to create a very unattractive character. However, in my view, Lear's subsequent ordeal at the hands of his two sadistic daughters is not only unjustified, it is disgraceful. I think Cordelia said it best: 'Mine enemy's dog, / Though he had bit me, should have stood that night / Against my fire ...'

I saw Lear as vain and needy right from the beginning when he conducted the absurd love test: 'Which of you shall we say doth love us most? / That we our largest bounty may extend / Where nature doth with merit challenge?' His two older daughters rise to the challenge and try to outdo each other with false declarations of love. Lear fails to see the irony in Goneril's opening statement: 'Sir, I love you more than words can wield the matter ...' If words cannot express her love, her words mean nothing. Lear, however, hears only what he wants to hear. Rather pathetically, he just wants to be told he is loved. So, even at this early point, I felt Lear was misguided rather than malicious. And part of me wished that all of his daughters had just humoured the old man.

But the plot is complicated when Cordelia, Lear's youngest daughter, refuses to patronise her father with false sentiments. 'Unhappy that I am, I cannot heave /

My heart into my mouth: I love your Majesty / According to my bond; nor more nor less.' Lear cannot see that Cordelia is being honest and sincere. He feels humiliated in front of his peers and lets his volatile temper get the better of him: 'Here I disclaim all my paternal care, / Propinquity and property of blood, / And as a stranger to my heart and me / Hold thee, from this, for ever.' Because Cordelia did not play the ridiculous game, she is banished in a rash moment Lear will live to regret. He quickly follows this with the banishment of Kent, his loyal servant of long standing: 'Come not between the dragon and his wrath.' There is no doubt that Lear exercises poor judgement, and that he himself is the catalyst for his own downfall.

Goneril and Regan find it easy to torment their father ('Yet he hath ever but slenderly known himself'), and his suffering really begins the moment he abdicates. While Lear is staying first with Goneril, she bullies him in a disturbingly underhanded way, simply by provoking his uncontrollable temper by telling her servants to neglect him: Goneril doesn't have to dirty her hands with throwing her father out; he does that all by himself. Yet even by the end of Act I, he has begun to realise his mistake: 'I did her [Cordelia] wrong.'

Throughout Act II, the Fool performs the important function of making Lear see the mistakes he has made: 'The hedge-sparrow fed the cuckoo so long, / That it had it head bit off by it young.' Yet Lear never rebukes the Fool for anything he says, and his silence indicates that he at least thinks about the Fool's words, even if they are hard to swallow: 'Fathers that wear rags / Do make their children blind; / But fathers that bear bags / Shall see their children kind.' In many ways the Fool seems to be articulating Lear's interior monologue. Lear knows that Goneril and Regan loved his money,

not him. He also knows that he was blinded to this fact by their protestations of love. And despite the Fool's lowly stature, as he says himself, at least he has a role: 'I am a Fool, thou art nothing.'

A still hopeful Lear journeys to Regan's house thinking that he will get a better reception there, but she and Cornwall have fled to Gloucester's castle to make sure that they cannot receive him. At first, Regan refuses to even see her father. She blames her travel fatigue, and already, by Lear's willingness to believe this ('Infirmity doth still neglect all office / Whereto our health is bound'), we see that as his domestic circumstances change from being the king of a huge kingdom to being the unwanted aged father of two devious daughters, Lear himself starts to change. He is not as rash with Regan as he was with Goneril and gives her every chance to take him in. Indeed, he begs her with a humility I, at least, would not have considered him capable of: 'on my knees I beg / That you'll vouchsafe me raiment, bed, and food.' When this fails, he scrapes his last remaining shreds of dignity together and journeys out into the storm: 'you unnatural hags, / I will have such revenges on you both / That all the world shall – I will do such things – / What they are, yet I know not, but they shall be / The terrors of the earth.'

The storm scenes of Act III are hugely important in Lear's development as a character, and they mainly focus on the theme of learning through suffering.

'I tax not you, you elements, with unkindness;
I never gave you kingdom, call'd you children,
You owe me no subscription …
… here I stand, your slave,
A poor, infirm, weak, and despis'd old man.'

In poverty, Lear starts to share and to demonstrate

compassion and a capacity for self-analysis: 'My wits begin to turn. / Come on, my boy: how dost, my boy? art cold? / I am cold myself.' Instead of a royal retinue, he is surrounded by the poor and the dispossessed: Poor Tom, the Fool and Caius. Yet he appreciates their loyalty and acknowledges the truth of the Fool's many comments about his mistakes. He sums up his situation perfectly: 'I am a man / more sinn'd against than sinning.'

In madness, Lear discovers the truth about his own flawed character. It is ironic that he shows his most attractive traits when he has lost his reason and stops putting on an act: 'the tempest in my mind / Doth from my senses take all feeling else ...' When Lear's intellect fails, he begins to engage with his senses. This primal, simple approach serves him much better than his previously complex, 'kingly' one. Soaked by the pouring rain and frozen by the chill winds, he realises that there are many even worse off, and that this, in part, is also due to him: 'Poor naked wretches, whereso'er you are ... defend you / From seasons such as these? / O, I have ta'en too little care of this!'

In Act IV, Lear's transformation is complete. Naked, bedecked in flowers, he has learned self-awareness and humility. When he encounters another blind, foolish old man, Gloucester, he acknowledges his own role in his downfall: 'They told me I was everything; 'tis a lie, I am not ague-proof.' Lear has finally acknowledged that he is just a man and that he should not have believed Goneril's and Regan's tributes, not because they weren't true, but because they could not have been true. 'A man may see how this world goes with no eyes.' Lear knows the only thing you need to see is what is in your own heart.

At this stage in the play, it really seems as though Lear has suffered enough, and Shakespeare wisely stages the long-anticipated reunion with Cordelia, just as Lear is discovering the rawness and vulnerability of newly awakened emotions: 'burning shame / Detains him from Cordelia.' Lear does not need anyone to tell him what is true now, so the Fool (presumably) dies, and Kent fades into the background. He tells Cordelia how sorry he is and how he feels he needs to be punished even more:

'If you have poison for me, I will drink it.
I know you do not love me; for your sisters
Have, as I do remember, done me wrong:
You have some cause, they have not.'

I think his new-found humility is really seen in the lines: 'Pray you now, forget and forgive; I am old and foolish.' I wouldn't have believed that Lear could ever admit to vulnerability from his behaviour in Act I.

Just as we see that Lear does not deserve to be sinned against any more, he and Cordelia are taken prisoner, and Cordelia is hanged. The old man musters his last bit of strength to kill his daughter's killer. He has truly come full circle. He dies having learned the inestimable value of Cordelia's love. His own subsequent death is at least that of a fully realised man, a true tragic hero, who has understood that you cannot quantify love. *King Lear* is arguably one of Shakespeare's finest plays and is certainly one of his deepest. Lear's suffering is undoubtedly self-inflicted to a degree, and this makes it even harder to endure, but he does not deserve to suffer to the extent he does. Yet when Lear is forced to plumb the very depths of his soul, he finds personal strengths that he never knew he had, such as kindness, bravery and humility. So, in a way, the sins committed against Lear do lead to his spiritual rebirth.

SAMPLE ESSAY 6

The Theme of Learning through Suffering

I found the theme of learning through suffering to be the dominant theme throughout *King Lear*. This was an especially relevant idea to Shakespeare's audience. Their lives were harder than we could ever imagine, and they had to believe there was a point to all their pain or they would simply have given up. Yet this theme is also a universal, timeless one. We all need to believe that we gain something from the bad times. Perhaps it is wisdom, strength or courage, but I certainly believe we do learn through suffering, and that every human experience, no matter how devastating, teaches us something worthwhile.

Lear is the character in whom we see this theme played out most vividly. But many of the other characters learn through suffering too. Even Cordelia, the most exemplary of the characters, learns through her harsh exile. I realise I am probably in the minority here, but I found Cordelia's refusal to 'heave' her heart into her mouth rather frustrating: 'I love your Majesty / According to my bond; nor more nor less.' Doubtless, this shows great integrity, but part of me felt she should just humour an old man, a man who obviously favoured her: 'I lov'd her most, and thought to set my rest / On her kind nursery.' Would it have been so hard to give him what he wanted?

When Cordelia returns to the play in Act IV, her speech is not so taciturn. Now, after suffering herself, and missing her father, she can articulate her love easily: 'O, look upon me, sir, / And hold your hands in benediction o'er me: / No, sir, you must not kneel.' Perhaps Cordelia has learned that the truth is sometimes less important than not hurting someone you love.

Lear undergoes a profound transformation in the play. The love test was an ill-thought-out attempt to fish for the ultimate compliment of his daughters' love. Lear's anger at Cordelia's refusal to play the game ('Here I disclaim all my paternal care, / Propinquity and property of blood, / And as a stranger to my heart and me / Hold thee, from this, for ever') is absolutely shocking. His temper, once ignited, is ferocious. Lear, a king, surrounded by sycophants and yes-men (aside from Kent), has been refused nothing. In the face of Cordelia's bluntness, he throws a despicable tantrum. And yet, deep down, I think Lear is mortified and hurt, rather than angry. I think he is trying to save face more than anything. But to take back Cordelia's dowry, and to let Burgundy or France take her as if she were worthless, are the sins of an egotistical man who values himself more than anything or anyone else.

The story could have ended there, and Lear might never have learned anything, were it not for the characters of Goneril and Regan. They have no use for the father they professed to love 'more than words can wield the matter' once he has given them everything. But it is their disgraceful treatment of Lear which is the catalyst for his spiritual journey. Lear's fatal flaw is his rashness. Goneril knows this when she instructs her servants to 'put on what weary negligence' they wish, and criticises his entourage. She knows exactly how to press his buttons, and predictably Lear loses his temper: 'Detested kite! thou liest.' But, while I was quite shocked at Goneril's filial ingratitude, I was repulsed by Lear's diatribe against her: 'Into her womb convey sterility! / Dry up in her the organs of increase …' There is something very disturbing about a father wishing his daughter's womb would shrivel up and die. At this point, Lear still has very much to learn.

Lear's rejection by Goneril kickstarts the process of learning. Journeying to Regan's house, he confides to the Fool about Cordelia – 'I did her wrong' – but he still thinks he can live out his days in comfort with Regan. When he finds her home empty, and Kent in the stocks, it starts to dawn on him that he has lost everything ('Oh how this mother swells up toward my heart!'). The Fool reminds him that Lear himself set this tragedy in motion: 'Let go thy hold when a great wheel runs down a hill, lest it break thy neck with following it'. Like her sister, Regan does not just admit she doesn't want her father; she baits Lear to the point where it is he who severs all ties with her, using the exact same technique as Goneril: 'I entreat you / To bring but five and twenty: to no more / Will I give place or notice.' There is no justification for Regan's behaviour, but it is disappointing to see that Lear has learned nothing from his last altercation:

'No, you unnatural hags,

I will have such revenges on you both,

That all the world shall – I will do such things –

What they are, yet I know not: but they shall be

The terrors of the earth.'

Yet Lear also shows how sad it all makes him, and for the first time I saw humility in his words: 'I have full cause of weeping; but this heart / Shall break into a hundred thousand flaws, / Or ere I'll weep. O Fool, I shall go mad!'

In a similar fashion to Lear, Gloucester also learns through suffering. Like Lear, he exiled his own child, but unlike Lear, Gloucester had some excuse because one son had turned him against the other. Gloucester's suffering is physical and tangible, whereas Lear's is spiritual for the most part. The blinding of Gloucester is full of vivid images of suffering ('Out, vile jelly! / Where is thy lustre now?'), but afterwards he confesses: 'I stumbled when I saw.' This showed me that he had learned through suffering. Gloucester is ashamed of thinking so ill of Edgar: 'O dear son Edgar, / The food of thy abused father's wrath!' I think that Shakespeare is saying that, deep down, we always know the truth even if we don't want to always acknowledge it.

Even Edmund, the anti-hero, learns through suffering. It takes his being fatally wounded by his brother to finally learn what he has done: 'What you have charged me with, that have I done; / And more, much more; the time will bring it out / 'Tis past, and so am I.' Edmund also tries to right the wrong he did in ordering the deaths of Lear and Cordelia: 'I pant for life. Some good I mean to do, / Despite of mine own nature. Quickly send, / Be brief in it, to the castle; for my writ / Is on the life of Lear and on Cordelia. / Nay, send in time.' In contrast, Goneril and Regan don't really suffer, and so never learn anything, and I found both of them to be very depressing characters because of this.

But to return to Lear, it is in Act III that Lear suffers the most and also learns the most. Homeless, naked and vulnerable to the harshness of the winter storms, Lear starts to become a truly good man. We see this in his concern for the poor: 'O, I have ta'en / Too little care of this!' We also see it in the tender way he cares for the Fool and Poor Tom ('how dost, my boy? art cold?') and for anyone who is suffering: 'Poor naked wretches, whereso'er you are, / That bide the pelting of this pitiless storm …'

However, I think it is the humility Lear displays to

Cordelia which shows how much he has changed. It is a stark contrast to the hot-headed, arrogant man he was: 'I am a very foolish fond old man'. Their reconciliation is one of the most tender, uplifting parts of the play, but it would not have happened had Lear not learned who he really was and what really mattered. It was heartbreaking to see Lear losing Cordelia so soon after reconciling with her, just as he has learned the value of her love, but it was heartening to see how utterly transformed as a character he is by the close of the play. With nothing to his name, Lear is a king in the best sense of the word.

In conclusion, as I have demonstrated throughout my essay, *King Lear* is indeed a play which has, at its heart, the central message that suffering can change us on a very fundamental level. Often considered quite pessimistic, I think this theme is actually optimistic. Lear may die broken-hearted, his dead daughter in his arms, but he has realised his potential as a human being. Ultimately, isn't that what we are all here for: to become the best possible versions of ourselves? Therefore, I found this theme inspirational.

PAST LEAVING CERTIFICATE EXAM QUESTIONS ON KING LEAR

(2010)
'In *King Lear* honour and loyalty triumph over brutality and viciousness.' Write your response to this statement, supporting your answer with suitable reference to the text.

(2010)
'In *King Lear* the villainous characters hold more fascination for the audience than the virtuous ones.' Discuss this statement with reference to at least one villainous and one virtuous character. Support your answer with suitable reference to the text.

(2006)
'In the play *King Lear,* the stories of Lear and Gloucester mirror one another in interesting ways.' Write a response to this view of the play, supporting your answer by reference to the text.

(2006)
'Reading or seeing *King Lear* is a horrifying as well as an uplifting experience.' Write a response to this view, supporting the points you make by reference to the text.

(2002)
'Powerful images heighten our experience of the play, *King Lear.*' Write your response to this statement. Textual support may include reference to a particular performance you have seen of the play.

(2002)

'Cordelia plays a very important role in the play, *King Lear.*' Discuss this view of Cordelia, supporting your answer by reference to the play.

(2001)

What, in your view, are the most important changes that take place in the character of Lear during the play *King Lear*? Support your points by reference to the play.

(2001)

'Scenes of great suffering and of great tenderness help to make *King Lear* a very memorable play.' Discuss this statement, supporting your answer with reference to the play, *King Lear.*

(Marking schemes are available on www.examinations.ie)

CLASSROOM ACTIVITIES AND GROUP WORK

Imagery Group Work:

Divide the class into five groups, and allow each group ten minutes to find as many examples of animal imagery as possible. The group with the most animals wins.

The Hot-seating Game:

Allow one slip of paper per student. Write out the names of the main characters on the slips. The class will divide into groups – the 'Lear' group, the 'Goneril' group, etc. Allow students time to discuss and prepare their character. One student per group will 'become' that character, and the other students in the class can ask them questions, e.g. you could ask the Fool what life as a court jester is like.

The Courtroom Game:

The premise of this game is that there is only one place left in hell, so, by default, either Goneril or Regan is going to get in to heaven. Set up the class as a courtroom. Pick one student to play God, who will be the judge. Pick two students to play Goneril and Regan, and select students to play their lawyers. Then try both women, to discover who is the least evil. The other students in the class can play characters who are going to be called as witnesses, or they can form part of the jury.

Prequel Game:

In groups, write a short prequel to *King Lear*. This prequel can take place at any point in time before the Love Test, be it hours, days or years beforehand. This exercise will offer some insight into the characters' motivations.

The author and publisher wish to thank the Utah Shakespeare Festival, Cedar City, Utah, USA, for permission to reproduce photographs of their 2007 production of *King Lear* in this book.

Photographer: Karl Hugh, © Utah Shakespeare Festival

Cast:

Lear	PAGE 22	Dan Kremer
Goneril	PAGE 22	Carole Healey
Regan	PAGE 74	Anne Newhall
Cordelia	PAGE 181	Shelly Gaza
Gloucester	PAGE 142	Kieran Connolly
Edmund	PAGE 41	Raymond L. Chapman
Edgar	PAGE 86	Shawn Fagan
Kent	PAGE 68	James Newcomb
Fool	PAGE 65	Tim Casto
Cornwall	PAGE 74	Phil Hubbard
Albany	PAGE 152	John Oswald

Royal Shakespeare Company productions

Photographer: Manuel Harlan, © Royal Shakespeare Company

Fool	PAGE 62	Kathryn Hunter (2010)
Lear	PAGE 111	Greg Hicks (2010)

Actors featured in illustrations:

PAGE 59	Ray Reinhardt – *San Francisco Shakespeare Festival (2001)*
PAGE 113	Graham Smith – *Collaborative Arts (2011)*
PAGE 144	Christopher Hunt – *University of Calgary (2011)*
PAGE 171	Derek Jacobi – *Donmar Warehouse / National Theatre (2011*